ERNEST BEVIN

ANDREW ADONIS

ERNEST BEVIN

LABOUR'S CHURCHILL

Biteback Publishing

First published in Great Britain in 2020 by
Biteback Publishing Ltd, London
Copyright © Andrew Adonis 2020

ISBN 978-1-78590-598-8

10 9 8 7 6 5 4 3 2

A CIP catalogue record for this book is available from the British Library.

Set in Adobe Caslon Pro and Futura

Printed and bound in Great Britain by
CPI Group (UK) Ltd, Croydon CR0 4YY

MIX
Paper from
responsible sources
FSC
www.fsc.org   FSC® C020471

In memory of Roy Jenkins:
friend, mentor, inspiration,
for whom Bevin was one of the greatest.

'A working-class John Bull.'
SIR WINSTON CHURCHILL

'He could neither read, write nor speak,
and he did all three triumphantly.'
ANON.

'Ernest Bevin was not a working man who became a statesman.
He remained a working man who added statesmanship.
In this he was the first of his kind.'
NEWS CHRONICLE

'I like to build, brothers.'
BEVIN TO HIS UNION DELEGATES

'They say Gladstone was at the Treasury from 1860 to 1930.
I'm going to be Minister of Labour from 1940 to 1990.'
BEVIN IN CHURCHILL'S WAR CABINET

'When you strip all these things down which produce political ideologies
and get down to the masses, what do they want? They want to live! They
want to be free, to have social justice, to have individual security, to be
able to go home, turn the key in the lock and not be troubled by a secret
police. Why not let them live? Why set them at each other's throats?
That is the basis of my approach to the problems of a war-scarred
Europe and world.'
BEVIN AS FOREIGN SECRETARY

CONTENTS

Ernest Bevin

'A working-class John Bull.' © *New Statesman*/David Low/The Print Collector/Print Collector/Getty Images

INTRODUCTION

Ernest Bevin was one of the greatest and most inspirational leaders of the twentieth century. He was Labour's Churchill.

As Foreign Secretary in Attlee's post-war government (1945–51),
Bevin was largely responsible for keeping communism and Stalin
out of Western Europe. He took the lead in creating West Germany,
NATO and the transatlantic alliance, all of which underpin European democracy and security to this day. As Minister of Labour
during the Second World War (1940–45), he was at Churchill's right
hand, masterminding the home front while Churchill commanded the battle front. In the process, and by design, he brought the
labour movement into government and put industrial partnership
and Keynesian collectivist ideas and institutions at the heart of the
British state until they collapsed in the era of Margaret Thatcher.
As leader of the Transport and General Workers' Union (1922–45),
he created the free world's then biggest and most formidable trade
union.

It was three decades of almost unparalleled productivity and constructive achievement.

To my surprise, after living with him for a year, I have come to see

Bevin's greatest interlocutor not as Churchill but Stalin. Bevin got the full horrific measure of the brutal Soviet megalomaniac better than any other leader of his generation and did more to defeat him than anyone else in the seminal six years after 1945. For the future of Europe and Western civilisation, these six years were as crucial as the previous six, which saw Churchill lead the defeat of Hitler and Nazism.

Bevin stood up to Stalin and largely outmanoeuvred him in Western Europe. He painted and partly achieved a vision of a far better, fairer democratic society that refuted the cruelty and abominations of communism and the Stalinist war of all against all. This is the biggest story in the following pages.

At home, Bevin did more than anyone in British history to turn the working class into a political force and Labour into a governing party. By doing so, he transformed the lives of working people. He was decisive in ensuring that the post-Second World War era was one of social progress and international security, in stark contrast to that which followed the First World War when Britain and Western Europe went sharply backwards. He had been a trade union leader in the thick of it after 1918 and he showed that he had learned the lessons well after 1945.

To understand modern Britain, warts and all, you need to understand Ernest Bevin. That's what this book seeks to do. He is fascinating as an extraordinary human being, rising from extreme poverty and disadvantage to become an international leader of unique charisma and authenticity, larger than life and full of contradictions, these latter characteristics also putting him in the Churchillian league.

Churchill, Attlee, Truman, Keynes and Marshall were among the partners with whom Bevin shaped the second half of the twentieth century. Indispensable to these partnerships were his extraordinary leadership, ideas, pragmatism and staying power. Serving in high executive office for nearly thirty continuous years, his career at the top of twentieth-century British public life was of a duration matched only by Churchill, Lloyd George and Harold Wilson.

Just as Bevin's successes shaped post-war Britain and the West, so did his failures. He was an unreconstructed imperialist, which made him all too literally Labour's Churchill. The disastrous post-war handling of Israel/Palestine and the failure to take seriously the initiation by France and Germany of the European Union were rooted in his imperialism, casting shadows that loom large in the twenty-first century, particularly over Brexit.

Living with Bevin for a year, I am seized by his ambivalence. He was a committed democrat yet a tough authoritarian; a socialist yet an imperialist; a fervent patriot as well as an ardent internationalist; a trade union leader and working-class icon who became thoroughly middle class, even pan class. By the 1930s there was no cloth cap but instead a bowler hat, cigars, well-cut suits and an art deco apartment in Kensington. During the war he even joined the Garrick Club. Yet, to the end, he was unseduced by money and status. The Garrick membership was mostly to hob-nob with actor managers from the world of entertainment like J. Arthur Rank, Basil Dean and Seymour Hicks, pan-class impresarios like himself, who became his friends and even family connections.

Bevin has receded in public consciousness, which is another reason for writing this book. His surname is routinely mixed up with Bevan, whom he called his 'namesake'. Wikipedia even notes under 'Ernest Bevin', 'Not to be confused with Aneurin Bevan.' Yet whereas Bevan has become a Labour household god for founding the National Health Service ('the closest thing the English people have to a religion'),[1] Bevin went out of fashion as just a man of power. 'Nye' Bevan was a romantic, mythologised by Michael Foot, while Bevin was a pragmatist whose admirers wrote no hagiography. In fact, 'Ernie' Bevin had social democratic principles and passions every bit as profound as Bevan's, and without Nye and Ernie together, we would not today celebrate the Attlee government.

Bevin was first and foremost a working-class trade union leader. This too cast him in the shade after his death, as a breed apart from many literary and political people, including the increasingly large proportion of middle-class Labour politicians. Meanwhile the trade unions themselves, too often unpragmatically led in the decades since Bevin, allowed his legacy to wither. Bevin would probably have been aghast that the most recent leader of his own union, incongruously renamed 'Unite', is Len McCluskey, patron of Jeremy Corbyn, the most unsuccessful Labour leader since George Lansbury, whom Bevin ousted in the dramatic Labour Party conference of 1935 before he had even fought an election. Lansbury's replacement was Clement Attlee, sustained and partnered as Labour leader by Bevin for the next sixteen years, eleven of them in the two most transformational governments in modern British history between 1940 and 1951.

'My relationship with Ernest Bevin was the deepest of my political life,' Attlee said in retirement. 'Ernest looked, and indeed was, the embodiment of common sense. Yet I have never met a man in politics with as much imagination as he had, with the exception of Winston.'[2] Attlee saw in Bevin a constant quest for action, not the fatalism of inaction, in the face of social and economic crisis. This impregnable Attlee–Bevin partnership underpinned the extraordinary strength and success of both the Churchill and the Attlee governments of the 1940s. It was in some ways the golden age of the British state.

In an arresting assessment of Bevin a few months after his death, Attlee's alter ego and adviser Francis Williams wrote of him thus as leader of the Transport and General Workers' Union in the turbulent aftermath of the 1917 Russian Revolution and the First World War:

> There is no doubt that he appeared to many at this time the most likely leader of the British working-class revolution which they hoped – or feared – would follow in due course on the heels of the Russian revolution – and not too far behind it...
>
> I have sometimes thought that if it were possible ... to conceive of Bevin's becoming a member of the British Communist Party in the militant years of 1919 and 1920, as some others of a like background did, then it might have been British Communism would have found its Stalin. There are indeed curious similarities between some – although only some – aspects of what we know of Stalin's character and Bevin's which perhaps go to explain their very different pre-eminence as working-class leaders in this age. Bevin had the same peasant shrewdness as Stalin, the same patience, the same power of stillness. His humour, brutal and genial by turn with its roots deep in the earth, was not unlike what we know of Stalin's. Both men forced their way to the front because they took care to gather into their own hands the controlling strings of organisations in which power rested. Each was in his own way ruthless in setting aside any who stood in the way of his advance. And it may be that when the moment came the mercurial Tillett with his quicksilver power of oratory was hardly less surprised – although with less dangerous results to himself – than Trotsky to

find how fallible was reliance on a gift of words when confronted with a genius for organisation. It would be absurd to press the comparison too far. It is valid only to the extent that it indicates the part played in the characters and careers of both men by a single quality and comparable understanding of the machinery of power.[3]

In the event, a Stalinist understanding of the working class and the machinery of power led Bevin to defeat Stalin, not to emulate him. Bevin was revolutionary about ends, democratic about means. He was a liberal social democrat. Humanity was his mission not his curse.

CHAPTER 1

ORPHAN

Two Foreign Secretaries were brought up in the remote Somerset village of Winsford on Exmoor: Boris Johnson, born in 1964, and Ernest Bevin, born in 1881.[1] Chronologically, they are eighty-three years apart. An eternity separates them in other respects, but the significant fact is that Winsford made them both quintessentially English.

The Winsford they knew was as different as their pedigrees. 'God was palpably present in the country and the devil had gone with the world to town,' wrote Thomas Hardy of rural Wessex in *Far from the Madding Crowd* (1874). But there wasn't much sign of the Almighty in Somerset when Ernest was born to a poor single mother just seven years later. Still less when he was orphaned at the age of eight. 'I'm sure there's no one in this wide world who was ever poorer than he and his mother,' recalled a neighbour.[2]

There was barely a scintilla of rural bliss in 1880s Somerset, only depopulation and depression. Winsford was not just remote, it was virtually isolated, nine miles from the nearest railway station. Bevin later described his life there as 'a form of slavery'.

Ernest's mother, Mercy, hailing from a family of labourers from time immemorial, was calling herself a 'widow' by the time Ernest, her last son, was born on 7 March 1881. She wasn't a widow: husband William had deserted her, or she him, a few years before. But she might as well have been, for she did not remarry and her last child, much younger than the others, never knew his father.

Prior to Ernie's birth, Mercy and William's ten-or-so years of marriage, a desperate struggle for security and survival, had taken them on the popular Victorian migrant trail from impoverished Somerset to the mining valleys of South Wales. For reasons unknown Mercy returned alone to Winsford with her six children, who never saw their father again. Ernest, her seventh child, was born thereafter, when she was forty.

Ernie, as he was always called, adored his mother; her picture was on his desk the day he died. His siblings had all left home by the time he was five or six and he was effectively an only child. Mercy eked out enough to support the two of them as a midwife and domestic help, with intermittent parish relief to avoid destitution. There was never much money, but there was happiness, respect, fun and a home 'spotlessly clean though, poor soul, she worked hard throughout the day away from it'.[3]

There was also lots of religion. Mercy was 'a fanatical Dissenter, at a time when to be so was to risk the displeasure of the local farmers and gentry'.[4] She helped lead a campaign to build a new chapel in the village and was equally fanatical about a cause allied to Methodism: temperance, banishing the evils of the bottle. From the age of three her little boy was sent to Winsford's Methodist Sunday School run by Mrs Veysey, the village postmistress. The earliest photograph of Ernie is of a solemn child in a velvet suit and straw sailor hat in the front row of her village class. Like Mrs Veysey, Mercy

Bevin 'hated the domination of Church and Squire' and was determined to worship God and live life in her own way, as was her son.[5] The temperance also rubbed off: Ernie was a teetotaller until his mid-twenties, although he more than compensated thereafter.

Ernie's years with his mother were happy and boisterous but tragically brief. Mercy succumbed to cancer when he was eight and she forty-eight. His childhood was devastated, and her funeral was to be the last time all the Bevin children gathered. It was Victorian England at its best and worst. Mr Anderson, the Tory parson of Winsford, tried to refuse to bury Mercy on consecrated ground for her loose morals and for consorting with Methodists. It was probably the latter he most resented. But the village turned out in force, views were forcibly expressed, reputedly at the church door, and Mercy was eventually laid to rest in the churchyard. It was a negotiation worthy of Ernie Bevin in his prime.

After his mother's death Ernie went to live with his 25-year-old half-sister Mary and her husband, a railwayman, thirty miles across the north Devon border near Crediton. First they lived in the village of Morchard Bishop, then in neighbouring Copplestone. It was a traumatic period for the young boy, which he rarely mentioned in later life. At Winsford, with his mother, he had been chubby, cheeky and outgoing; at his sister's home he became thin, withdrawn and angry. Five decades later, interviewed for a profile of the new Foreign Secretary, Morchard Bishop's long-retired postman recalled a boy of ten who was 'pale-looking and bullied'. He remembered 'seeing that young boy getting water for the house or cleaning potatoes. The water came from an icy cold stream and his hands were all covered with broken chilblains.'[6]

Ernie's education was par for the course for a late-Victorian labourer's child, featuring a few primary schools inculcating the 'three Rs', then out to work by the age of eleven. Most accounts of Bevin, however, fail to stress two key points about his education. First, he had one. At school level it was basic, but it was a huge improvement on what most village children had experienced only a few years previously, before Gladstone's 1870 Education Act. Had Ernie been born at the time of his eldest siblings, he might not have received an education at all. Several of his older relations were illiterate, and at his sister's cottage he read aloud by the fireside from each day's *Bristol Mercury* about some of the doings of the wider world. The *Mercury* was a Gladstonian Liberal paper, pro-Irish Home Rule after 1886, supporting the Grand Old Man but strongly critical of the 'ingratitude' of 'the Irish'.[7] Maybe that rubbed off too.

Furthermore, the 'three Rs' were not the end of Ernie's formal education. In his late teens and twenties, he went to extension lectures in Bristol, given by distinguished university lecturers, which equipped him with a good grounding in politics and economics. This, too, was a late Victorian and Edwardian trait: basic schooling followed by determined self-improvement, including adult education, of which Ernie made the most. Although in later life he liked calling himself 'a turn up in a million', there were plenty of others who had made successful, even brilliant, careers from a similar standing start. Charlie Chaplin, eight years younger, was another 'turn up in a million' from an equally poor and disrupted childhood, and millions of others – one or more in most working-class families – turned up in skilled or professional careers from working-class roots, including teaching and trade union administration. Ernie Bevin was a representative of his age just as much as he was a genius.

From school at the age of eleven, Ernie had no choice but to be a farm boy, 'scaring birds, stone picking, following the dibble, hoeing, twitching, cutting up mangels and turnips for cattle fodder, or doing odd jobs'.[8] He hated it. For the young teenage Ernie, manual labour in a village with no autonomy and little society was 'a form of slavery' and a life unfulfilled. News of his older brothers in the big city of Bristol, about which he read every day in the *Mercury*, made him desperate to escape, and within two years he had found his way there with little more than the clothes on his back.

There is a vivid portrait of Ernie's boyhood in a 1946 issue of *Picture Post*, written by a journalist who visited the villages where he grew up. Ernie's cousin Jack was still a gardener at the Royal Oak in Winsford, where his mother had worked 'in the stag hunting months'. Mercy Bevin was remembered as 'jolly, energetic, unconventional and brave'. He was told that the parish relief from Mr Anderson, the Tory vicar, hadn't amounted to much, 'not much more than sixpence a week and bread'.[9] It was literally life on the bread line.

The village postman took the journalist to Beers Farm, Copplestone, where Ernie had worked from dawn to dusk for sixpence a week. And to the barn where he 'fought the farmer and ran away to face life on his own' after Farmer May had thrashed him for not picking enough turnips. At least, that is one version of events; another has him 'trembling with fear and white with anger' rushing at the farmer with a billhook. Francis Williams, a friend in the 1940s, said Ernie denied the incident even took place and it may be apocryphal 'as so many Bevin stories are, for he was a man about whom legends gathered'. Another example is his reputed reply to King George VI, on being sworn in as Minister of Labour in 1940. The King asked him how he had acquired so wide a knowledge of public affairs, to which Bevin replied: 'Sir, it was gathered in the 'edgerows of experience.'[10]

The *Picture Post* journalist also met an older farm hand who had worked alongside Ernie at Beers Farm, 'old John Perkins, who could neither read nor write'. It was Perkins, impressed by little Ernest's argumentative powers, who made the remark that a biographer might have invented if it weren't attested by others: 'That boy will never work on a farm, but he'll be in Parliament yet.' The *Picture Post* portrait is one of a boy who knew his own mind, and it wasn't on a farm. The article ends with a picture of the bridge and lane leading out of Copplestone, with the caption: 'The road down which little Ernest marched, after leaving Beers Farm. The road which eventually led him where he is today!'

Bevin really had been a Bristol barrow boy. His company, Brooke & Prudencio,
c. 1890. © Amoret Tanner/Alamy Stock Photo

It was a long and winding road. And it led next to Bristol.

Ernie's elder brothers, Jack and Albert, had found jobs and digs in Bristol, the great port metropolis of the south-west. At the age of thirteen, Ernest joined them. However keen he was to escape from Beers Farm, his first days in Bristol 'had a frightening loneliness about them. He knew one or two people in the city, but they were not helpful.'" He lodged first with Jack, getting a casual job in a butcher's shop in affluent Clifton. At the age of thirteen and fourteen, Ernie was constantly in and out of jobs, including spending weeks unemployed. At one point he was a van boy on the mineral water wagons of Brooke & Prudencio: he really had been a Bristol barrow boy.

Albert was a pastry cook at a restaurant in the city centre and soon found his youngest brother, now aged fourteen, a better-paid job there: six shillings a week plus meals, in return for twelve hours' work a day, six days a week. The teenage Ernie may have had no mother or father, but the young siblings stuck together and helped each other with jobs and lodgings as they made their way in the great cities, another Victorian and Edwardian trait. He didn't do it all alone. Sixty years later Albert recalled:

> He became a general factotum and made himself useful and in time he became very popular. After a time they made him a sort of glorified page boy and dressed him up and he used to wait at table and in the shop and run out for errands and I think it was then that he became conscious of the two sides of the people. First there was the people who came in and had full courses, dinners, who he waited on, and just out in the street there were always a great crowd out of work, sixty or seventy always to get one job,

and wages were fifteen shillings to £1. He became so obsessed with this difference in people's lives that he used to talk to us by the hour of the unhappy conditions that people lived in.[12]

By fourteen Ernie was a big, broad-shouldered boy with a square jaw, streetwise and, with his brothers, well able to look after himself. He was proudly working class but not remotely downtrodden. Think Alan Johnson. He scrubbed up well in his Sunday best: just look at that bow tie, waistcoat, watch chain and smart parting in the plate section of this book.

Aged sixteen, Ernie became a horse tram conductor at twelve shillings a week. But he hated the routine and confinement and was soon back with Brooke & Prudencio as a drayman at fifteen shillings a week. He called it his first 'man's job'.[13] Then, at eighteen, he joined his third brother Fred as a horse driver of mineral water wagons for another Bristol firm, John Macy's. Ernie liked this job as he worked independently, driving around the city and surrounding villages, drumming up his own business on commission, grooming his horse every evening. He stuck at it for eleven years until becoming a trade union official at the age of twenty-nine. It gave him something approaching security, until politics intervened. On top of his basic pay of fifteen shillings, he typically made another seven shillings a week in commission. His main outgoing, rent, was five shillings and sixpence when he married and rented in the artisan district of St Werburghs.

Although unskilled, Ernie's pay and work from his late teens gave him status comparable to that of a skilled man. Here again, Bevin as myth and as reality are not quite the same.

Notably, at no point in all these jobs did the teenage or

twenty-something Ernie Bevin join a trade union. For most of these unskilled trades there wasn't a union to join. But even after he became politically active in his mid-twenties, he didn't do so until he in effect created his own union. Even in collective action, Ernie was an individualist and only really content when he was himself in charge.

A lot of young Ernie's self-confidence, and readiness to preach, came from nonconformist chapels. Continuing where he left off in Somerset and Devon, he became a Baptist Sunday school teacher soon after arriving in Bristol, joining the Bible classes of a local celebrity preacher, the Reverend James Moffat Logan of Newfoundland Road Chapel. Moffat Logan, a pacifist and socialist who had opposed Lord Salisbury and Joe Chamberlain's imperialist Boer War of 1899, had a big impact on Ernie coming into his twenties. His Sunday afternoon Bible class was a meeting place for young men of all kinds of faith who discussed politics as much as religion. Bevin's first biographer 'met two old cronies' from his early Bristol days, John Winter, a tobacco salesman, and Tom Ellison, foreman in a paper works.

> They were talking about those old days in Logan's classes. John enthusiastically asked Tom, Do you remember that afternoon when young Bevin shouted, 'If the Lord returned to Bristol now His rejoicing would be near the slums where poverty can be beaten only by the personal bravery of mothers whose faith is the only hope of their children.'[14]

Aged twenty, in 1901, Ernie was baptised by full immersion at the Baptist mission at Bethesda Chapel in Great George Street. For the next three years he was a tub-thumping local preacher, in common with many other Labour politicians of the era who, like him, 'owed more to Methodism than to Marxism'. Politics took over as Bevin approached his mid-twenties, but until well into his forties he attended St Mark's Baptist Church in Easton. Thereafter he largely stopped going to church but never renounced his faith. And he never stopped preaching: his audiences and messages just changed to politics.

Until her death in 2000, Ernie's daughter kept two of his Bibles. In one was the following inscription: 'Ernest Bevin entered into the fulness of Christ,' signed by a minister and dated 10 February 1904, with 200 Bible verses underlined. In the other, in Ernie's unmistakably halting hand, is written: 'I This evening Sept 18th 1907 I have resolved By the Grace of God to serve him where ever he may call me. May God keep me an gaurd till he shall call me home. Singed Ernest Bevin. [sic]'[15]

The chapel was to Bevin what Sandhurst was to Churchill: a university of life, as powerful in its mission-inducing legacy as Oxford or Cambridge. It took his ebullience and physical presence and taught him to speak, harangue, inspire and persuade, to impose and be imposing. It also gave him social standing. Chapelgoers were respectable, and the Bevin family, even when seriously poor and out of work, were respectable. 'It was an age when appearances accounted for everything,' wrote an early biographer. 'The congregations which he addressed as a lay preacher were, in the main, self-satisfied, particularly among the middle-aged. Men in rags were regarded as outcasts.'[16] Bevin was rarely self-satisfied and never disdained men in rags. But he was always respectable. The absence of a university education may also have been an unspoken bond between Churchill and Bevin as close colleagues in later life. In this and other respects, including stature, vigour and sheer willpower, they were peculiarly similar in their dissimilarity. One of the most moving incidents of their service together was one of Churchill's very last wartime acts, in his capacity as Chancellor of the University of Bristol: the conferring of an honorary degree on his trade unionist colleague, the ex-Bristol barrow boy. 'In Mr Bevin,' Churchill eulogised in brilliant gold-braided robes, 'I have found a colleague who has handled most intricate and difficult problems in the maintenance not only of our armies, but of the vast effort of our factories, and who has laid a heavy but not in many cases an unwelcome hand upon every human being in the Kingdom.'[17]

While living in Bristol in his twenties, Ernie went to evening classes at the Bristol Adult School Movement and the Workers' Educational Association (WEA). The lecturers were good, including the Bristol university economist H. B. Lees-Smith, who was to become a Liberal MP in 1910, switching to Labour in 1919 before serving as a minister under Ramsay MacDonald and as chairman of the Parliamentary Labour Party. Lees-Smith proposed a Prevention of Unemployment Bill in 1926 and pioneered the building of Ruskin College Oxford for adult trade unionists: very Bevinist.

The Bristol classes gave Ernie the wherewithal for dealing with political discourse and 'intellectuals', one of his life-long bugbears. One contemporary wrote, 'My impression is that it was in the Adult School that Ernest Bevin learned how to stand on his hind legs and express himself in public. He got the name for being extravagant in voicing social and industrial injustice.' This isn't quite correct: long before then Bevin's lay preaching gave him the capacity to 'stand on his hind legs', but the WEA helped give him new political texts to preach from. The same witness remembered him at a WEA trade union study session on agriculture where he was 'vocal, sitting with papers and books bursting from his pockets'.[18] The WEA was only founded in 1903, so Bevin would have been one of its first and most successful students.

Now in a steady job, Ernie settled down with his girlfriend Florence Townley. Flo, as she was always called, was the daughter of a Bristol wine taster whose family included artisans about the docks. They met at the Bristol Socialist Society and married when Ernie was twenty-five. Flo never worked after their marriage: she saw his career as a joint project. Still, contemporary accounts make only one reference to a specific political intervention by her as Mrs Bevin: when she urged Ernie to set up day nurseries for working mothers as Minister of Labour during the war and visited some of them.[19] She was always in the background, portrayed in memoirs of her husband as the supportive, slightly bored wife whose only recorded passions were music hall and shopping.

The Bevins had one daughter, Queenie, born just before the outbreak of the First World War. Q, as she was known, was in 1935 to marry Sydney Wynne, a journalist on the Labour paper the *Daily Herald*, of which Ernie was then a director. Sydney later became an executive with J. Arthur Rank, the film company, whose leading lights were friends of the Bevins during and after the Second World War. It was worlds away from the insecurity and manual labour of Ernie's childhood. But there was continuity as well as change. Until he joined the cabinet in 1940, Ernie went to the music hall with Flo most Saturday nights when he wasn't working all weekend. For their summer holidays they took cottages in seaside towns like Hove, although the couple appear to have taken only one holiday during the entire Second World War, in Scotland.

The young Bevin was a hybrid of Victorian and Edwardian. Victorian imperialism shaped him for life, as it did Churchill and Attlee, but Edwardian radicalism was equally formative. Ernie was twenty in March 1901, six weeks after the death of Queen Victoria and the accession of the more unbuttoned Edward VII. The metropolitan ferment of Edwardian Bristol radicalised Bevin's social gospel, redirecting his energies from the chapel into politics and trade unionism. Like all of Britain's great Victorian and Edwardian cities, Bristol was a cauldron: some of the richest people and places in the world alongside a mass of the poor and unemployed surging migration. Bristol's population nearly trebled in the half-century before the First World War as rural migrants, like the Bevin brothers, flooded in.

Ernie's conversion from Methodism to socialism was progressive, not damascene. As late as 1910, aged twenty-nine, after losing his election to become a socialist member of Bristol city council, he talked of becoming a missionary. But this was more an emotional response to the setback and, really, he was now embarked on a political journey. Apart from singing hymns to himself, sometimes out loud on his horse and cart, socialism and social action was now his New Testament, drawing on all he saw about.

The story goes that on his horse and cart one day, Ernie encountered an open-air meeting of the Bristol Socialist Society on the Downs. He stopped to listen, liked what he heard about ending the division between rich and poor and mobilising the masses, and went to more meetings. But he was already largely converted to socialism as an extension of Christianity, thanks to the Reverend Moffat Logan. The Bristol Socialists even had their own song sheet for Methodist-style sing-alongs after the sermon. A favourite was William Morris:

On we march then, we the workers, and the murmurs that ye hear
Is the blended sound of battle and deliverance drawing near
For the hope of every creature is the banner that we bear
And the world is marching on.

It was the same sentiment as the great Victorian hymn that Flo chose for her husband's memorial service in Westminster Abbey in 1951, one of his favourites:

Judge Eternal, throned in splendour,
Lord of lords and King of kings,
with your living fire of judgment
purge this land of bitter things;
solace all its wide dominion
with the healing of your wings.

Still the weary folk are pining
for the hour that brings release,
and the city's crowded clangor
cries aloud for sin to cease,
and the homesteads and the woodlands
plead in silence for their peace.

The Bristol socialists had a more radical and practical social gospel than the nonconformists, which attracted Ernie. 'He contrasted the attitude of the chapel folk and the "revolutionaries" to this same problem of unemployment,' wrote an early biographer. 'To the chapel folk the great panacea was Samuel Smiles' *Self Help*. It was always placed next to the Holy Bible.' Bevin and Flo were soon calling themselves socialists. They were never revolutionary in the sense of wanting to overthrow parliamentary institutions but 'attracted by the earnestness of men like Frank Sheppard, Watts Treasure and the leading lights of the Bristol Socialist Society. Most of them became, a generation later, aldermen of their city.'

The highlight was a visitation by Ben Tillett, hero of the dock strike of 1889 and founder of the 'New Unionism' that Bevin was dramatically to reinvent and expand. Tillett 'roared that the salvation of the workingman was to be achieved not through political revolution but through industrial organisation'. An ex-Bristolian as well as an ex-Risley boy circus performer, Tillett was soon to be Bevin's mentor in the dockers' union. It was Tillett who urged a mass meeting of dockers on Tower Hill during the London dock strike of 1911 to take their hats off and pray to Almighty God to strike dead Lord Devonport, the chairman of the Port of London Authority. Devonport was to become a bugbear of Bevin's.[20]

Young Ernie Bevin wanted practical action, then as at every phase of his life. Responding to a call from the Social Democratic Federation to its socialist branches in 1905 to set up 'Right to Work' committees to lobby MPs, councils and employers, the 24-year-old drayman made himself organising secretary of the Bristol Right-to-Work Committee. One of his early successes, after stunts including a silent procession of the unemployed into a Sunday morning service in Bristol Cathedral, was to persuade the city council to construct a lake in Eastville Park as an unemployment relief measure. Known for years afterwards as 'Bevin's Lake', it was Keynesianism before Keynes – public investment to create jobs in a recession – as Bevin was fond of saying in later life when he struck up a remarkable rapport with the great economist.[21]

The backdrop was a national political scene moving rapidly from the Boer War and imperial high Toryism of Queen Victoria's last Prime Minister, the third Marquess of Salisbury, to the Edwardian liberalism of Herbert Henry Asquith, David Lloyd George and his Tory-turned-Liberal disciple Winston Churchill. The 'Khaki election' of 1900, a Tory landslide in the middle of the Boer War, was followed only six years later by a Liberal landslide. The 1906 election also returned twenty-nine Labour MPs, thanks to a Lib–Lab electoral pact negotiated by William Gladstone's son Herbert and Ramsay MacDonald, secretary of the recently formed Labour Representation Committee.

Asquith's government made Britain's first serious moves towards a welfare state and progressive taxation. Dubbed 'New Liberal' for its departure from the Gladstonian orthodoxy of keeping taxation and state intervention to a minimum, it introduced old-age pensions for the over-seventies, national insurance for sickness and unemployment, land reform and labour regulation.

The defining battle between the Liberals and the still hugely powerful Tory aristocracy was Lloyd George's 'People's Budget' of 1909. Lloyd George's actual measures were a far cry from socialism. His new 'super tax' was a mere 7.5 per cent on incomes above £400k in today's money, but it shocked the sensibilities of the Edwardian aristocracy and plutocracy. The old-age pension of seven shillings and sixpence a week for the destitute over-seventies – 37.5 'new pence' – were to the fifth Earl of Rosebery, Gladstone's successor as Liberal Prime Minister in 1894 who married a Rothschild heiress, 'So prodigal of expenditure as likely to undermine the fabric of the empire.'

The aristocracy's thin-end-of-the-wedge paranoia was stoked by Lloyd George, who began pushing liberalism to new boundaries.

The House of Lords was 'five hundred men chosen at random from among the ranks of the unemployed' and 'their day of reckoning is at hand', he declaimed at Limehouse in July 1909. 'A fully equipped Duke costs as much to keep up as two Dreadnoughts [battle-ships], and Dukes are just as great a terror, and they last longer!' This alarmed Edward VII, who branded Lloyd George 'a menace to property and a Socialistic spirit'.[22] It was Liberal radicalism pointing the way to Labourism and social democracy.

Thus provoked, the House of Lords rejected the budget. Asquith thereupon won two 'Peers vs People' elections in 1910, aided by the continuing Lib–Lab electoral pact, which saw Labour advance further. The second election was required by the new King, George V, before he would agree to create enough new Liberal peers to force the House of Lords to limit its own powers by passing the Parliament Act 1911. This gave a further lease of life to Lib–Lab collaboration until the First World War was precipitated by an assassin's bullet killing Austrian archduke Franz Ferdinand in Sarajevo on 28 June 1914. A large part of British liberalism proceeded to die in the bloody carnage of the Somme, Gallipoli and Passchendaele, and over the following decade Labour was to replace the Liberals as Britain's main non-Tory party, thanks in no small part to Bevin.

However, this Edwardian battle between the Tory aristocracy and a middle-class Liberal Party was a world away from the streets of Bevin's Bristol, where conflict was just as fierce between middle-class Liberals and working-class Labour, exposing the huge gulf separating the upper, middle and working classes in early twentieth-century Britain. Then, as now, politics took some visceral forms, particularly jingoism and xenophobia, including bitter anti-Irish prejudice among the working class, stirred up by Tory and elite populists like Joseph Chamberlain and Lord Randolph Churchill, Winston's erratic aristocratic father who died of syphilis at the age of forty-five.

For socialists and trade unionists, the Edwardian Liberals engendered more animosity than admiration. Asquith and Lloyd George may have been better than Tories, but only just. Westminster and its stylised political debates were a world away to the young Bevin fighting for better pay and conditions in Bristol's docks, tramways and casual labour markets. There, the world of Charles Dickens and *Hard Times* was alive and well, with intense poverty and discontent underpinned by rigid separation, incomprehension and real hatred between the classes.

In Bevin's Bristol, Labour wasn't the junior partner of the Liberals, it was no partner at all. Despite the national Lib–Lab pact, the city did not elect its first Labour MP until 1923, and only a handful of Labour members were elected to the city council before the First World War. Before 1914 there was no question of working men or trade unionists being selected as Liberal candidates for any of the city's four parliamentary seats.

Soon after the Liberals were elected nationally in 1906, 26-year-old Bevin, by now secretary of the Bristol Right-to-Work Committee, led a delegation to lobby Augustine Birrell, Liberal MP for Bristol North. Could there be a programme of public works and house building to tackle unemployment, Bevin asked Birrell, a successful barrister like his friend Asquith and one of England's first ministers of education. According to the minutes: 'Mr Birrell shook his head and said they must think of the opposition and whether they would agree; and that it might mean the disruption of the Liberal party and they would then again have the Conservative party in power.' He wasn't even sympathetic in principle. 'Mr Birrell was fain to admit that the remedy for unemployment could only be brought about by the upset of the current commercial system. The deputation formed the opinion that it seemed plainly evident that the government had not seriously considered the question.'[23]

It was this do-nothing mindset in the face of mass unemployment and poverty that drove Bevin, like most Edwardian trade unionists, from Lib–Labbery towards socialism and an independent Labour Party.

The Right-to-Work Committee gave Bevin a taste for local politics, and in 1909 he stood for the city council. He deliberately called himself a 'socialist' rather than a 'labour' candidate; it was the same year as the People's Budget and his campaign was a mini-Limehouse. 'Vote for Bevin, who fought for the unemployed,' was his slogan for the deprived city centre St Paul's ward. 'Think!' he wrote in his election address, which called for the nationalisation of the docks:

> Last winter in Bristol there were 5,000 heads out for work, 20,000 human beings suffering want and 10,000 paupers, and you will realise the chaos, misery and degradation brought upon us by the private ownership of the means of life. I claim that Socialism, which the common ownership of those means, is the ONLY SOLUTION OF SUCH EVILS.[24]

In a fit of candidate-itis Bevin thought he was going to sweep the poll, but it didn't happen. He lost by nearly 400 votes to a Liberal businessman whose slogan was 'Vote for Gibbs, the progressive candidate, and save the ward from Socialism.' The total vote was sharply up but the defeat was decisive.

Bevin's reaction was intense anger. The campaign had been wounding: Liberal hecklers took to shouting 'apron' at him after the short sack-cloth apron he wore to protect his clothes when carting mineral water from his wagon. He hated losing, to the point of impounding the electoral register and claiming the Liberals had broken the law. The aftermath was still more ugly. Some Bristol employers, including big hotels, boycotted Bevin's water: there was an organised campaign against him which caused real bitterness. Fortunately, his employer John Macy, although a Liberal, stood by him and he kept his job, though his sales and commission fell sharply and so did his income.

On several occasions in later life Bevin claimed that he had had to steal food to live in his Bristol years. 'I found myself walking the streets, unemployed, and having to steal for my living,' he told one rally.[25] If this was true, it was of his much earlier years when he first arrived as a thirteen-year-old boy, not of his Right-to-Work years as he claimed. But it testifies to his precariousness even when he was in work, particularly once he ventured into politics – and to the bitter lifelong memories. Struggle and oppression were, for Bevin, very personal.

Bevin kept going to socialist meetings and kept up his work with the unemployed. This and his daily delivery round brought him into contact with the Bristol dockers during the Avonmouth dock strike of June/July 1910, when the whole port was brought to a standstill. Bevin was put in charge of the strikers' relief fund, although not a docker. He immediately grasped the need for joint union action between different trades and workers in the ports and its suppliers. As a carter (driver) himself, he urged the hundreds of carters around the docks to join a union, and for solidarity and impact to do so as a branch of the dockers' union, or, to give it its full title in the trades-based union world of the early twentieth century, the Dock, Wharf, Riverside and General Workers' Union.

After arguments as to whether to join the dockers' union or to set up a separate union, Bevin carried the day with his fellow carters on joining the dockers. He won by persistence and force of personality, which also got him elected founding chairman of the Bristol carters' branch of the dockers' union. It foretold the same argument about the power of building a single big union, rather than many smaller unions, which he was to win decisively at national level after the First World War in creating the Transport and General Workers' Union. Six months later, in the spring of 1911, the Bristol organiser of the dockers' union agreed that a full-time organising secretary was needed for its new and fast-expanding carters' branch, and the job went to Bevin for £2 a week.

So, having only just joined a trade union, Bevin became a full-time union official. To the end of his life his framed certificate of membership, dated 27 August 1910, with its old-fashioned Victorian illuminations and scrolls, took pride of place over the fireplace at home.

The penniless thirteen-year-old orphan who arrived in Bristol from Beers Farm with nothing more than his brothers' addresses was now embarked on the career that would take him to fame and political fortune beyond his wildest boyhood dreams. It chimed with Bevin's favourite poem, Oliver Goldsmith's 'The Deserted Village':

> Far, far away, thy children leave the land.
> Ill fares the land, to hastening ills a prey,

Where wealth accumulates, and men decay:
Princes and lords may flourish, or may fade;
A breath can make them, as a breath has made;
But a bold peasantry, their country's pride,
When once destroyed, can never be supplied…
Teach erring man to spurn the rage of gain;
Teach him, that states of native strength possest,
Tho' very poor, may still be very blest;
That trade's proud empire hastes to swift decay,
As ocean sweeps the labour'd mole away;
While self-dependent power can time defy,
As rocks resist the billows and the sky.

CHAPTER 2

DOCKERS' KC

Most politicians date their rise to power from when they won their first parliamentary seat or Cabinet post. For Bevin, it was when he created his own trade union. Not just any trade union, either, but what started as the third largest in the country and became, by his death, the largest in the free world. 'Everything that happened before the formation of the Union led *to* it. Everything that developed after it led *from* it.'[1]

The Transport and General Workers' Union (T&G) gave Bevin national power; the power to speak for the working class in a way no labour or trade union leader had done before or since. It was a case of 'cometh the hour, cometh the man': after the First World War democracy was proclaimed and British politics and society were turned upside down, but without leaders to credibly represent the numerically dominant working class, which lacked voice, unity and organisation. Bevin came to provide all three, or more of it than existed before or since, and he did it on the platform of his union. What started as a trade union in 1922 became, in the 1940s, the vanguard of a labour movement that briefly outclassed even the Conservative Party as a political vehicle. In spite of the Tories' still potent social, commercial, religious and aristocratic elites, Bevin was able to overwhelm them and wield national power. No one else in the union movement has done anything like it in England since.

It all began with Bevin's £2-a-week job as secretary of the new Bristol carters' branch of the Dock, Wharf, Riverside and General Workers' Union in the spring of 1911. It took eleven years for Bevin to get from this first trade union post to creating and leading the T&G. In 1913, two years after starting as a branch official, he became an assistant national organiser of the dockers' union, then a national organiser a year later. Six years into this job, in 1920, a single event turned him into a public figure overnight: his extraordinarily extrovert and brilliant presentation of the dockers' case for a pay rise in the Royal Courts of Justice. He became a celebrity, known as 'the Dockers' KC' – 'King's Counsel', the most elite of legal advocates – amid the vast industrial turmoil in the aftermath of the First World War. This triumph gave him the break he needed to found the Transport and General Workers' Union, an amalgamation of the dockers' union and thirteen others. Thereafter, he was to be not just the leader of the T&G but its personification until his death in 1951, if not until its name ceased to exist in 2007.

Leaders often come almost from nowhere. In Bevin's era, Stanley Baldwin rose from junior minister to become leader of the Conservative Party and Prime Minister in 1923 after just twenty-five months. Walter Citrine became general secretary of the Trades Union Congress in 1925 only twenty-one months after joining its staff. However, like most rapid ascents, both Baldwin and Citrine stepped into dead (or nearly dead) men's shoes; and, again like most leaders, they rose through established institutions and hierarchies. What makes Bevin's rise so extraordinary is that he created both the post and the institution that made him a national leader. In talent and creative genius his achievement is of the order of William Gladstone fashioning the Liberal Party in the 1860s: a new institution that advanced social progress and representative government in the nineteenth century as surely as the T&G and the Labour Party did in the twentieth century.

Keir Hardie and Ramsay MacDonald were the founders and early leaders of the Labour Party. But their creation was weak and MacDonald, tragically, sought to destroy his offspring. Bevin, like Gladstone, stayed true to his founding mission and changed Britain fundamentally.

As organiser of the Bristol carters in 1911, Bevin showed immediate flair. Within a year he had more than two thousand members in his new branch of the dockers' union and had won negotiating rights from the Bristol employers and a notable pay rise. Bevin was a pragmatist from the start. 'He was always insistent at group meetings that any claims to be made should be realistic,' a Bristol union friend recalled. 'It was no good asking for the moon. It was no good asking for something that you could not possibly visualise getting.'[2]

From the outset Bevin ventured beyond Bristol, engaging energetically in virtually every dockers' dispute in the south-west, South Wales and right across to Southampton. Dockers' union membership tripled in 1911 as industrial militancy rose in response to an economic slump and a trade union impulse that, with Lloyd George preaching democracy to the House of Lords, the working class should get its just deserts.

The Cardiff Port Strike of 1911 was especially fraught and became a crash course for Bevin in strike leadership. Non-unionised 'blackleg' labour, intended to break the strike, was literally shipped into the port of Cardiff by the shipowners on a vessel named *Lady Jocelyn*. Pickets from the dockers' and railwaymen's unions stopped the 'blackleg ship' from docking and foiled an attempt to bring in 'blacklegs' by land. It was akin to a siege. Violence erupted on the picket lines and police and troops were sent in by then Home Secretary Winston Churchill. Fortunately for the union, ports strikes were spreading nationwide 'like prairie fire', most notably to London, and the employers could not fight on so many fronts. Even the diehard Lord Devonport, of Tillett's invective, was forced to settle in London. After two years of almost constant struggle Bevin became a hero of the South Wales dockers, who in 1913 'signified their appreciation of the services rendered by presenting Brother Bevin with a gold watch and chain'.[3]

Bevin spent a lot of time and energy creating new branches of the dockers' union virtually from scratch across the south-west. Despite Dorset's legendary Tolpuddle Martyrs of 1834, sentenced to transportation to Australia for daring to create a union, there was still no West Country trade union movement worth the name eighty years later. In 1913 the dockers' union had fewer than 500 members in Plymouth; Bevin doubled this number by the outbreak of war in 1914. He scored an unlikely success in Bridgwater's brick, timber and coal yards, recruiting 2,500 members by 1914 and holding a May Day procession there at which, according to the *Dockers' Record*, 'Brother Bevin was in splendid form'.[4]

Bevin was not starting from scratch. He had long ago learned from the Reverend Moffat Logan and Ben Tillett, and perhaps originally from his mother and Mrs Veysey, how to harangue and to cajole, if not always to charm. He had learned from his Bristol university lecturers the political and economic texts to quote and mis-quote as well as any Oxford PPE-ist. He had also honed his keen eye for stunts, which after the war made him the Dockers' KC. Just as he had led Bristol's unemployed into the cathedral to protest unemployment, so one of his early stunts in the union was to lead a demonstration, brandishing two apples on a stick, in protest at a drayman being sentenced to prison for taking two apples from a bin on the wharf. It made the front pages of the Bristol papers and there was a retrial.

Bevin built his union organiser credentials through hard grind: endless slow journeys by train, overnight in cold and damp lodgings, sandwiches and hasty station meals, meetings of half a dozen or a dozen people, week after week and including many weekends. He had two serious breakdowns in these early years and had to take several weeks off work both times. But all this earned him an 'action man' reputation and got him the job of assistant national organiser in 1913, and then, a year later, on the eve of the First World War, promotion to become one of the three national organisers. He was now one of the half-dozen men at the head of the union, although he carried on living in Bristol.

Bevin's early speeches were full of invective and denunciations. He sang amen to Ben Tillett, proclaiming to the dockers' union conference in 1912, 'Capitalism is capitalism as a tiger is a tiger; and both are savage and pitiless towards the weak.' However, even in these early years, Bevin abhorred political violence. The philosophy of 'direct action' to seize power on a national scale through mass strikes – called 'syndicalism' at the time – was the gospel of many union and socialist activists in those years, but it was only Bevin's up to a point. He believed in concerted industrial action to improve workers' conditions, even to coerce the government, but not to bring down the government or to launch class war.

Bevin was revolutionary about ends, democratic about means: a constant theme of this biography. His revolutionary goal was what he came to call 'economic democracy': an ideal of a classless society based on the equal value of each citizen, but brought about peacefully and not by dictatorship in any form, including the dictatorship of one class over another. As he put it in the *Dockers' Record* in 1920, his Methodism in full flow: 'A new life of liberty and love will take the place of the master-class oppression; men and women will walk in a newer and purer world.' He addressed the syndicalist issue directly when standing as a Labour candidate in the 1918 general election. 'I cannot see how you are going to build up a higher civilised state unless there is a fundamental change in the present organisation of society. If my principles are accepted it is a revolution,' he said, but he immediately added: 'I stand for a social revolution brought about by a freely elected Parliament.'[5]

Bevin was against the First World War, like many Labour and trade union leaders, although most of their rank-and-file disagreed. MacDonald resigned the Labour Party leadership rather than support war, while Bevin spoke on the Downs in Bristol, 'calling for action by the workers in all countries to prevent war'.[6]

Bevin was never a pacifist and was contemptuous of the 'intellectual' MacDonald even in those early days, but he was deeply suspicious about the Asquith government's justification for the war. 'Personally I decline to cast another vote in this business until I know what really happened,' he told the first TUC annual conference he attended, in his home city of Bristol in September 1915. Indeed, he was contemptuous of almost all political leaders in these years. He was in the hall when Lloyd George addressed the conference and urged stronger labour support for the war effort, a performance memorably described by Beatrice Webb as 'exactly like a conjuror'. Bevin's first

TUC speech was made on the final day of the conference. It was a call for a Minister of Labour to be included in the Cabinet, the post he was to hold in the next world war. But Bevin was vehemently against Labour joining Lloyd George's coalition in 1916, when the party was offered the new Ministry of Labour. In his first Labour Party conference speech in 1917 he vitriolically attacked Arthur Henderson, who had taken over as party leader from MacDonald, and other Labour MPs who joined Lloyd George's coalition.[7]

Francis Williams put it elegantly: 'Bevin followed a well-established pattern of emotional demagogy the advantages of which to a newcomer set upon forcing his way to the front of a left wing movement have not been overlooked by others before or since.'[8]

Bevin strongly opposed conscription too. Fortunately for him, as a full-time union official in a key industry, he was exempt from it, perhaps the best unintended consequence for him of becoming a trade unionist. Bevin's war was constant union meetings and negotiations, mostly in the south-west but playing a part in national wartime innovations too, including the first national wage agreement for transport workers. He was also appointed a member of the Port and Transit Executive Committee, set up by Lloyd George to deal with the serious hold-up of traffic at the docks. This gave him his first experience of interacting with government departments, reinforcing his view that 'the power to negotiate is the most valuable thing that we can have'.[9] It also brought him to Lloyd George's personal attention. There was even an intriguing invitation to serve as a labour adviser in No. 10, which he turned down.

Bevin's wartime theme was his by now trademark plea for solidarity behind majority decisions, including the decision to prosecute the war itself. 'Tillett and I had some discussion and I came to the conclusion that I would do my best to preserve the economic unity of the men I represent and accept passively the opinions of the majority of men,' he told a transport workers' conference in June 1917. The war intensified his hostility to the 'ruling class' and the 'corrupt' status quo. 'The other class are not superior to us in brains' became his refrain, and 'if an industry can be socialised for war it can be socialised for peace'.[10] Disdain for the old 'governing class' was now outright contempt.

Apart from sheer survival, maybe the best thing that happened to Bevin during the war was his selection, on Ben Tillett's recommendation, to go to the United States as one of the TUC's two fraternal delegates to the annual convention of the American Federation of Labor, in 1916. Given the wartime hazards of the transatlantic crossing – the *Lusitania* had just been sunk – there was little competition for the privilege, so while most of his fellow working men were in the trenches on the Western Front, Bevin was embarking on a six-week tour of America. It was his first trip overseas and, unlike many of his compatriots on the Somme, he came back alive, and with constructive experiences.

America made a huge impression on the 35-year-old union official, who had only recently discovered London, let alone the New World. There was the ten-day voyage from Liverpool; Grant's tomb and Grand Central Station in New York; a ceremony in Washington to mark the start of construction for the American Federation of Labor's new eight-storey headquarters, which gave him the inspiration to build the equally imposing Transport House a decade later; the five-day rail journey to San Francisco, crossing the Rockies with stops at Denver and Salt Lake City; the Golden Gate and an exhibition to celebrate the opening of the Panama Canal; all this as well as visits to the headquarters in Buffalo of the International Longshoremen's Association, the American dockers' union, and the film-makers' 'Universal City' in Los Angeles, which began a bedazzlement with Hollywood.

This 1916 American tour was an electric, overwhelming experience for Bevin and it made a huge impact on him. He never had much truck thereafter with anti-Americanism, which loomed large with many Labour politicians of his generation. He also became seriously knowledgeable about international labour practices, even more so as he engaged in European and imperial industrial visits and trade unionism between the wars. He became not just a trade union leader but a genuine expert in international industrial relations and organisation. This gave him a new stylistic USP of invariably, in any dispute or debate, painting a rhetorical 'big picture' of what was going on abroad, which always added something interesting and arresting, even when only half true or tendentious. Few others in Bevin's manifold committees or meetings had been, like him, to New York and Washington, let alone to Denver and Buffalo. While others made their stock references to 'workers of the world', Bevin had actually participated in the largest representative assembly of workers in the largest industrial nation in the world. 'It broadened my views in conception of the great world problems ... how akin we were in human desires, weaknesses and ideas; it emphasised that the need of the workers was a common one, and the struggle a common one,' he wrote in the *Dockers' Record* on his return.[11] All of this began to equip him, idiosyncratically, to become not only leader of the Transport and General Workers' Union but also Foreign Secretary in a Labour government.

The highlight of Bevin's 1916 tour was meeting the genial, dictatorial Samuel Gompers, founder and president of the American Federation of Labor (AFL). First elected AFL leader thirty-four years previously and president continuously since 1895, 'the stumpy, flamboyant yet shrewd cigar-maker from London exerted a personal power unknown in the TUC or its constituent unions' – until Bevin, that is. Gompers was the greatest trade union boss in American history, the apostle of 'business unionism'. Part of Gompers and the 1916 trip stayed physically attached to Bevin until the end of his life. As a fraternal present, the AFL president attempted to place a gold ring decorated with the figure of a naked woman on his English visitor's hand. The ring was too small. 'What's that you got – a bunch of bananas?' Gompers joshed. The ring was enlarged and Bevin wore it for the rest of his life. In 1949 he used it to seal the North Atlantic Treaty that created NATO.[12]

Bevin returned to Bristol and sought to become the Gompers of Britain.

The times were favourable. Unions were ascendant at the end of the 'war to end all wars'. So was industrial and political pugilism. Bevin's knack was pugilism in pursuit – usually – of common sense, even when it was initially unpopular on his own side. At the 1916 TUC conference in Birmingham, for example, he argued for a postwar international labour peace congress including the Germans, a proposal that was greeted by protests. 'You have got to take the Germans into consultation after this war. You have got to reckon with the Germans as an economic factor,' he persisted.[13] He was voted down, but he was clearly right and was soon seen to be so.

Bevin stood for Labour in Bristol Central in the 1918 general election. It was another khaki election; Labour was by now in opposition to peak Lloyd George, so Bevin was never going to win, and the experience just reinforced his trade unionism.

It is hard to exaggerate the dislocation and sense of impending social revolution in the months after the armistice in November 1918.

The Spanish flu pandemic was raging. Crowns and empires were toppled Europe-wide. Elites everywhere, including in Buckingham Palace, feared the Russian Revolution might be coming their way fast. The two years after the war saw the fiercest civil conflicts Britain has ever known short of civil war, alongside a real and terrible war of independence in Ireland. Between 1911 and 1914, itself a turbulent period of industrial strife, the days lost to strikes had been an annual average 17.7 million, falling to 4.2 million during the First World War. In 1919 and 1920, though, the figure was about 40 million each year, an astronomic scale of social and industrial breakdown. Much of the country was barely functioning. Lloyd George told fellow world leaders at the Versailles peace conference:

A feeling not of depression, but of passion and revolt reigns in the breasts of the working class against the conditions of life that prevailed before the war. It is expressed in strikes and a certain aversion to work. All signs go to show that the striving is as much for social and political changes as for increases in wages.[14]

We saw in the Introduction how Attlee's lieutenant Francis Williams regarded Bevin as a potential revolutionary leader after the First World War. Maybe Lloyd George did too; he said to his confidant George Riddell in March 1919: 'He is a powerful fellow, with a bull neck and a huge voice – a born leader. If there is trouble, mark my words. You will hear more of Bevin.'[15] However, the 'bull neck born leader' was focused on wages not revolutions, and it was this that would gain him lasting national prominence and respect.

As the post-war strike wave intensified, the dockers' union made a claim for a sixteen-shillings-a-day minimum wage for Britain's

125,000 dockers. This was hardly a king's ransom, and it was far less than Bevin had been earning with his horse and cart delivering mineral water in Bristol twenty years earlier. Pre-war, the employers would nonetheless have rejected such a claim with contempt. They dared not do so in the revolutionary ferment of October 1919, but they were loath to concede. Instead, they latched on to legislation just enacted, in a bid by Lloyd George to contain industrial disputes, making it possible for a quasi-judicial Court of Inquiry to be established at the request of both sides to an industrial dispute. The wealthy ship owners thought this would inevitably favour them, once their expensive barrister dominated the courtroom.

However, they didn't count on Bevin, who sensed the opportunity to seize a national stage. He persuaded his reluctant union executive committee to agree to a Court of Inquiry rather than launch yet another strike. Then, he appointed himself as legal counsel for the union, presented the case personally in court and ran rings around the expensive counsel for the employers. He took complete charge of the courtroom, not only on the facts and arguments, but also in his emotional range and the oratorical tricks of the barrister's trade, which he deployed better than the men in wigs and gowns.

This alone, however, did not catapult Bevin to prominence. What made him, and what he intuited when going for the inquiry in the first place, was that the performance was taking place in the Royal Courts of Justice on the Strand, with all the panoply of the law in its inner sanctum in Central London. This was the chance to take on the Establishment face to face and on fairly equal terms. He was dubbed the 'The Dockers' KC', the sobriquet that made him, because he was up against one of the grandest KCs in the land, Sir Lynden Macassey KC, in a court presided over by a Law Lord, Lord Shaw of

Dunfermline. It was David vs Goliath in the palace of the Philistines. There was also novelty value: this was the first such Court of Inquiry held under Lloyd George's new legislation to mitigate major trade disputes, which attracted a lot of attention as well as giving Bevin maximum scope for defining the rules of engagement. It helped that Lord Shaw, while impeccably Establishment, was also a former Liberal MP and gave the 'Dockers' KC' latitude in conducting the case.

Bevin's opening statement to the court was epic. Starting on 3 February 1920, it lasted eleven hours, spread over the first three sittings of the inquiry. There was a long applause when he finished and a commendation from the judge. Although legally untrained, Bevin had spent weeks preparing meticulously with a team of researchers and submitted a mass of supporting documents culled from official reports and statistics.

Bevin was unintimidated by the formalities. He had long since lost stage fright and deference and he was used to performing in public. 'The Court will appreciate that this is an unusual environment for me to be in and also that the proceedings are very novel for the whole Labour movement of this country,' he began with mock trepidation.

> We have agreed as transport workers to submit our claims to the test of public inquiry, first because we are convinced of the justice of our claim, and secondly because we have no objection to the whole question of the standard of life being open for public inquiry. We hope it will serve not only to obtain what our men desire but to influence public opinion to a higher conception of what that standard of life ought to be.[16]

He was playing the media from the start.

The eleven hours following alternated between close factual argument and emotional descriptions of the poverty and precariousness of the dockers' existence. 'The dockers have had one of the highest death rates in the country due to their irregular life and the horrible slum conditions,' he said in one graphic passage, likening the morning call for labour at the dock gate to a modern slave market.

> Men were injured and it was a common thing for the bullying foreman to say: 'Throw him in the wing and get on with the work...' If the men dared to protest ... it was: 'To the office and get your money and clear out.' And then they might stand on the stones for weeks ... as an example to other people for obedience.[7]

Sensing the mood of the court and the media, Sir Lynden Macassey did not attempt to patronise his opponent. 'I think we may predict for Mr. Bevin in the cause which he has so much at heart a very great future,' he said after the union official's opening statement. But Bevin's best was yet to come. When Sir Lynden sought to demonstrate that the employers were right to say that wages were adequate at three pounds four shillings and two pence a week, and that they did not need six pounds a week, Bevin pulled a brilliant stunt. With his secretary, Mae Forcey, who before working for Bevin had been a publicity agent for a 'theatrical impresario', he went to Canning Town. There, taking Macassey's wages figure and dividing this into what it allowed a docker to spend on food for a family of five per meal, they spent this sum on ingredients. The following morning, he presented to the court five plates with paltry, shrivelled quantities of bacon, cheese and vegetables. 'I ask the Court, my lord, to examine the dinner which counsel for the employers considers adequate to sustain the strength of a docker hauling seventy-one tons of wheat a day on his back,' said Bevin as the journalists crowded around and later took photos of the scraps on the plates.[18] One of the photos is among the illustrations to this book: a photo is worth a thousand words, as Bevin well knew.

When Sir Lynden then unwisely called a Cambridge economist to argue that calorific value could be maximised better than on those plates, Bevin produced more plates the following morning with measly 'rations' of fish to show that the particular choice of food made little difference. The docker's wife, 'the greatest Chancellor of the Exchequer that ever lived', couldn't make 'something from nothing', noted the Dockers' KC drily. 'I want to ask any employer, or you, or the Court, whether a Cambridge professor is a competent judge of a docker's breakfast?'[19]

Then the coup de grace: Bevin produced the lunch menu for the Savoy Grill, to show that the shipowners had rather different ingredients for their own dinner.

'People thought all that business with plates was just a clever stunt,' he told Francis Williams years later. 'It wasn't. These fellows quote statistics but they forget about human beings. I had to make 'em remember they were dealing with human lives – it's terribly easy to forget that when you're sitting in a Court or on a Government Commission.'[20]

The cross-examination of witnesses was done with equal flair. Bevin pressed Sir Alfred Booth, chairman of Cunard Steamship Co., on the existing rate for dockers in Liverpool:

BEVIN: Do you seriously suggest that [three pounds four shillings and two pence] is a living wage?

BOOTH: I do.

BEVIN: I put it to you very straight. Could you maintain your family on it?

BOOTH: No, I could not.

BEVIN: Then are you any more to the community than the docker who handles your ship?

BOOTH: That is a matter of opinion. As an individual, certainly not.

BEVIN: Do you think it right to ask a man to live and maintain himself on what you would not dream of asking your own family to live upon?

BOOTH: It is not a question of what I ask him to live upon; it is what the economic conditions render possible.[21]

After twenty days of this, Lord Shaw made his ruling. He accepted the dockers' wage claim in full. It was a famous victory. The judge even publicly congratulated Bevin on his 'cogent and impressive' case.

After the final hearing there was a procession, complete with banners and a band, from the Royal Courts of Justice to the Royal Albert Hall for a huge rally. 'In the whole history of our movement,' said Harry Gosling, a veteran of the 1889 dock strike, 'there has never been a case put more clearly and with greater ability than your case has been put by Ernest Bevin.'[22] The victor rose to the occasion. The dispute was about 'something bigger than merely an inquiry into sixteen shillings a day', he said. It was 'a platform to unfold the great human tragedy of men and women fighting year in and year out against the terrible economic conditions with which they have been surrounded,' and to give 'those who toil the mastery of their own lives'.

Revelling in personal triumph, and turning it into a triumph of the working class, Bevin told the dockers' union conference a few weeks later:

> I have been praised for the case in the court and now they are be-ginning to say I have been to the university. The great struggle of my own people has been my university. I do not decry education. I lament the lack of it and I curse the other class for monopolising it … Before our movement developed, you responded to the whip of the master. I want you to respond to the call of liberty.[23]

In the event, the call of liberty was soon silenced. Within three years the employers had drastically cut the new pay rates from sixteen shillings to ten. Faced with mounting unemployment, and by now a Conservative government in office with the semi-revolutionary ferment ended, there was little the union could do to resist. No one blamed Bevin, though. His reputation as 'the Dockers' KC' did not devalue: it was the prestige on which, within two years, he clinched the formation of the Transport and General Workers' Union.

Bevin's national profile was to rise further in another controver-sy immediately after the Shaw Inquiry: the 1920 crisis on war with Russia. This pitted him directly against Lloyd George.

After the end of war with Germany in 1918, Lloyd George and his belligerent lieutenant Churchill had engaged Britain, by proxy, on the Polish side in the Russo-Polish war, hoping to bring down Lenin's new and apparently fragile Bolshevik regime. This had seemed possible in 1919, sharpening still further the industrial strife in Britain, which was partly communist inspired. But by the summer of 1920, following a brilliant defence and counter-attack masterminded by Trotsky, the Red Army was threatening Warsaw, and Lloyd George moved towards direct intervention against Soviet Russia. In early August, a British ultimatum demanded an immediate cessation of hostilities by Lenin, with the threat of war. 'We must face [the imperative to defeat Russia] with the same unanimity and the same courage with which we faced the crisis of 1914,' thundered *The Times*.[24]

Labour and the trade unions, scarred as they were by the headlong rush to war in July 1914, were staunchly opposed to a war with Russia, let alone to seeking to destroy its new communist regime. Much of the left was positively on the side of Lenin and the Bolsheviks, while the rest – including Bevin – did not deny their right to rule Russia. A Council of Action was set up to mobilise against war. The crisis flared up for Bevin personally when dockers in London's East India Dock discovered crates to be loaded on the *Jolly George* labelled 'On His Majesty's Service: Munitions for Poland'. They sent for the 'Dockers' KC'. Bevin declared that if the dockers refused to load the boat, he would support them 'to the hilt'. Indeed, at the dockers' union conference in Plymouth the following week, he was uncompromising: 'Whatever may be the merits or demerits of the theory of government of Russia, that is a matter for Russia, and we have no right to determine their government, any more than we would tolerate Russia determining our form of government.'[25]

The *Jolly George* left London for Poland without the munitions.

Brightly painted in his *Jolly George* and 'Dockers' KC' triumphs, Bevin led a Labour and trade union delegation to see Lloyd George on 9 August, decrying war and war by proxy against Russia. It was his first visit to 10 Downing Street and his first exercise in national leadership beyond his union. He was only thirty-nine but showed no great deference to the Prime Minister. 'We know our people are with us. This is not merely a political action but action representing the full force of Labour,' he told Lloyd George. 'We believe also, judging by the enormous support we enjoy from other classes of the community, that we are representing the desire and will of the great majority of the British people.'[26] He then sought, pretty effectively, to nail Lloyd George down on 'war or no war':

PRIME MINISTER: Do you mean to say that Labour will not permit the Government to send a single pair of boots to people who are fighting for their liberty [in Poland]?

ERNEST BEVIN: Labour will consider the position when that occasion arises.

PRIME MINISTER: Very well. That is quite good enough for me.

ERNEST BEVIN: But I want to make this perfectly clear – that that condition has not arisen.

PRIME MINISTER: No. You do not need to make that clear to me, because I agree with you.

ERNEST BEVIN: But, suppose the Polish people themselves agreed upon a constitution which did not suit the allied powers?

PRIME MINISTER: What have we to do with that? That is their business, not ours.

ERNEST BEVIN: It is their business?

PRIME MINISTER: Certainly. What have we to say to that? I do not care what the Constitution is. If they like to have the Mikado there, that is their business.

ERNEST BEVIN: That is what we wanted to know.[27]

Bevin did not stop there. He put plans together for a general strike if the government moved towards war with Russia and he organised a huge rally of more than a thousand trade unionists and Labour members in Central Hall Westminster on 13 August, making a passionate speech for 'peace and the unity of nations in place of the terrible struggles of the past years'.[28] He also met the Soviet government's representatives in London several times, urging respect for Polish independence, as well as meeting Lloyd George again in Downing Street to discuss the proposed peace terms between Poland and Russia. Soon afterwards there was a Russo-Polish ceasefire and armistice, and no British intervention. Another 1914 had been averted.

Alan Bullock believes Bevin's diplomacy with the Russians and his warnings to Lloyd George 'had some effect' in stopping direct British intervention and securing the Russo-Polish armistice in October.[29] Bevin had threatened a general strike to bring about a radical change in government policy well beyond industrial relations and it had worked, giving lie to the notion that he would never countenance such a move or that it couldn't work in 'constitutional' Britain. Maybe the circumstances were unique, but so are all circumstances. Since Lloyd George did not persist with war, the implications for the labour movement encroaching on constitutional government were never tested. Bevin had calculated coolly, bid high, led strongly and won, as he was to do time and again as union leader and Foreign Secretary in the years to come.

Stopping a war with Russia in 1920 was a victory for Bevin. 'Ironically enough, this first incursion into foreign affairs was almost his last which pleased the British communists,' recalled Christopher Mayhew, his junior minister at the Foreign Office in 1945.[30]

However, this was not an isolated incursion into European affairs. By now Bevin was making regular working visits to the Continent and they continued until 1939. The year 1920 saw him in Oslo at the

International Transport Federation conference, where he promised British financial assistance for dock strikes in Rotterdam and Amsterdam. In 1921 he was at the federation's annual conference in Geneva, taking Flo with him for a holiday too. In 1922 he was in Vienna with the federation, speaking strongly against reparations and the Versailles Treaty in a debate on reconstruction ('This incitement to nationalist feeling in the various states is in reality a crime'). Also in 1922, he went to Berlin for a conference of international socialists beset by arguments about engagement with Lenin. This stoked Bevin's growing antipathy to communism. 'Up to the time I attended the Berlin conference I did not understand the Russian position as well as I did when I came away. It is contrary absolutely to our conception of democracy,' he told the T&G's first conference in 1923, opposing a communist-led move to affiliate to the 'Third International', the Moscow-led international alliance of communist parties.[31]

However, a coda to the *Jolly George* crisis chipped away some of Bevin's newfound prestige. He had just become a director of the *Daily Herald*, the Labour newspaper. This itself was testament to his growing stature in the labour movement, although he was not yet even a union general secretary. However, in a clumsy, stupid manoeuvre, the left-wing firebrand MP and future party leader George Lansbury and his son got involved in a backdoor deal in September 1920, by which the *Herald* ended up taking Soviet money. It was straight out of John le Carré: go-betweens ostensibly negotiating supplies of paper for printing presses, while a mysterious package of Russian jewels was converted into cash in London. Bevin was uninvolved, but when the farrago started to become public Lloyd George, still smarting from the *Jolly George* incident, wrote him an open letter and got the better of the subsequent exchanges when

Bevin equivocated on what he knew and when. To me, the striking point is that Bevin now merited such prime ministerial attention. Equally significant was Bevin's reaction when he properly understood what had happened. He was adamant the *Herald* should not take the Soviet money. He forced the go-between to resign as a director of the newspaper and instead raised its price to cover the shortfall.[32] He did not equivocate and he acted decisively.

Bevin's transformational manoeuvre, in the wake of the Shaw Inquiry and the *Jolly George*, was to promote the creation of an amalgamated union from the existing dockers and transport unions, with himself in charge. 'Joint action and autonomy are impossible,' was his motto.[33] And *sotto voce*: joint action without him in charge was inaction.

The idea of an amalgamated dockers' and transport workers' union dated back to before the First World War. At Ben Tillett's initiative, the National Transport Workers' Federation was created in 1911, nominally covering some 150,000 members. It had a secretary and a committee but the dockers' union and the other unions in the federation surrendered no real decision-making power. Some were bitter rivals for members, and much of the committee's time was taken up dealing with recriminations. Another attempt at amalgamation was initiated in 1914 but fell on the outbreak of war. Bevin had given strong support at the time in a speech remarkable for its self-confidence even then. He had only been a national union organiser for a year, yet was already boasting that what he'd done in Bristol was a national template. Or, as he put it: 'I happen to be where the dockers and carters are in one union and there the carters have been more successful than in any other town in the country.'[34]

Immediately after the war, in the crisis years of 1919 and 1920, amalgamation was relegated as a priority behind building up the 'triple alliance' of transport, miners and railway unions. The 'triple alliance' was pushing towards what was called a 'general strike': a co-ordinated strike of all the unions in these three sectors on the back of bitter disputes in Britain's then biggest industry, coal mining, and the wider post-war industrial unrest. There was critical ambiguity, including in Bevin's speeches, as to whether such a general strike would be essentially industrial or political in purpose. This equivocation persisted until the collapse of the actual General Strike of 1926.

However, already showing a good grasp of the realities of power, Bevin saw the triple alliance as both too much and too little. It was too much to attempt a workable federation across three vast trade union sectors, each of which, including his own, was itself a weak hotchpotch federation of dozens of unions. Yet it was also too little, in that the triple alliance did virtually nothing to promote greater unity within each of its three constituent sectors. Bevin saw clearly that the key to leveraging the strength of the dockers was the creation of a single 'amalgamated' union from the numerous existing dock and road transport unions, focused on common demands for better pay and conditions, rather than investing in a loose and fragile alliance with unions in radically different industrial sectors – particularly the miners, whose leadership, with strong communist elements, was focused on maximum political disruption. The temporary collapse of the triple alliance on 'Black Friday', 15 April 1921, was Bevin's opportunity to propel the dockers' union towards amalgamation, and he seized it with alacrity.

Black Friday presaged all the elements that bedevilled the General Strike five years later. Faced with a crunch decision on support for the miners following big wage cuts in the intensifying recession of 1921, which was exacerbated by the post-war privatisation of the

coal mines that had been nationalised during the war, the railway
and dockers' unions backed away. The miners' federation executive
was itself divided on a strike once Lloyd George, to divide and rule,
offered the miners a Court of Inquiry on the model of the Shaw
Inquiry. Once this became known, the other unions were still less
inclined to support the miners. 'Why,' asked Bevin in a fractious
meeting with the miners' leaders, 'seeing we had to use considerable
influence to get our people to accept a Court of Inquiry, [do] we
now have to use our influence to get them to strike because you will
not accept a Court of Inquiry?'[35]

A key issue was who would have the power to call off a general
strike: the triple alliance or the miners? The miners would not accept
a triple alliance decision, while the dockers and railwaymen would
not mortgage themselves to the miners. Crucial for Bevin was the
avowedly communist miners' leader A. J. Cook and his revolutionary agenda. 'If I had to live through that Friday again in exactly the
same circumstances, with exactly the same machine, I should take
exactly the same action,' Bevin said unrepentantly after Black Friday.
To his mind, the triple alliance had shown itself to be 'a paper
alliance'.[36]

Seizing on growing anxiety within his own union about the recession and employer backlash, at the end of 1920 Bevin convinced
his dockers' union executive, and a critical mass of eighteen allied
unions, to start amalgamation negotiations. 'We need fewer unions
and more trade unionists,' was his mantra.[37] He quashed an earlier
amalgamation initiative from outside the dockers' union, which he
feared might marginalise the dockers – and himself. Bevin denied
that he was to blame for its collapse, but it failed to get the support
required in a ballot, with a suspiciously high abstention rate among

members in his fiefdom of Bristol and the south-west. The existing Transport Workers' Federation meanwhile sought to reinvent itself, which Bevin also strongly opposed as a talking shop not under his control, with a communist general secretary in Bob Williams.

A key ally in Bevin's ultimately successful move towards an amalgamation led by his own dockers' union was Harry Gosling, secretary of a smaller riverside union, the London Society of Watermen, Lightermen and Bargemen. Since the Shaw Inquiry, Gosling had become an ardent fan of the younger Bevin, who he saw as a protégé. Gosling was well liked and put the case in personal and emotional terms to the amalgamation conference held at Leamington Spa in September 1921:

All the time [throughout the Shaw Inquiry] we were trembling in case we had to expose the weakness of the solidarity of those whom we represented. Bevin had to consult this body and that body which said he had not said enough for them but had said too much for somebody else, because he had no Executive behind him that represented the whole thing.[38]

Bevin's dockers' union voted for amalgamation by 117,500 votes to 1,463 in early 1921; the second largest dock labourers' union, with 80,000 members, also voted heavily for amalgamation and only three of the seventeen others in these initial negotiations voted against. Bevin had the threads of the amalgamation negotiations in his hands from the outset. He was elected provisional general secretary, over the general secretary of the United Vehicle Workers union by 225,000 votes to 130,000 at a delegate conference of the constituent unions in the St Pancras Hotel on 11 May 1921. Harry Gosling was elected provisional chairman. In the all-members ballot for the general secretary's job proper at the end of 1921, Bevin crushed the communist Bob Williams by 96,842 votes to 7,672. Gosling became president unopposed.

Except that Gosling wasn't really unopposed, and therein lies a tale of Bevinist ruthlessness and guile. Ben Tillett, outgoing general secretary and continuing patron saint of the dockers' union, wanted to be president of the amalgamated union and would probably have won the post in a ballot. Bevin stopped him. He wanted Harry Gosling, partly because Gosling came from a different union and demonstrated diversity, but also because he didn't want competition at the top. He told Tillett bluntly that he could not stand, using the diversity argument to convince this potential threat to his leadership. Tillett knew the score and complained that he had been 'elbowed out'. However, he ultimately went along with it, not least because Bevin sweetened the pill considerably. Tillett kept his previous salary and was appointed international and political secretary of the T&G, which gave him lots of freebies.[39]

It was clientelism too for the 250 full-time officers of the fourteen unions joining the amalgamated T&G. They all got jobs in the new union and none lost out financially. 'You would not be in this room today as you are if I had not been congenial personally,' Bevin the Boss told them at the T&G's first delegate conference.[40] But none of the 250 was allowed to occupy a position that rivalled his. No one formally deputised during Bevin's breakdown in exhaustion at the end of 1922, when he was off work for two months, and it was two years before an assistant general secretary was appointed. Furthermore, both occupants of this post before 1945 were under Bevin's thumb. Even when Arthur Deakin, assistant general secretary from 1935, took over the running of the union when Bevin became Minister of Labour in 1940, it was only as acting general secretary: Bevin did not formally resign the leadership until he became Foreign Secretary in 1945.

Apart from Gosling's position as president, no other official of the union was elected by the whole membership. All other paid officials were appointed by the executive or its smaller General Purposes Committee, invariably on Bevin's nomination. Gosling himself was not replaced when he died in 1930, and he was lucky to survive that long as Bevin had tried to retire him in 1924 but was overruled by the executive in a rare rebuff.

Bevin took great care with the constitution of the amalgamated Transport and General Workers' Union. According to Francis Williams he applied lessons from the American constitution 'which continued to fascinate him from the days of his first visit to the United States'.[41] To avoid the Balkanisation of a union covering two large occupational sectors, docking and road transport, Bevin set up five 'trade' groups representing the principal occupations, but overlay on this an 'area' structure that obliged officials dealing with the different trades and occupations to collaborate. The union's executive, conceived as a kind of Parliament, comprised lay elected representatives of both the groups and the areas, plus the general secretary as the only directly elected national official. Unusually for large unions of the time, paid officials could not be voting members of the executive but were 'in attendance', which again strengthened Bevin's position vis-à-vis his subordinates.

The allocation of functions between the various tiers was also carefully defined by Bevin. Negotiations and disputes were the prime responsibility of the trade groups, which had far more autonomy in these respects than in most previous union amalgamations.

But crucially, the power to call strikes, and call them off, was vested in the central executive – i.e. largely in Bevin, who thereby had the power to intervene in negotiations, and take them over, whenever he saw fit, but to stand back when he didn't. It was a sophisticated constitution that stood the test of time, being barely reformed for the next thirty years apart from through the addition of more groups and areas as the union quadrupled in size and the number of unions amalgamating with the T&G more than doubled.

AMALGAMATION

Transport and General Workers

FELLOW WORKERS:—

The great scheme of Amalgamation will be submitted to you for ballot forthwith.

The scheme has received the considered judgement of the Executives of each Union that are parties to it, and at a great Delegate Conference in London it was endorsed unanimously. (See Resolution overleaf.)

We are convinced this is the right step to take to secure the necessary power and efficiency to deal with the problems that must be solved by the Movement.

Our Unions have, in their respective sections, played a wonderful part in the past, but PROGRESS DEMANDS that existing methods shall give way to new.

CAPITAL IS WELL ORGANISED—EVERY TRADE IS INTERWOVEN AND INTERLINKED.

The great industries on the employers' side stand together ! !

Labour must do likewise. Whoever stands in the way of this great change in methods of organisation is doing a grave injustice not only to the present generations, but to the children yet unborn! The scheme allows for the creation of a GREAT and POWERFUL UNION.

It pools its financial resources.
It gives opportunity to create efficient methods of negotiations and handling disputes.
It gets rid of jealousy between Unions.
It allows for the rank and file to co-operate in port, waterway, road transport and factory.
It gives the officials greater scope; a greater opportunity of acquiring knowledge—placing them on an equal footing with employers in dealing with your problems.
It provides for each section to have its own National Committee.
It allows opportunity to shape its program and policy, at the same time bringing to the assistance of any one section both the moral and financial strength of the remainder.
It proposes to organise the whole of the workers engaged in the respective industries covered by the new Union—administrative, clerical and manual.
It is the creation of a NEW MACHINE.
It will ultimately not only talk of wages, but exercise greater power and control.

WE MOST EARNESTLY APPEAL TO EVERY MEMBER OF THE AMALGAMATING UNIONS TO SECURE THEIR BALLOT PAPER AND UTILISE THEIR VOTE IN ITS FAVOUR.

NOTHING CAN PREVENT IT — only two things can hinder it — namely — VESTED INTEREST and APATHY.

If vested interest stands in its way, then vested interest will be swept aside by force of events.

If, owing to apathy of the rank and file, the necessary power is not given to the Committee to go on immediately, then the RANK AND FILE WILL BE GUILTY of a crime against themselves, their wives and their children.

It is said it's the duty of Leaders to lead—We now give you the lead—Don't fail to respond ! !

Signed on behalf of the Delegate Conference,

HARRY GOSLING,
Chairman.

ERNEST BEVIN,
Hon. Secretary.

'We are going to lead,' Bevin told the union's first delegate conference with the regal plural.

However, it wasn't the T&G's ingenious constitution that made it such a success after its launch on 1 January 1922. It was the leadership of its founder, Ernest Bevin. 'We are going to lead,' he told the union's first delegate conference, using the regal plural. 'But if you do not follow, if you place your pettiness, your personality in the way of the consummation of this scheme you will have committed a crime against the men who are compelled to go forward.'[42] In 'Bevin's union', as the T&G was known by friend and foe from the start, the congeniality of the boss came in an iron fist. It was trade unionism meets Tammany Hall.

After 1922, the T&G grew organically and through further amalgamations. The key play was the Workers' Union joining with its 100,000 members in 1929. This was largely due to Bevin. In dire straits because of poor leadership and recession, the workers had a choice to either join the General and Municipal Workers or the T&G. They went with Bevin, wrote the union's historian, because the T&G was 'clearly the more successful' with its 'forceful reputation'.[43] This amalgamation was crucial to the T&G's resilience in the Great Depression of the 1930s.

Like every leader, Bevin was a combination of remote and intimate. 'He was known as Ernie to almost everyone, but he made friends more readily with crowds than with individuals,' said Francis Williams.[44] Although over the following decades he forged strong and enduring working relationships, including with Winston Churchill, only one turned into a genuine friendship in his entire career at the top: his partnership with Clement Attlee. Tellingly, this friendship was cultivated and fully reciprocated by Attlee, and they both saw it – at the time, not just in retrospect – as vital to their acquisition and exercise of power. Bevin had what François Mitterrand called the supreme quality of leadership: *indifference*. In French the word means more than just 'indifference', including connotations of cold calculation irrespective of consideration for other persons. In strength of public personality, Bevin was matched only by Churchill and Lloyd George in the 1930s and by Churchill alone in the 1940s.

Within the T&G, Bevin rarely intervened when he could not win. In extreme cases this could lead to him going deliberately AWOL, as in the early stages of the London bus strike of 1937. There, he judged that he could not stop the strike at the outset, so he let the communist-dominated strike committee overreach and implode in its initial weeks until he seized control. It was a crisis situation badly handled, but Bevin sensed that it could have destroyed him entirely if he had tried to assert control early on and failed. His interventions, and his non-interventions, came from pointillistic personal knowledge of people and local contexts. Constantly on the road, as in his earliest days as a dockers' organiser, he knew personally a high proportion of the T&G's 1,500 branch chairmen: the people who *were* the union on the ground and who mostly came to respect, even to worship him.

Bevin had courage, energy and resourcefulness. 'At the first signs of disturbance he put on his hat and went down to the docks or the transport garage or the factory gates, climbed up on a lorry or a bench and used his voice,' said Williams.[45] Walter Citrine, a vital colleague over two decades as TUC general secretary but a not uncritical admirer, gave this balanced judgement a few years after Bevin's death:

> He was creative in his thought always. I never knew the circumstances in which Bevin couldn't, given reasonable time, make a constructive proposal. He was never negative. But he was a very strong personality; he was a man who could not brook opposition.

He always personalised opposition. If a person put an argument, Bevin always saw the opponent and not the argument, which was sometimes extremely embarrassing.[46]

There was a good deal of rough personal experience in that remark, as we shall see. Within the T&G, the executive met only quarterly and the full union conference, originally specified to be annual, was reduced to taking place every other year after its first meeting in 1923. Yet the T&G was not a dictatorship, and Bevin would probably have been toppled at some point had he tried to make it so. It was 'government by discussion', as Attlee said of democracy at large. The quarterly meetings of the executive lasted for several days, including a comprehensive written report by Bevin and long debates. At critical junctures, when he felt acutely vulnerable or vindictive, notably after the unofficial 1922 dock strike and the 1937 London bus strike, Bevin expelled (mostly communist) firebrands. But generally he kept his opponents close, and this was his prevailing tactic to prevent or limit breakaways and threats to his position. During strikes and controversial negotiations he invariably called frequent delegate conferences of the union groups and areas concerned, to keep the troops with him and to calibrate his action at every stage. 'His whole life was spent in an atmosphere of discussion and uninhibited argument,' Bullock observed.[47]

In Bevin's entire twenty-three years as T&G leader there was never a serious attempt to oust him. Periodic cries of 'Napoleon Bevin' never coalesced. The closest attempt at mutiny was a motion at the 1931 conference in Blackpool, modelled on Dunning's famous parliamentary resolution condemning King George III in 1780: 'That the powers, the inaccessibility and independence of the General

Secretary have increased, are increasing and ought to be restricted and defined.' Bevin's response was not a blunderbuss but a carefully crafted refutation:

> I helped to build this Union in groups and I have religiously re-fused to attend Group meetings unless it is a crisis ... I don't think I should be at every meeting. I will tell you why ... I recognised the danger, in the first inception, of this Union becoming a one-man show. I don't suppose it is egotistical for me to say I have a forceful personality. I should be no good to you if I hadn't, but I recognise the dangers of it as much as you do, and I have tried to avoid exploitation of it as much as I can. When the national secretaries have had a problem, I have said 'For your own sake, try to get through yourself in order to develop responsibility.'[48]

The motion was overwhelmingly defeated.

The T&G could hardly have come into being at a tougher time, in the trough of the first deep post-First World War recession. In six of its first ten years, it lost members; as late as 1932, there were only 75,000 more members than in 1922. Although by the late 1930s it became the biggest union in the country and the free world, the T&G's growth was not linear, and it never became hegemonic within the wider trade union movement. Even within the transport sectors Bevin failed to secure an amalgamation with the seamen, and he never seriously attempted amalgamation with the highly self-conscious and organised railway workers' unions. In both cases he judged the price of any viable amalgamation to be too great, and he appears to have sensed, although he never actually stated, that he already possessed sufficient critical mass for his own industrial and political purposes. Leadership is about avoiding over-reach as well as under-reach, and Bevin judged this like an artist. He was to do the same in his relations with Attlee and Churchill in the 1940s.

The labyrinthine detail of the two decades of industrial affairs and disputes of the Bevin era have today receded into the mist, and apart from the General Strike, recounted in the next chapter for its seismic importance to Bevin and his world, a description of them would be tedious and add little to understanding the spider at the centre of the web. However, immersing myself in them, I have been struck by Bevin's sheer command: command of detail, command of negotiations, command of his followers, command of respect among his interlocutors. It is equally striking that, socially and intellectually, he treated everyone as essentially an equal, from Lord Ashfield, the big boss of London Transport in the 1930s, to the doorkeepers and secretaries at Transport House. He only had two personal secretaries in his entire time at the T&G, and the second stayed with him as his constituency secretary when he became an MP and minister in 1940 right through until his death in 1951. He had a supreme talent for giving and commanding loyalty.

Bevin's work ethic was extraordinary, even among Stakhanovites. Apart from some evenings and parts of weekends with Flo, and occasional sporting events, he had no life outside work. Day-in day-out it was a litany of wage claims, complex agreements, sixpence a shift here, a shilling more over a year rather than eighteen months there, forty-one hours a week rather than forty-two hours, the first paid holidays. It went on and on, interspersed with speeches and interviews about the state of Europe, the world, and trends in international shipping and bus design. His only serious relaxation, besides football matches and the music hall, was talking about his work and politics.

As a negotiator Walter Citrine said: 'I never met Bevin's equal.'[49] His constant quest was to secure not only good deals but machinery for future deals too. This was an era in which employers routinely locked out workers who didn't accept wage cuts or changes to working conditions and brought in new staff to replace them. It was a time when employers regarded unions as fundamentally illegitimate, even if forced periodically to negotiate with them. Bevin grasped that a negotiating process could be worth a hundred agreements, particularly one that put the two sides on a basis of negotiating equality. Bevin's days and weeks were spent in bodies like the Dock Labour National Joint Council, negotiating even with the infamous Lord Devonport. Vital to this was Bevin's cardinal belief in the sanctity of agreements. Unofficial strikes were anathema to him, and he ruthlessly stamped them out wherever he could: they undermined agreements and the incentive for employers to negotiate with him.

Bevin was an inveterate moderniser. In the words of a labour correspondent of the day: 'He has been outstanding among British trade union leaders for his readiness in discussing improved technique and productive processes to insure greater returns to industry and safety to workers. He has not objected to these greater returns so long as a fair share of the improvement was given to the workers.' A constant Bevin quest was to take the T&G into new and expanding sectors like chemicals and road haulage, as well as unionising the broad mass of unskilled and unionised workers. 'In one town I organise the midwives, and in another the gravediggers, and everything between is the Transport Workers,' was a favourite quip.[50]

He also pioneered the provision of services as a key benefit of the T&G as a modern mass union. This included the building of union retirement homes, which literally had the T&G organising the gravediggers. There was a poignant episode after Bevin received an honorary doctorate from Cambridge University as Foreign Secretary. After the grand ceremony he went to visit a T&G retirement home he had established north of Cambridge more than a decade earlier. He knew many of the residents personally.

Bevin was the fiercest critic in his day of unions being behind the times and needing to catch up. One of his favourite yarns, recalled by the actor-writer Peter Ustinov, sums up the Bevin worldview.

There was three men in a boat, see, a communist, a fascist, and a good union man. All of a sudden the boat sinks and the three men are thrown into the water. There's people on the river bank. The fascist salutes at them, but finds it impossible to swim with one arm, and 'e drowns. The communist begins shouting slogans at them, exhausts 'imself, and 'e drowns. This leaves only the union man, swimmin' towards the bank in strong easy strokes. 'E's almost within 'is depth, when the factory siren goes and 'e drowns.[51]

Part joke, part parable.

Bevin was seeking not just to represent the working class; in a fundamental sense he was forging it as a class.

For Bevin, trade unionism was a vocation. He had no desire whatever to use trade union leadership as a stepping stone out of the labour movement, unlike for example Frank Hodges, the miners' federation leader at the time Bevin was forming the T&G, who ended up a wealthy businessman. Power never corrupted Bevin: he had no desire for riches and a lavish lifestyle. This was in sharp contrast to the American union bosses he half admired, like Samuel Gompers and the equally expansive John Lewis, leader of the American

Mineworkers. Harry Truman was reminded of Lewis when he first met Bevin at the Potsdam conference in 1945. Yet Bevin's salary as general secretary of the T&G was £650 a year in 1922, the same as when he was a dockers' union organiser. It rose to twice that level over the next two decades, but it remained a small fraction, for example, of the Prime Minister's salary of £10,000 a year. Bevin's expenses were modest and on the same scale as other national T&G officials.

There is not a hint, even a scintilla of a hint, of corruption at any stage of Bevin's career, which is remarkable given its length, power and temptations. On his death in 1951 he left little besides a flat and his union pension to his wife Flo. He turned down all honours, although almost everything was offered, including a peerage, a knighthood and the Companion of Honour (CH). Many fellow union and Labour leaders accepted honours, notably Attlee who became both an earl and a knight of the garter. Citrine accepted a knighthood and a peerage. Even Jack Jones, ostensibly a left-wing firebrand when Bevin's successor as leader of the T&G in the 1970s, accepted the CH. But when Churchill offered Bevin the CH in 1945, he replied: 'I prefer not to accept. The job I have undertaken, like thousands of others, during the war has been in the interests of the Nation and I do not desire special Honours.'[52]

Bevin had a shrewd sense that co-option to the titled elite would damage his brand and his power. Had he gone to the House of Lords, as MacDonald proposed in 1930, this alone would probably have made it impossible for him to become Minister of Labour in 1940 and Foreign Secretary in 1945. Oliver Cromwell's injunction that 'I had rather have a plain russet-coated captain that knows what he fights for, and loves what he knows, than that which you call a gentleman' was never more honoured than by plain, russet-coated Ernie Bevin.

While an inveterate pragmatist, Bevin never sought to counter the 'Boss Bevin' image in the Tory media. At times he even revelled in it, cultivating a hint of menace, true to Machiavelli's *The Prince*: 'It is better to be feared than to be loved if you can't be both.' Indeed, Bullock writes, 'His [strike] activities in 1924 had made Bevin the most hated and most abused man in the country.'[53] His strategy wasn't to try and get a better press from Beaverbrook and the right-wing media but rather to build up the labour movement's own media and propaganda machine. This is why he invested so much time and energy in turning the *Daily Herald* into a successful Labour paper.

Bevin was especially Cromwellian in his attitude towards Ramsay MacDonald, who led the first two Labour governments in 1924 and 1929, both of which ended in sharp conflict with Bevin. MacDonald and Bevin had much in common: both were working class, poor, 'illegitimate', with no father. They were both labour political organisers who made it from the bottom to the top of England's power structure in its first decade of full democracy. Yet Bevin's contempt for MacDonald was prodigious – and mutual.

It wasn't just that MacDonald resisted Bevin's dockers and tram workers in major disputes and strikes in 1924, even threatening to use wartime emergency powers, only to ride even more spectacularly roughshod over trade union opposition to the welfare cuts he sought to impose in his second government in 1931. Bevin also thought MacDonald was socially on the make, trying to escape his class, not to represent it, which was just as contemptible. He saw MacDonald's socialism as a pose floating on a cloud of woolly sentimentality. He particularly resented MacDonald's frequently expressed contempt for 'the whirlpool of class-conscious trade unionists'.[54] Bevin never respected or liked MacDonald and tried hard to remove him as Labour leader in 1925. When MacDonald's remark that he was 'a swine' was relayed back to him, Bevin retorted: 'Ah, you've found him out then? We all do sooner or later.' With some bitterness he wrote in the T&G newspaper after the fall of MacDonald's first government in 1924: 'I have not much faith that the middle-class politician will give us socialism; the type of mind revealed in the last Government indicated a mid-Victorian outlook.'[55] In truth, Bevin was by now himself pretty middle class in his lifestyle, but his self-belief and self-promotion, accepted by most observers without question whether they liked or loathed him, was that he was still the real working-class deal, and he was certainly more so than Mac-Donald in the 1920s, even before the Marchioness of Londonderry took hold of the Scotsman.

Bevin's patience and staying power were elephantine. Not until 1925 did he seek election to the TUC General Council and he never served on the Labour Party's National Executive Committee, although he was clearly the party's most powerful leader in the 1930s and was second only to Attlee in the 1940s. In an era when prominent union leaders were often MPs, including Frank Hodges, Jimmy Thomas, the railwaymen's leader, and Harry Gosling, president of his own T&G, Bevin wasn't elected to the House of Commons until he became a minister in 1940. He was pressed hard by union and Labour colleagues to run in the east London Whitechapel by-election of December 1930 caused by Gosling's death, but he refused to divide his energies and only stood (and lost) in the 1931 general election as an act of solidarity in a moment of existential crisis for the entire labour movement. Bevin is a wholly exceptional twentieth-century case of a political leader whose ascent to power led him to join the House of Commons, not vice versa.

There was virtual unanimity among his contemporaries that Bevin was the greatest trade union leader of the twentieth century. Among the other large unions, the best-known leaders of the miners, A. J. Cook and later Arthur Scargill, were communists who led their followers to catastrophic defeats, while no leader of the railway workers left a great legacy. Tellingly, among the next most successful, by general agreement, were Bevin's successors as leader of his T&G, particularly Arthur Deakin and Jack Jones. Deakin, his deputy and immediate successor, was an extension of Bevin himself, right down to the cigars and speech mannerisms and in taking on Bevin's long-serving secretary Ivy Saunders after his death.

Is Bevin in the same league internationally? There are a few trade union leaders of romantic appeal as figures of national liberation, most famously Ireland's Jim Larkin, whom Bevin knew well from the 1913 Dublin transport workers' strike. Of those who made a big impact in big countries, the master is often held to be Samuel Gompers, Bevin's inspiration from San Francisco in 1916. Gompers was another larger-than-life practical idealist seeking the transformation of the condition of the working class by democratic means, remembered today for his inspirational 'More' reply when asked what he wanted: 'What does labor want? We want more schoolhouses and less jails; more books and less arsenals; more learning and less vice; in fact, more of the opportunities to cultivate our best natures, to make manhood more noble, womanhood more beautiful, and childhood more happy and bright.'

Yet Bevin had a far greater impact than Gompers on the society and politics of his day. This was not a matter of chance but of strategy. Gompers rejected participation in government and in the leadership of the Democratic Party. He turned this rejection into a doctrine: 'Wherever the political movement is predominant, as against the industrial movement, there the Labour movement is weakest, wages lowest and general conditions the worst to be found.'[56] Bevin took the opposite view and refuted Gompers. For all his frustrations with the Labour Party, Bevin believed that trade unionists would only be socially transformational when they and their representatives were also leading the state.

From the moment Bevin became leader of the T&G, his mission was to make the trade unions a pillar of the state. This he did, in no small part, by making himself a pillar of the state. As Francis Williams put it: 'Bevin was an organiser in the sense that some men are writers or artists. He found in organisation his mode of self-expression.'[57] He was the Picasso of twentieth-century trade union power.

THE FIGHT FOR THE FAVOURITE.

Mr. Lloyd George. "HERE, I SAY, THIS IS MY MOUNT."
Mr. Winston Churchill. "NO, IT ISN'T. I THOUGHT OF IT FIRST."

Churchill and Lloyd George outdoing each other to be anti-labour in the early 1920s. Bevin had other ideas. © *Punch Magazine*

CHAPTER 3

GENERAL STRIKE

The General Strike of 1926 was a disaster for the unions but a qualified success for Bevin. It propelled him to national leadership and sealed his reputation as tough, pragmatic, serious and in a class of his own – a 'leader of leaders'.[1]

The Tory media turned Bevin into a bogey man, but most of the Tory leaders with whom he dealt were more nuanced, especially Stanley Baldwin, Britain's dominant politician between Lloyd George and Churchill. If Bevin had been in charge of the union side from the outset of the crisis leading to the General Strike, it would probably not have taken place; there would probably have been a deal with Baldwin. But, equally, had there been a general strike with Bevin in charge, it would have been better prepared, better led, and might have resulted in a deal too.

There is a myth that 'just as the German War was inevitable so was the General Strike inevitable', in the words of F. E. Smith, by now ennobled as the Earl of Birkenhead, the Boris Johnson-esque Tory extrovert of the day.[2] It is true, as we have seen, that talk of a general strike was constant in the bitter industrial strife after the First World War. But looking back, it is remarkable how intense were the negotiations between Baldwin and union leaders to avoid a general strike. In the run-up to its outbreak on 3 May 1926, TUC negotiators were constantly in No. 10.

Intensive government/union bargaining was not only a feature of the 'beer and sandwiches' 1960s and 1970s: it went back to Lloyd George and the big industrial disputes before, during and after the First World War. The problem in 1925–26, though, wasn't a lack of negotiations but the failure of the unions to unite behind a viable union strategy in the face of a Tory government that was conflicted between a genuine desire for social peace and an instinctively *laissez-faire* attitude to unemployment and economic dislocation. The situation was complicated further by a Labour Party whose leader, Ramsay MacDonald, shared similar *laissez-faire* instincts and disliked union leaders as a class. Bevin was to learn comprehensively from these failures and apply the lessons in the 1930s and 1940s.

The General Strike grew out of the debilitating crisis in Britain's largest early twentieth-century industry: coal mining. It was a crisis that was to flare repeatedly until the end of large-scale mining at the close of the century.

Coal mining was terrible, dehumanising, yet vast. In an industry employing more than a million people in 1920, equivalent to the entire population of Birmingham today, there were many hundreds of fatalities each year and tens of thousands of people seriously injured, as well as an appalling toll on the health and families of the millions living in mining communities. One South Wales mining explosion alone killed 440 miners in 1913. The industry was chronically badly managed, with unions to match. In 1889 more than a dozen unions came together to form the Miners' Federation of Great Britain. But this was a weak organisation akin to the loose federation of transport unions before Bevin forged the T&G, and it never had a leader remotely of his calibre. A. J. Cook, the miners' leader in the crucial years from 1924 to 1931, called himself 'a humble disciple of Lenin'.

The economics of mining collapsed after the First World War, with the rise of oil and too much coal chasing too few buyers. When the price of coal halved between the end of 1920 and mid-1921, owners in the re-privatised industry sought big cuts in wages and longer working hours. The collapse of the 'triple alliance' of miners, railwaymen and transport workers on Black Friday 1921 was described in the last chapter. Four years later, on 31 July 1925, came 'Red Friday': the victory of the triple alliance against Baldwin's newly elected Tory government. The government feared a general strike, partly because it was unprepared and partly because its 'peace in our time' Prime Minister recoiled from conflict. Baldwin granted a nine-month government subsidy to halt a miners' pay cut while a royal commission took stock, headed by the former Liberal minister Sir Herbert Samuel.

Bevin played a part in Red Friday. With the National Union of Railwaymen, the T&G worked up and announced a plan, short of a general strike, for an embargo on coal distribution, designed to bring heavy industry and power generation to a halt. This alarmed Baldwin, since coal stocks were low, and it helped persuade him to grant the nine-month coal subsidy at the last minute. The same technique of halting coal distribution brought down Edward Heath's Tory government in the miners' strike of 1974.

Shortly after Red Friday, Bevin was elected to the TUC General Council for the first time. He was soon at the centre of the looming crisis of what to do when Baldwin's nine-month coal subsidy expired on 30 April 1926.

The government used the nine-month respite to make intensive preparations to counter a general strike. Volunteers and staff were recruited to keep essential supplies and services going, including new 'independent' agencies like the shadowy Organisation for the Maintenance of Supplies. Meanwhile, the unions did little besides crow about Red Friday. Beatrice Webb noted in her diary on 16 September 1925: 'A.J. Cook on behalf of the T.U. Left, and Wheatley on behalf of the Clyde, talk about immediate revolution, whilst George Lansbury thunders threats of the immediate dissolution of Capitalist civilisation.'[3] Bevin was more circumspect: 'The other side has studied the recent movement and will organise against us,' he told his T&G executive in August. 'The one essential thing to concentrate upon at this stage is to discipline our movement.'[4]

Bevin's position on a general strike before May 1926 was ambivalent. He had no truck with communist tactics or principles, even after Red Friday. As he told the Labour Party conference in Liverpool in September 1925: 'Communists cannot conscientiously reconcile the Communist basis with the basis of evolutionary democracy that the Labour Party represents. Working class men in this country want people to be straight with them.'[5] But he wasn't in principle against a general strike in support of industrial goals or even, as we saw with the *Jolly George* and Lloyd George's march to war with Russia in 1920, to fundamentally change government policy. He judged, however, that it had to be a last resort, it had to be for a reasonable cause (without ever being too explicit about what that might be), and there had to be a very good prospect of winning. Bevin didn't go in for glorious defeats.

Tellingly, one of Bevin's main projects in 1926, apart from the General Strike, was the building of Transport House, an eight-storey edifice in Smith Square, Westminster, modelled on the American Federation of Labor headquarters on Massachusetts Avenue, Washington DC, whose opening he attended on his US visit of 1916. Ramsay MacDonald opened Transport House in 1928 with what Bullock calls 'a moving speech, astonishingly empty of meaning', although for him that was hardly unusual.[6] Transport House was, literally, a monumental vision of the labour movement. It was the first trade union headquarters in the vicinity of Parliament, and it also housed the TUC and Labour Party headquarters. It even impressed the Tories, who in 1958 took possession of an equally grand building almost next door. For half a century, until Labour moved out in 1980, Transport House was a metonym for the Labour Party itself. These were most of the fifty years for which, Bevin quipped at the end of Churchill's wartime coalition, he would be known as Minister of Labour. They encompassed four of the six Labour governments there have ever been.

A critical moment leading to the General Strike was the report, on 10 March 1926, of the Samuel Commission on the future of the mining industry, set up by Baldwin as part of his climbdown on Red Friday the previous July. It was seven weeks before the end of the government's coal subsidy. Sir Herbert Samuel gave something to both sides, although more to the employers. He recommended significant rationalisation of the industry, in order to reduce the need for pay cuts or longer working hours. But wage cuts were implicit because three-quarters of British coal was produced at a loss and subsidies could not, Samuel recommended, continue indefinitely. In a careful balancing act response to the report, Baldwin declined to take responsibility for a modernisation plan but raised the possibility of further subsidy if a viable plan was agreed to by the two sides.

The mine owners immediately gave notice of big pay cuts for 30 April. Coal hewers in South Wales, for example, would see their pay nearly halved from seventy-eight shillings to forty-six shillings a week. The obvious next move for the miners and the TUC was to seek to engage Baldwin directly in negotiations over the comprehensive modernisation plan envisaged by Samuel. There would probably have been pit closures and job losses as part of such a deal, but these were almost inevitably going to happen anyway, and with the right deal they would have been reduced and delayed, even just possibly avoided, particularly if the government was obliged to become so engaged that it underwrote the resulting modernisation plan. Bevin urged this course before, during and after the strike. And negotiations were clearly what Baldwin expected to happen, because he readily engaged in them weeks later when the strike was imminent, and the TUC General Council called for talks. The government was divided between hawks and doves: Churchill, as ever, was chief hawk, but Baldwin was a dove in dove's clothing, which is what mattered since he was the unions' chief interlocutor.

Negotiations didn't start until the last minute because the miners' leaders would not enter into them unless pay cuts were taken off the table before they even started. Unlike A. J. Cook, the TUC's leadership was careful not to absolutely rule out pay cuts after the publication of the Samuel Report, but when it came to the crunch in late April they initially drifted towards a general strike rather than seeking to force the miners into negotiations. With Bevin not yet fully in charge, the TUC leadership wasn't strong or united enough to stand up to Cook, who just wanted a general strike.

At this stage Bevin's influence was not strong because he had only recently joined the TUC General Council. He didn't sit on the key industrial committee, led by Arthur Pugh, leader of the Iron and Steel Trades Confederation and president of the TUC for 1926. The dour and unimaginative Pugh was supposedly engaging with the miners and the government, but it was only on 14 April, five weeks after the publication of the Samuel Report and barely a fortnight before the expiry of the coal subsidy, that he even asked Baldwin to bring the two sides together. Baldwin agreed but without committing to make any proposals himself. The result, inevitably, was deadlock when the two sides eventually met, but the fact that talks were ongoing under the aegis of the government led observers, including Bevin, to think that a process was in train to 'play it long'.

On Wednesday 28 April, at an emergency conference of nearly a thousand union delegates attended by Ramsay MacDonald, Bevin made the most rousing speech. 'In twenty-four hours from now,' he declaimed, 'you may have to cease being separate unions; for this purpose you will have to become one union with no autonomy.' This statement was greeted with cheers. But Bevin was evidently rallying the troops to strengthen the hand of TUC negotiators, for Pugh gave a measured account of the talks underway and said that he was seeing Baldwin again with fellow TUC negotiator Jimmy Thomas, the railwaymen's union leader and Colonial Secretary in MacDonald's 1924 Cabinet, who was contemptuous of A. J. Cook's communist posturing and known to be against a general strike. So, again, a general strike did not seem imminent.[7] (Jimmy Thomas, popular on all sides in the Commons in the 1920s, not least as a raconteur, left Labour to form the National Government with MacDonald in 1931. His son became a Tory MP, a mirror image of Baldwin, whose own gay son Oliver became a Labour MP in 1929. It is wrong to see inter-war Labour–Tory politics, even amid the General Strike, as an unbridgeable divide. Baldwin had staked his whole leadership in 1925 not just on Red Friday but on resisting backbench Tory legislation to harass the unions. This was when he made his famous 'peace in our time' speech in the House of Commons.)

Pugh and Thomas's talks with Baldwin the following day lasted until 1.30 on the morning of Friday 30 April. On the table now was a 13 per cent national pay cut alongside a proposal for yet another royal commission on coal industry reorganisation. It was obviously unacceptable to the unions that there should be a large pay cut before agreement on any plan for reorganisation that might reduce or obviate the need for it. Since Baldwin would not shift further in these talks, a general strike now looked possible and the government declared a state of emergency.

However, there was still an expectation of further negotiations. As Bevin told the reconvened conference of union delegates on Saturday 1 May, which resolved on a general strike from Tuesday 4 May, workers in the affected categories should come out 'on Tuesday morning, that is to say, if a settlement has not been found'. He made another big rallying cry: 'Even if every penny goes, and every asset is swallowed up, history will write that it was a magnificent generation that was prepared to do this rather than see the miners driven down like slaves.'[8] But immediately afterwards Pugh and Thomas wrote to Baldwin offering to resume negotiations, with Bevin's strong support. Crucially, Pugh believed that the TUC, not the Miners' Federation, was now in charge of seeking and agreeing a settlement. He would hardly have written to Baldwin on behalf of the unions otherwise.

A. J. Cook and Herbert Smith, the Miners' Federation president, claimed to believe that a general strike was now decided, and they immediately left London, probably to avoid any further negotiations or discussions. Afterwards it was an article of faith by Cook that they had not known about the subsequent talks in No. 10. 'I heard quite by accident, at about 9 p.m., that the negotiating committee of the TUC were closeted in Downing Street with the Prime Minister,' he wrote in his bitter retrospective account.[9] But of course he was only unaware because he had left TUC headquarters in central London. Had Bevin been in charge it is hard to think he would have tolerated Cook behaving like this.

As soon as Baldwin had received Pugh and Thomas's letter on the Saturday afternoon, he agreed to further negotiations. The three men met at 8.30 p.m. in No. 10 together with other ministers and advisers including the new TUC general secretary Walter Citrine. Another negotiating marathon ensued into the early hours of Sunday 2 May. It produced a promising formula: there should be a two-week negotiation on coal industry reorganisation without preconditions. Crucially, there was no explicit mention of pay cuts and there was to be no lock-out while the talks were ongoing. It was agreed that Pugh and Thomas would put this to the General Council and the Miners' Federation and return with a reply before lunchtime on the Sunday.

Baldwin accordingly summoned the Cabinet for noon on the Sunday. However, Pugh could not make contact with A. J. Cook or Herbert Smith, when, to his surprise, he discovered they had fled London. He felt unable to make any reply in their absence, and in sending a message to No. 10 to say he would not be returning at noon, he does not even appear to have said why. These were negotiating blunders utterly inconceivable from Bevin. When the Cabinet met at noon, Baldwin and his colleagues thought there was some kind of ruse afoot. Opinion hardened. Churchill 'was characteristically impatient to stop talking and get to war'. With the wily Lord Chancellor Birkenhead now holding the pen, a tougher negotiating formula than Baldwin's of the night before was agreed. This made explicit that any deal 'may involve some reduction in wages'.

Birkenhead, a drinking friend of Jimmy Thomas, gave a contradictory retrospective account of Baldwin's policy, except insofar as it had him, Birkenhead, at the centre throughout. He said that Baldwin wanted to force a showdown with the miners on terms on which the government could triumph; yet he also said that Baldwin gave too much ground in the key overnight negotiations with Pugh and Thomas on Saturday and Sunday 1 and 2 May.[10]

All accounts, however, including Birkenhead's, agree that the Churchill group of hardliners in the Cabinet were aghast at Baldwin's concessions in the overnight talks. Baldwin had no reason to think that Pugh and Thomas would not agree to the start of negotiations the following morning on the basis of his proposed 'without preconditions' formula, so it seems clear to me that Baldwin did indeed make a vital concession to the TUC on 1 and 2 May in pursuit of a settlement. He was genuinely anxious to avoid a general strike, not just on logistical grounds but also in search of social peace, and he made the 'without preconditions' concession as a pragmatic gesture to the equally pragmatic Pugh and Thomas. Had formal negotiations started on this basis, there might have been a deal, albeit with acute difficulty. But once talks failed to start immediately, Baldwin lost ground to his right, and he anyway had little choice but to act tough once A. J. Cook became the public face of the unions.

The TUC leaders did not return to No. 10 until 9 p.m. Even by then, incredibly, Pugh had not received a response from A. J. Cook and Herbert Smith, who were reportedly somewhere on a slow Sunday train back to London.

What happened next was pure fiasco-to-farce. While Pugh and Thomas were with Baldwin in the Cabinet room, A. J. Cook, Herbert Smith and the entire TUC General Council, including Bevin, arrived at No. 10 and were shown in to the Chancellor of the Exchequer's drawing room on the first floor of No. 11 next door. Pugh and Thomas left Baldwin to join them. A heated argument ensued in No. 11 as to what to do while Baldwin and the entire Cabinet waited downstairs.

Bevin set about drafting a negotiating remit on the lines of the earlier Baldwin formula while emissaries went back and forth to No. 10. Leo Amery, a member of the Cabinet, takes up the story:

> We kicked our heels for hours. Presently after 11 p.m. an exhausted Baldwin came in and collapsed in an arm chair leaving it to Birkenhead to state the very inconclusive results ... Opinion had hardened very much in view of the fact that notices ordering the General Strike to begin the next day had been sent out, regardless of the negotiations the night before. While we were discussing, the news arrived that Monday's *Daily Mail* had been suppressed by the printers who disliked the leading article. This tipped the scales... [The Cabinet agreement] was now stiffened to make it quite clear to the trade union leaders that negotiations could not be continued until the interference with the press was repudiated and the General Strike called off. We dispersed about 12:30 leaving Baldwin to hand the note to the trade union leaders and go to bed.[11]

The dénouement is recounted by Alan Bullock, a surreal picture of the events leading to the greatest strike in British history, which has Bevin pragmatic and constructive throughout:

> Bevin had got seven clauses [of his draft] down on paper and one o'clock had struck when the Prime Minister's secretary came up and asked the negotiating committee to return. With agreement

so near, the committee were reluctant to go, but on a second request, Pugh, Thomas, Swales and Citrine went down ... Baldwin
was alone and ill at ease. He handed them the letter [setting out
the new Cabinet position] and briefly informed them that the
Cabinet took so serious a view of the *Mail* incident that it had
decided to break off negotiations forthwith.

The union leaders had known nothing of the *Mail* incident, however.
It was an unofficial strike by the compositors, who refused to print
Monday's *Daily Mail* when they saw its anti-union leading article.
Pugh and colleagues thereupon returned to the union delegation in
No. 11.

As soon as Pugh finished reading the Cabinet communication,
a confused clamour broke out, everyone trying to speak at once.
It was Bevin's powerful voice which made itself heard. 'I propose
that we depute someone to draft a reply and that in the meantime
we continue our discussion where we left off when the message
came, for a basis of settlement has to be found sooner or later,
and as we have made good progress on the job we had better go
straight on and finish it.'

Bevin's proposal found immediate support and for two hours
the General Council and the Miners' executive continued their
discussion in the Chancellor's room while the lights were put out
in No. 10 and the Prime Minister went to bed. A reply to the
Government's ultimatum, protesting at the sudden rupture of the
negotiations, was drawn up but, when Pugh and Citrine went
downstairs to deliver it they found the Cabinet room and the rest
of the house in darkness. There was nothing to do but return to

Eccleston Square from which the General Council dispatched its reply dated 3.30 a.m. on Monday 3 May.

Bevin was still anxious to get agreement on the terms of a settlement and, after a few hours' sleep, met Pugh, Citrine and the miners' leaders in his own office at Central Buildings, Westminster. Only one point of substance remained to be settled. In his original draft Bevin wrote that, after the proposed National Mining Board had completed their proposals for the reorganisation of the coal industry, 'they shall determine what adjustments shall be made, if any, by all parties, necessary to cover the interim period, subject to the maintenance of a national minimum [wage] and the Seven Hours Act'. 'A' national minimum or 'the' national minimum wage? It was the old issue in a new form. The miners' leaders wanted to rule out any wage reduction even if reorganisation was guaranteed: hence their insistence on *the* national minimum, i.e. the minimum accepted in the 1924 agreement. On that Monday morning, Smith and Cook finally agreed to substitute 'a' for 'the'. But when they took the draft to their full executive, meeting in a room in the House of Commons, the change was repudiated by twelve votes to six.

Bevin had attended the meeting of the Miners' Federation. Defeated there, he brought the draft back to the General Council, arguing that the miners had handed over their powers and must accept the General Council ruling as final. The draft was adopted by the General Council with the original wording of '*a* national minimum'. Hurriedly stuffing the papers into his pocket, Bevin walked back to the House of Commons – it was then four in the afternoon – and saw the proposals delivered to MacDonald. Not content with this, Bevin got in touch with Frederick Leggett, of the Ministry of Labour. Handing Leggett a copy of his proposals, he urged him to get the

Prime Minister to put them forward in the House that evening. If he did, Labour would be supportive, Bevin assured Leggett.

Leggett went to Sir Horace Wilson, the permanent secretary of the Ministry of Labour. Wilson's only response was to ask if the TUC were prepared to accept a reduction in wages. As they were not, the Government was not interested. Bevin still expected that MacDonald would produce his proposals in the House, but when he spoke, the Labour leader made no reference to them. Possibly MacDonald hesitated to do so in view of the miners' objections to the change the General Council had made. [More likely, he wanted to avoid becoming engaged personally, as was his wont in relations with the trade unions. He went on essentially to sit out the General Strike.]

Whatever the reason, Bevin never changed his opinion that, if the draft negotiating remit had been made public by MacDonald in the debate that Monday evening, before the strike began, the course of events might have been different. But the chance was lost and within a matter of hours the men came out.

As the evening shifts ceased work on the night of 3 May, the whole transport system of the United Kingdom came to a standstill.[12]

As a chapter of accidents, incompetence and amateurism, this was a 1920s production of *The Strike That Goes Wrong*. It explains why Bevin thereafter got to the top of the TUC so quickly: there was a leadership vacuum and he filled it.

Bullock's account is pretty far removed from the Churchillian and Tory sabre-rattlers' picture of the strike leaders as all 'reds under the bed'. But the TUC leadership could hardly have been more maladroit and there were elements of extreme militancy among the miners' leaders. To win, the government played fairly rough, but so too did the unions, including Bevin who never played to lose. There were some ugly scenes on the ground, particularly in mining communities, although none as bad as the bloody 'Battle of Orgreave' in the depths of the miners' strike under the Thatcher government in 1984. Roy Jenkins told me the story of his father Arthur Jenkins, cerebral autodidact secretary of the South Wales Miners' Federation in the 1920s, and later a Labour MP and parliamentary private secretary to Attlee, who was imprisoned by magistrates for 'inciting' pickets outside a Welsh colliery during the strike. Arthur and his family bitterly resented what they saw as this trumped-up charge and sentence imposed by the coal owners' friends on the bench. It was years before he even told his son that he had gone to jail.

Bevin was last in, first out of the General Strike. As he well knew,
All was not Well! From *The British Worker*, the TUC's paper.

Having called the General Strike, the best decision the TUC General Council took, with Bevin in the lead, was to call it off after nine days. Similarly, the best decision taken by Baldwin was to keep the troops in their barracks and not turn a bitter industrial dispute into an armed conflict, as Churchill did when he sent in troops to the 1910 Tonypandy riots, also during a miners strike. Baldwin wisely set Churchill on to editing the pro-government newspaper the *British Gazette*, whose patriotic anti-union bombast didn't kill or injure anyone.

Bevin was 'last in, first out' among the leaders of the General Strike. But when he was in, he was in. He made it his first job to get his dock and transport members out on strike as solidly as possible. Apart from the miners and railwaymen, no other union responded so totally. This remained true until the end of the strike.

His next job was to try to turn the General Council into a general staff, from a standing start. The TUC headquarters in Eccleston Square, near Victoria, had only a handful of staff and became a scene from Bedlam, disorganised and unable to cope. Bevin persuaded Pugh to set up a small strike organisation committee. This was chaired by Alf Purcell, chairman of the General Council, but Bevin was the prime mover, as one eyewitness wrote afterwards:

> The reputation of many of Britain's budding Lenins has been badly bruised by their conduct during the Strike. The fire-eaters were the first to feel the weight of the forces arrayed against them.
>
> The big man of the strike, if anyone was entitled to that epithet, was Ernest Bevin. It was his quick brain and natural genius for organisation that saved the strike from being a complete fiasco. He could be called 'the Dictator of Eccleston Square', to whom all applied and sought advice. His word was absolute.[13]

Bevin's dynamism earned plaudits even from A. J. Cook, who said that, of those who tried 'to bring into machinery to cope with the requirements', Bevin was foremost. Bevin's secretary Mae Forcey acted as secretary of the committee as he improvised from hour to hour. 'Could anyone doubt that with his unrivalled experience of strikes, the Deity had specifically ordained him to run the first General Strike in Great Britain?' Citrine noted edgily in his diary. In the verdict of Francis Williams, Bevin's reputation was enhanced because 'it was as the organiser not as the policy-maker he was judged and in its organisation the General Strike had been as successful as any such strike could ever hope to be'.[14]

Long before the strike started, Bevin could see that the problem was how to bring it to an end. Citrine too had warned months before that 'nothing would more surely lead to the disintegration of the trade union movement than a reckless abuse of power' and a general strike was 'a literal impossibility as the country could not cease to function'. As soon as it became 'The General Strike' and was successfully presented as a challenge to parliamentary democracy there could be only one victor, short of an implosion of the government itself. Such an implosion is what essentially happened to Edward Heath in the miners' strike of 1974, which also brought the country to a near standstill. But Heath lacked Baldwin's shrewdness and guile, and the TUC he confronted was wiser than to turn a miners' strike into a General Strike, not least because it had learned the lessons of 1926. The Baldwin government's preparations also paid off, particularly the use of road transport to move essential supplies despite the rail stoppage.

On day three of the strike, Citrine wrote gloomily in his diary: 'I sit in the committee and wonder how it is all going to end. We are constantly reiterating our determination not to allow the strike to be diverted into an attack on the constitution but while there is any suspicion of this it seems impossible for the government to capitulate.' By day five he was in despair. 'Even the most ardent advocates of the general strike have usually reasoned on a few hours or days stoppage at the most.'

Bevin knew 'it was time something was done to get negotiations going somewhere' and he contacted Sir Herbert Samuel among others to try to restart negotiations. But the miners' leaders refused point blank to make any compromises – 'the miners had had plenty of Sir Herbert Samuel, we knew him quite well and did not want any further dealings with him', said Miners' Federation president Herbert Smith – so the initiative broke down.[15]

By the second week of the strike relations between the miners' leaders and the other main strike unions, the railwaymen and the T&G, had broken down. 'Not a minute on the day, not a penny off the pay,' was the miners' absolutist slogan. At the end of the first week, the railwaymen's leaders threatened to send their members back to work unilaterally if the strike was not called off by the TUC. The collapse came on day nine at a bitterly acrimonious meeting of the General Council. 'A hullabaloo took place,' Bevin wrote afterwards.

Everyone on the General Council felt that there would be no solution in conjunction with the Miners' Executive but that it had become necessary to reach a decision without them. We were responsible for four times as many people as they had in the field and therefore the question of whether the miners accepted it was disregarded altogether.[16]

The following day, 12 May, the General Strike was called off. Bevin and other General Council leaders saw Baldwin in No. 10 at 11.45 a.m. They put out a statement calling for the lock-out of the miners to be raised and the protection of strikers from victimisation, which, as Baldwin had offered neither, was a fig leaf. The miners were 'left alone in their struggle', A. J. Cook put it bitterly, until they were forced back to work by destitution in December.[17] It was abject defeat. Union membership fell sharply, and rival unions to those striking were set up in the coalfields.

The acrimony was indescribable. Arthur Pugh told Herbert Smith that better terms could not be obtained if the strike went on for ten years. 'The miners were impossible,' wrote the economist and political theorist Harold Laski, which was significant from him as he was rarely outbid on the left. 'They never budged an inch throughout. They have no plans, and if they had their own way, the TUC would be out until Domesday.' Even the sober Citrine, who thought that 'the worst thing' about the strike was 'the implication that class bitterness and class hatred are essential to trade unions', felt a frisson of genuine class war. 'I looked at them with mixed feelings, bitterness,' he wrote of his and Bevin's meeting with Baldwin and the Cabinet to call off the strike on 12 May.

> I reflected one of them at least would have butchered our people without compunction or any pretext which offered. I thought to myself what an anomaly it is that there should be such a thing as a governing class. I comforted myself with the reflection that some day that would be altered.[18]

Bevin had similar thoughts – and did the altering, as we shall see.

Cook had a sad end, breaking first with Bevin then with the Communist Party, before signing the proto-fascist Oswald Mosley's Manifesto for a New Party in 1930 and falling prey to cancer in November 1931 at the age of just forty-seven. At the 1928 TUC conference, attacking Bevin, 'he shouted with his face deeply, dangerously flushed' before collapsing and crying: 'Have I beaten them? Have I beaten them?' In a memoir of the strike he fantasised, like Arthur Scargill in the 1980s and Jeremy Corbyn in the 2010s, of the imminent collapse of the Tory government and all it stood for. 'A few days longer and the Government and the capitalist class, financiers, parasites and exploiters, would have been compelled to make peace with the miners. We threw away the chance of a victory greater than any British Labour has ever won.'[19] Bevin – last in, first out – was not remotely so deluded. He recognised frankly that Baldwin had defeated the General Strike comprehensively, and that had it gone on longer the defeat and suffering would have been worse still.

Having won, Baldwin tacked right with anti-union legislation in 1927. This was largely declaratory as far as the banning of general strikes was concerned, and he deliberately kept out provisions, supported by the Tory right, that would have made it much harder for unions to function. But it was nonetheless penal. The provision that really rankled was replacing the 'opt out' regime for the political levy for union members with a requirement to 'opt in'. This badly hit the Labour Party's finances until it was reversed by the Attlee government.

Bevin grudgingly acknowledged that Baldwin had won not only the war but the peace. It was a victory that extended to Bevin personally. Four months after the strike, the government invited the T&G leader to join an official delegation to study industrial conditions in North America. Arthur Steel-Maitland, Baldwin's Minister of Labour, told No. 10 that Bevin should be cultivated as 'the ablest leader in the Trade Union movement, with a combination of practical ability and imagination greater than that of any other'.[20] Baldwin agreed and Bevin accepted the invitation.

Triumphalism was subdued among the more sensible employers. They knew that unless a *modus vivendi* could be reached with pragmatic union leaders like Bevin, industrial relations would be in perpetual crisis. A few months after the General Strike a group of business leaders proposed a formal dialogue with union leaders in what became the Mond–Turner talks of 1928–29. The employer side was led by Sir Alfred Mond, a former Tory minister in the Lloyd George coalition and founder in 1926 of Imperial Chemical Industries, one of the world's biggest conglomerates. Bevin was the dominating figure on the union side, both in getting the talks going – their genesis was an approach directly to Bevin by Lord Weir, a business magnate, after the two met in New York during Bevin's industrial tour of the US in late 1926 – and in the formal discussions themselves. But, astutely conscious of the union politics involved, he did not seek the titular leadership, which went to the consensual Ben Turner, president of the TUC for 1928 and a former Labour MP and weaver. 'Turner was impressed by Lenin but not by his revolutionary politics,' it was reported after he led a trade union delegation to Russia in 1920. 'Labour stands for cleanliness of mind, body and soul,' was his mantra.[21]

Mond–Turner did not yield any breakthrough or blueprint, with little bold or imaginative thinking on either side. Its significance was largely that it happened at all, bringing together the leaders of big business and the TUC on equal terms for the first time. Also notable was the acceptance by Mond and his colleagues that mass unemployment was an obscenity that had to be ended. It was from this point that Bevin often called himself an 'industrialist' or 'an industrial leader', not just a trade union leader. The mood was conciliatory and cautiously constructive, in the spirit of Baldwin. Church sermons were preached up and down the country over Christmas 1927 urging the success of the talks.

Bevin was now the trade union 'leader of leaders'. A. J. Cook branded the talks 'Mond Moonshine' but Bevin carried the TUC behind them. 'Is the strike the only way to fight?' was his robust response to Cook's attack on Mondism and co-operation with employers at the 1928 TUC conference, one ex-Baptist lay preacher to another. 'Cannot we fight by discussion as well as starvation? Cannot we fight by intelligence?' Then, in crystal-clear Bevinese:

> I have claimed from the beginning, and I have never apologised for it, that the general strike was a culminating point to that conflict for power which has been going on. In view of this invitation [Mond–Turner] and subsequent development – if it was not all that we desired – it proved that we had not lost the fight after all.[22]

Bevin's immediate priority after the General Strike was to shore up the T&G. By the end of May 1926 he had ensured that none of his laboriously negotiated national agreements was lost. Out of 353,000 members who had been out on strike, the union failed to get fewer than 1,500 back into their jobs. But the T&G lost one in seven of its members in the year after the strike and faced a huge £600,000 financial hole. Numerous expedients, including a sixpence weekly levy on members, helped repair the union's finances. Bevin

toured the country, speaking at more than a hundred meetings to rebuild morale. He also put down an October attempt by communist
London dockers to form a breakaway union.

Building up the TUC was the next task, which Bevin did in alliance
with Citrine. Although never friends – they were too wary and competitive of each other for that – Bevin and Citrine rubbed along. They
were united in opposition to communism and on a strategy to up-
grade the TUC, now based in Transport House alongside the T&G,
'Citrine lucid and methodical, drawing upon his famous notebooks for
the facts, Bevin ranging and impressionistic, throwing out ideas; the
one a master of exposition, the other of conviction and imagination.'
Mond–Turner was one initiative; another was hiring more staff for the
TUC. Citrine's headcount increased from fourteen in 1924 to forty by
1930. In 1928 they also set up an economic committee of the General
Council. Bevin was a member, telling the 1928 TUC conference:

> I look forward to the time when the General Council will be
> coming and laying down before this great parliament of its own
> creation annual reports on the discussion of great economic prob-
> lems, trying to direct your attention on lines of analyses, lines of
> investigation, not mere debating points blown by the wind. Thus
> and only thus will the movement be really intelligently dealing
> with the real economic problems of the age.[23]

Invitations to TUC leaders to serve on state bodies were also lobbied
for and accepted, particularly during the second Labour government
of 1929–31.

A key lesson Bevin drew from the General Strike was that the
trade unions and the Labour Party needed to be much better at

communication and propaganda, not least with their own followers. With his keen understanding of publicity, he played a big part in developing the *Daily Herald*, precursor of today's *Sun* in style and popularity although not in politics. In 1920, after the Lansbury debacle described earlier, Bevin raised the funds needed to relaunch the *Herald* as a daily paper. In 1922, the Labour Party took ownership of the broadsheet. When Baldwin's trade union legislation of 1927 drastically reduced the party's income, though, it had to cut its support. The paper's quality suffered, and by 1928 circulation had slumped to 301,000, way behind the *Daily Express* and the *Daily Mail*. Thanks to Bevin, in 1929 the TUC took a major stake in the *Herald*, in partnership with a commercial publisher, and Bevin became vice-chairman of the new holding company. The paper was relaunched and Ernie characteristically toured the country over thirty-five consecutive weekends to persuade Labour and trade union members to subscribe.

Bevin then threw himself into the launch of a northern edition of the *Herald*, printed in Manchester, including a further tour of the north. The first northern edition, published on 28 June 1929, was celebrated in Manchester by 'a procession three and a half miles long, preceded by more than a hundred tableaux mounted on carts and accompanied by twenty-five bands complete with all the delights of the fair from Blackpool and ending in a dazzling display of fireworks'.[24] By 1933 the *Herald* had become the first paper in the world to reach a circulation of 2 million.

What did not improve in these years, however, was relations between the miners and the rest of the labour movement. A. J. Cook accused Bevin, Citrine and MacDonald of being 'sickening'. They were 'traitors' and 'collaborators', he said. And relations between the TUC and the Labour Party leader were not much better. MacDonald blamed the TUC for blundering into the strike and called publicly for a 'thorough reconsideration of trade union tactics'.[25]

As ever, Bevin took on all comers, laying into Cook for not negotiating and MacDonald for 'stabbing us in the back'. 'Cook asked me if I hadn't economic theory to guide me in my settlements,' he told an away weekend of 250 full-time T&G officers in February 1927. 'I said "No, of course not." I have got a theory for society in substitution for the present one, but we have to deal with our business on business lines and whilst working under a capitalist system we have to have regard to it accordingly.'[26] However, we also need to take with a pinch of salt the lengths Bevin went to after the General Strike to attribute the failure of mediation during the strike to the refusal of the miners to budge. After a week of a general strike that was clearly faltering, Baldwin, and still less Churchill and the hard men, were never likely to agree to negotiations without the strike being called off unconditionally.

A key point to note about Bevin and the General Strike is that at no stage did he depart from, or even contemplate departing from, majority decisions by the TUC General Council. Even when not fully in control and when critical of TUC strategy, he was a man of majorities not minorities. When the majority was for the strike, he was in the vanguard. When a majority could be secured to call it off, he was in that vanguard too.

Furthermore, for all his fabled pragmatism, Bevin was only ever pragmatic up to a point. Whatever his disagreement with the miners' leaders over tactics and strategy, his greater contempt by far was for the Tories and the coal owners. Bevin saw the General Strike as essentially their fault. The root cause of the strike, he insisted, was Churchill's return to the Gold Standard in 1925, which, by over-valuing the pound, undermined coal exports. This wasn't just Bevin's retrospective view, and it long predated Keynes's *The Economic Consequences of Mr Churchill*. As far back as 1917, as a member of the Ministry of Reconstruction Committee on the economic transition from war to peace, Bevin had argued 'stubbornly and almost alone' against the orthodox view that there should be an early return to the gold standard.[27] From his earliest days in national politics his self-confidence knew few bounds, even when taking on economic orthodoxy.

As for the coal owners, it was hardly extremist to regard them as incompetent and often vicious. Birkenhead said of them: 'It would be possible to say without exaggeration of the miners' leaders that they were the stupidest men in England if we had not had frequent occasion to meet the owners.'[28] Bevin saw public ownership as the answer and was passionately committed to coal nationalisation for the rest of his life, including in Germany, where he sought to impose it in the British zone as Foreign Secretary after 1945.

When the TUC General Council debated future strategy in the autumn of 1927, Citrine tabled a paper with three options: the first – and it is telling that this should have been included – was to try for another, bigger general strike, 'in the hope of creating a revolutionary situation on the assumption that this might be turned to the advantage of the workers and to the abolition of capitalism'; the second option was to return to old-style trade unionism and 'pursue a policy of fighting sectionally for improvements'; the third 'was for the trade union movement to say boldly that not only was it concerned with the prosperity of industry, but that it was going to have a voice in the way industry was carried on'. Bevin was adamant for this third way, which he saw as a bold strategy of taking power and changing the system fundamentally, but only by democratic means and for democratic ends. As he put to the 1929 TUC conference in Belfast: 'Parliament will never lead the industrial system. Parliament will follow the industrial system.'[29]

Bevin was revolutionary about goals, democratic about means.

'The result of the General Strike altogether delights one,' Birkenhead wrote triumphantly to Lord Halifax, then Viceroy of India, when it was over. 'For it shows that this old England of ours retains its spirit unimpaired ... I thought of the Burghers of Calais approaching their interview with Edward III, haltered on the neck.'[30]

From the other end of the political spectrum, Bevin agreed that 'old England' was 'unimpaired'. But he saw the strike as a massive intellectual and organisational failure by the labour movement, and he applied his indomitable energy to reversing it. 'He swarmed with ideas,' as Bullock put it.[31] In the immediate aftermath he got renewed zest from the six weeks he spent on his government-sponsored tour of the US, including in Chicago, Detroit, Pittsburgh, Philadelphia, New York and Washington. There the raw energy and cruelty of American industrialism again appalled and amazed him, as it had on his visit in 1916.

In 1927 he again undertook his by now near annual gig at the International Labour Organisation conference in Geneva, followed by the International Transport Workers' Federation conference in Stockholm. The Swedish conference included a trip to Narvik across the Norwegian border in the far north. Bevin was awestruck by the Land of the Midnight Sun. Thirteen years later, in April 1940, it was to be the Land of the Midnight Defeat, a defeat far more serious than the General Strike, as Norway fell to Hitler. The war was to bring Bevin to power as the right-hand man of the same Churchill he had fought in the General Strike.

What drew Keynes to Bevin was 'a temperamental affinity in favour of action against mass unemployment rather than a timid quietism'.

CHAPTER 4

KEYNES

K eynes was to Bevin as Hayek was to Thatcher.
'Thatcher instinctively realised the need to regain the moral as well as the practical initiative from collectivism,' said Nigel Lawson. 'In this she was strongly fortified by the economist and philosopher Friedrich Hayek.'[1] Similarly, Bevin instinctively realised the need to regain the moral as well as the practical initiative from the prevailing *laissez-faire* policy. And in this, he was strongly fortified by the economist and philosopher John Maynard Keynes.

Leading an intellectual revolution, Keynes branded *laissez-faire* as a fundamental cause of mass unemployment in the 1920s and 1930s. 'Practical men who believe themselves to be quite exempt from any intellectual influence are usually the slave of some defunct economist,' he famously observed. So it was with *laissez-faire*. The verdict of the victorious Lord Birkenhead on the General Strike – 'on the absolute defeat of the strike came to depend failure or success in educating the working people of this country into the iron realities of the economic wage' – says it all.[2]

But the supposedly 'iron realities' of *laissez-faire* gripped the Labour leadership too, causing the collapse of Ramsay MacDonald's

1929 government. In August 1931 MacDonald abandoned trying to run a Labour government because he had no policy and philosophy with which to resist demands for big spending and welfare cuts from the City, the Bank of England, the Treasury and the media.

It is not unusual for governments to expire because they go politically bankrupt. It has happened several times besides 1931 in the past century: from Theresa May over Brexit in 2019 to Callaghan after the 'Winter of Discontent' in 1979, Eden after Suez in 1957 and Chamberlain after the fall of Norway in 1940. What makes 1931 unique is that MacDonald and his Chancellor Philip Snowden not only resigned, they defected to the other side and formed a government with the opposition. Within weeks they were fighting an election accusing their former comrades of 'Bolshevism run mad'.

The political bankruptcy of 1931 was total. Snowden, an ex-Inland Revenue clerk, was 'raised in an atmosphere which regarded borrowing as an evil and free trade as an essential ingredient of prosperity', writes his biographer.[3] His socialism was a mix of Methodism, pacifism, teetotalism and a rigid Gladstonian economy imbibed in the 1880s when he was in his twenties. It never changed thereafter.

For Snowden and MacDonald, what made Keynes's nascent ideas at once so potent, yet so resistible, is that they were championed by the mercurial Lloyd George. The ideas therefore attracted huge political attention and forced a response, but they ultimately held no sway over either Labour leader. On the contrary, MacDonald regarded Lloyd George with jealousy, fear and suspicion and was determined to keep him out. Stanley Baldwin had the same goal, becoming Tory leader specifically because he had led the Tory revolt that toppled Lloyd George in 1922. As he told the Carlton Club meeting that did the deed, he felt that Lloyd George was a 'dynamic force', which was 'a very terrible thing'.[4]

In 1929 MacDonald and Baldwin were in a spiritual coalition against Lloyd George. Baldwin called for 'Safety First', MacDonald for 'No Monkeying', both slogans aimed at the Liberal leader whom MacDonald dismissed as 'an old performer at familiar tricks' simply trying a repeat of his 'homes fit for heroes' con of 1918 in his new campaign to slash unemployment. MacDonald spent virtually the whole of the 1929 election campaign talking about disarmament and world peace partly so he could avoid talking about unemployment and Lloyd George.[5] Then, in August 1931, MacDonald and Baldwin formed an actual coalition together that deliberately excluded Lloyd George, who never again held office. Fittingly, his last vote in Parliament, cast at the age of eighty, was in support of the Beveridge Report in 1943.

The politics of the late 1920s and early 1930s was thus conservatives versus radicals: the Tory and Labour leaderships were the conservatives; Lloyd George, Keynes and Bevin were the radicals. 'They are always wanting to find reasons for not doing things,' Lloyd George said of MacDonald and Snowden with exasperation in February 1931, in reply to a private appeal from George Lansbury to join the Labour Party. 'They are too easily scared by obstacles and interests.'[6]

MacDonald and Snowden could not completely refuse to engage with Lloyd George and Keynes in 1929, being a minority government dependent on Liberal votes in the House of Commons. Snowden therefore took diversionary action. He 'consulted' for six months after the election, then, in November 1929, he set up a committee of inquiry to examine relations between finance and industry. He included Keynes on the fourteen-strong committee but surrounded the radical economist with an Establishment phalanx. As chairman he appointed an economically illiterate judge, Lord Macmillan, who had recently chaired a royal commission on lunacy. Bevin was put on the committee too, the only trade union representative and one of only three leftish members. The intention was clearly not to praise Keynes but to bury him.

What Snowden and MacDonald hadn't counted on, however, was that Keynes would be so assiduous on the committee, hunting as a pack with Bevin and converting others too. This Keynes–Bevin axis was a large part of the reason why Labour split in 1931 rather than accepting MacDonald–Snowden austerity. Bevin and those he influenced were convinced that MacDonald was wrong, fundamentally wrong, on the economics as well as the politics of austerity.

Keynes had been calling out *laissez-faire* since the mid-1920s. He inveighed against Churchill's twin errors as Baldwin's Chancellor of returning the pound to the gold standard at a grossly overvalued exchange rate and refusing to invest in public works at a time of mounting unemployment. 'I see no reason why, with good management, real wages need be reduced on the average. It is the consequence of a misguided monetary policy,' he wrote in *The Economic Consequences of Mr Churchill* (1925). Churchill's policy was, according to Keynes, a 'deliberate intensification of unemployment ... The plight of the coal miners is the first, but not – unless we are very lucky – the last of the Economic Consequences of Mr Churchill.'

The revolution brought about by Keynes overturned the *laissez-faire* view, propounded most trenchantly by Alfred Marshall in his *Principles of Economics* (1890) and *Money, Credit and Commerce* (1923), that the economy had a self-righting tendency towards equilibrium and full employment without state intervention. He also argued against the traditional doctrine that state investment was counter-productive because it simply 'crowded out' an equivalent amount of private investment.

In his *Tract on Monetary Reform* (1923), and his seminal lecture 'The End of Laissez-Faire' (1926), Keynes launched his intellectual revolution. Maybe there were self-righting forces in the economy, if allowed enough time, he accepted. 'But this *long run* is a misleading guide to current affairs. *In the long run* we are all dead.' From this insight flowed his opposition to the Gold Standard, with its promise of long-term self-righting benefits as a result of inflexibly pegging the pound. It also prompted his support for counter-cyclical public spending, or what became known as 'demand management': that in economic slow-downs the government should boost demand by spending more, particularly on employment-generating public works. Public investment had to come to the rescue when the market failed. Keynes's formal rationale for this, including the concept of a 'multiplier' yielding dynamic effects from wise counter-cyclical investment, was not set out until his *General Theory of Employment, Interest and Money* of 1936, but the key elements of it were at the heart of his evisceration of the orthodox 'Treasury view' a decade before.

By the mid-1920s Keynes was working hand-in-glove with Lloyd George, despite their celebrated earlier disagreement about the Versailles Treaty and its devastating reparations penalties on Germany. Attacked for this *volte-face*, Keynes responded characteristically: 'The difference between myself and some other people is that I oppose Mr Lloyd George when he is wrong and support him when is right' – a variant on his maybe apocryphal quip: 'When the facts change, I change my mind. What do you do sir?'[7]

Bevin and Lloyd George were strikingly similar as politicians of boundless action and ideas. They hardly read books, but they read people who read books, and they both had magpie minds that picked out glittering ideas from intense conversation, stashing them in their political nests with little concern as to how they fitted together. Few glittered as brightly as Keynes.

Until the end of his life Lloyd George, the 'Welsh Wizard', had something about him of the 'goat-footed bard', a 'half human visitor to our age from the hag-ridden magic and enchanted woods of Celtic antiquity' conjured by Keynes in *The Economic Consequences of the Peace*, complete with 'cunning, remorselessness, love of power' and 'existence outside or away from our Saxon good or evil'.[8] Bevin too was an outsider who, in becoming an insider, lost little of the 'working-class John Bull' that made him such an object of fear and fascination. Keynes too was a highly unusual mix of insider and outsider: an Etonian social insider *par excellence*, but an intellectual iconoclast with flashes of Martin Luther and Karl Marx.

What drew Keynes to Lloyd George, and after 1929 what drew him to Bevin similarly, was what the historian Peter Clarke calls 'a temperamental affinity in favour of action rather than timid quietism or doctrinaire inertia'. They had this in common with maybe the greatest democratic leader of the twentieth century: 'Like Franklin Roosevelt when he later launched his "New Deal", an instinctive belief that there was nothing to fear but fear itself can be seen as a defining political ingredient in policies that were in some respects incoherent.'[9] Even in his attacks on Lloyd George at Versailles, Keynes was magnetised by his 'six or seven senses not available to ordinary men', and he saw some of them in Bevin too. He accordingly cultivated the T&G leader when they were both members of the Macmillan Committee, much as he had earlier cultivated Lloyd George. Both were wise investments, particularly the one in Bevin, the man of the future, although this wasn't so clear at the time.

On gaining the Liberal leadership from Asquith in 1926, after the General Strike, Lloyd George set up his Liberal Industrial Inquiry. 'When Lloyd George came back to the party, ideas came back to the party,' said the Liberal turned Christian socialist Charles Masterman.[10] The inquiry reported in 1928 with ambitious plans for state-funded public works. Popularised as the 'Yellow Book', with Keynes's help this became *We Can Conquer Unemployment*, Lloyd George's radical manifesto for the 1929 election, by which time unemployment was escalating towards the 3 million mark it eventually reached in 1931.

Snowden was frank, in retrospect, that the Macmillan Committee was set up 'largely because of the impression made on public opinion by Mr Keynes' proposals'.[11] But the committee was also a response to Bevin, who was becoming Keynesian long before he met Keynes. The moment Churchill introduced the Gold Standard policy in 1925, Bevin grasped its practical impact on wages, exports and unemployment. Angry at the total lack of initiative and energy shown by MacDonald after the May 1929 election, he used the September TUC conference in Belfast and the October Labour Party conference in Brighton to call for public works to reduce unemployment. This included road building and the Severn Barrage (still not built in 2020). He demanded that Snowden investigate the banking system and why it was not doing more to support industrial investment, which is partly why, lethargically, Snowden set up the Macmillan Committee in November and put Bevin on it.

Keynes quickly took charge of the committee in alliance with Bevin and Reginald McKenna, chairman of the Midland Bank and

Asquith's former Chancellor. McKenna was another independent thinker, albeit a more cautious one, who became attracted pragmatically to an active industrial policy because he saw huge volumes of 'frozen savings' sitting idle in bank accounts at the Midland, which he thought could be put to better use.

Keynes dominated the Macmillan Committee in an unusual way. He became chief witness as well as chief interrogator. For nine hours he set out to the committee, with scintillating lucidity, the workings of the financial system, why it was broken, and how it should be reformed. 'The boom, not the slump, is the time for austerity at the Treasury,' was his constant message.[12]

Bevin kept fairly quiet in the early sessions, learning from Keynes's mega tutorials. But increasingly he rowed in behind the economic wizard, supporting his economic arguments with his own practical experience. Describing himself as an 'industrialist' sharing 'a common interest with the manufacturer and employer of labour against those who lived off industry', he argued that returning to the Gold Standard was 'the direct cause of upsetting every agreement with every employer in the country'. He went on:

> You return to the gold standard in 1925 and you give to a miner and a mineowner the job on adjusting industry. They do not know what has hit them. They have got to handle all the problems of a million men ... That was the thing that pushed us over the cliff.[13]

Bevin's passage of arms with Montagu Norman, the taciturn do-nothing governor of the Bank of England throughout the 1920s and 1930s, had shades of his 'Dockers' KC' performance at the Shaw Inquiry a decade earlier. One exchange cut to the quick:

'MR BEVIN: Is it possible to have some direction through public bodies, municipalities, of the whole operation of credit ... to prevent the blow falling upon the workpeople?

THE RT HON MONTAGU NORMAN: I should say it is impossible.'[14]

The radical historian A. J. P. Taylor said of Bevin's performance on the Macmillan Committee: 'He remained all his life a casual labourer, ready to turn his hand to anything and without much belief in the trained expert. An engine-driver or a maker of precision tools would never have challenged the bankers as ruthlessly as Bevin did.'[15]

The Macmillan Committee's report, largely drafted by Keynes, called for cheaper credit for industry, with an international fund to guarantee loans. In a minority report, Keynes, Bevin and McKenna went further and proposed major public investment to tackle unemployment and boost industry. This 'marked the start of the Keynesian revolution in policy making', writes Keynes's biographer Robert Skidelsky. '*Laissez-faire* as understood before the war can never be recreated,' said Bevin.[16] The 1944 Employment White Paper and the International Monetary Fund, set up in 1945, were both inspired by these Keynesian ideas.

Bevin, however, went further. In a minority report of one, he called for Britain to come off the Gold Standard and devalue the pound immediately, together with 'a large measure of state planning and reorganisation, particularly in the basic industries, with the provision of Transport and Power as basic services'. He concluded, 'I really cannot see how it is possible to maintain the gold standard and abolish unemployment at the same time.' This was almost immediately proved right: the Gold Standard collapsed in September 1931, a month after the formation of the National Government that was set up to defend it.[17]

Yet while Bevin was more Keynesian than Keynes in calling for an end to the Gold Standard, his support for wholesale nationalisation was distinctly un-Keynesian. Keynes believed in public and government spending to tackle unemployment and underconsumption, but he was a firm opponent of the state as the bureaucratic owner and manager of industries. Keynes never went in for the fashion, which was embraced by Bevin and extended even to Harold Macmillan as late as the 1950s, of praising Soviet five-year plans with their supposedly bold and effective schemes of economic mobilisation. Bevin wrote of Soviet economic planning, 'Whilst it may be impossible to introduce a similar form in this country, to leave our industries languishing and our people to the tender mercies of a worn out nineteenth-century system is an insane policy.'[18]

The unstated reason why Bevin conceded that Soviet-style planning 'may be impossible' in Britain was, of course, because of the degree of state direction and oppression required, a critique in accord with his own condemnation of communism as tyranny. Keynes saw this contradiction for what it was, a refutation of the five-year plans whose fabled 'tractor production' statistics and achievements were anyway bogus confections of a dictatorship that could no more compel their realisation than invade Mars. However, Bevin hankered after something at least halfway. He saw the nationalisation of heavy industry – 'the commanding heights of the economy' – as a good compromise, in Lenin's 1922 phrase which stuck in British Labour discourse, although he had a somewhat different view of 'commanding' and 'heights'. This policy was partly realised by the 1945 Labour government. Antipathy to the private owners of these industries, particularly the coal owners, was a powerful further motive. By contrast, Keynes's halfway house was a different one, which sought not a compromise with communism in nationalising much but not all private enterprise, but rather a compromise between public control and private control across the whole of industry, in order to deliver better on the democratically agreed objectives of high employment and public welfare.

It is a pity Keynes and Bevin never engaged in a dialogue on this crucial agenda of nationalisation versus public–private partnership. Keynes made a persuasive argument for partnership rather than nationalisation at the time. The government, he argued, should 'experiment with all kinds of new sorts of partnership between the state and private enterprise. The solution lies neither with nationalisation nor with unregulated private competition; it lies in a variety of experiments, of attempts to get the best of both worlds.' Tellingly, this was in an address to Liberal candidates. One historian calls it 'liberal socialism', which is a good description of both Bevin's and Keynes's broad political philosophy in the 1930s and 1940s.[19] It was this 'liberal socialism' that underpinned Bevin's break with MacDonald in August 1931.

Bevin was soon estranged from the do-nothing economic policy of the 1929 Labour government. MacDonald set up an Economic Advisory Council in January 1930, which he chaired and on which Bevin and Keynes sat, but it was all waffle, no action. MacDonald appointed a string of reactionary company chairmen to the council and it failed to agree on Bevin and Keynes's call for a public works programme even as unemployment hit 2.6 million in early 1931. Sir Arthur Balfour, a steel master from Sheffield, and Sir John Cadman, of the Anglo-Persian Oil Company, saw public investment as the path to inflation and national bankruptcy, and used such apocalyptic language constantly. MacDonald, at sea in economics, made no attempt to reconcile these wildly divergent views, still less to make constructive proposals on behalf of the government. Meanwhile Snowden explicitly supported Balfour and Cadman. Tellingly, as the economic crisis got worse, the Economic Council met less frequently. Its final meeting was in April 1931, six months before the collapse of the government, where Bevin predicted that unemployment would worsen until Britain came off the Gold Standard and devalued the pound.[20]

Bevin was also by now in favour of tariffs to protect British industry, an issue that fiercely divided all three political parties, particularly the Tories and the Liberals. On this, too, he was in opposition to Snowden, who was an out-and-out old-school free trader. So much so that, even after joining MacDonald in his Tory-dominated government in August, Snowden soon resigned when the new government decided to introduce tariffs.

The arguments for and against trade tariffs, and what was called 'imperial preference' to allow goods from the Empire to enter Britain with lower or zero tariffs, divided Keynesians and indeed Keynes himself, whose views oscillated. For Bevin, this became another case of 'action versus inaction', and he developed an argument of his own that was politically compelling if economically dubious: that a tariff wall was necessary to enable rationalisation – and in many areas nationalisation – to be carried through to make British jobs competitive. 'Friends,' he said to the TUC when debating tariffs in 1930, 'I believe in organising ourselves.'[21]

Bevin's support for tariffs with imperial preference was to have an important further consequence for his politics in the 1930s and 1940s. By definition, it prioritised the Empire over Europe. In the mid-1920s, Bevin had been in favour of a European customs union, an idea made flesh in the French Foreign Minister Aristide Briand's plan of 1930 and whose ideas were taken up again by Jean Monnet and Robert Schuman after the war. At the 1927 TUC conference, Bevin had deployed language similar to theirs and proposed a European customs union, leading to fuller economic and political integration. But by 1931 he had shifted from Europe to Empire as the means to promote jobs and trade. This was to have significant ramifications after the war for his policy and outlook as Foreign Secretary.

Unemployment escalated from 1.1 million when Labour took office in 1929 to 2.5 million by December 1930 and 2.8 million in July 1931. The sense of MacDonald 'fiddling while Rome burns' was dramatically captured by Sir Oswald Mosley in his resignation in May 1930. Mosley had been the minister responsible for tackling unemployment, but Snowden rejected all his proposals. His resignation speech in the House of Commons on 28 May 1930, setting out a bold plan to tackle unemployment, was an electric parliamentary moment. He gathered significant cross-party support before setting up his New Party in 1931 and going fascist. At the October 1930 Labour conference in Llandudno, a motion supporting Mosley won over a million votes and the sixth baronet himself was elected to Labour's National Executive Committee, ousting Jimmy Thomas, epitome of the 1920s union movement and the minister in MacDonald's government supposedly leading the charge against unemployment.

Bevin never toyed with Mosley. Tory-turned-Labour aristocrats weren't his thing and he remained publicly loyal to Labour. But Bevin's private criticism of MacDonald was biting. As early as August 1930 he told his T&G executive: 'The bankers and the industrialists are already manoeuvring for an attack on money wages

... This union must be organised. Every available penny must be put in reserve in order that we may be ready when the crisis comes.'[22]

The end game of the MacDonald government was dictated not by external forces but by self-imposed decisions in the weeks and months leading up to August 1931. A key moment was 11 February, when, faced with a Tory motion of confidence in the House of Commons on the government's 'wasteful expenditure', including borrowing to fund the unemployment insurance fund at a time of rocketing unemployment, Snowden accepted a Liberal amendment for an independent committee to recommend economies. (The Liberals of 1931 were as divided as Labour on Keynesianism, only in their case it was the leader who was Keynesian and many of his business followers who were *laissez-faire*.) Snowden then deliberately appointed an ultra-orthodox committee to recommend spending cuts, chaired by Sir George May, a former secretary of the Prudential Assurance Company. The committee included four representatives of business and industry but only two of labour. As Beatrice Webb noted in her diary after meeting Snowden at this time: 'Philip has completely changed ... from being a fervent apostle of Utopian Socialism, thirty years of parliamentary life and ten years of Front Bench politics have made him the upholder of the banker, that landed aristocrat and the Crown.'[23]

The ideological battle – Keynes and expansion versus Snowden and austerity – could not have been starker. Sir Laming Worthington-Evans, the Tory baronet and ex-Baldwin minister who moved the censure motion on 11 February, attacked Snowden for a 'deliberate and reckless policy of increased expenditure at a time when the most rigid economy is the greatest need of the nation'. Yet far from seeking to justify Labour's higher public spending as necessary during a recession, Snowden's response was to blame the 'extravagance' of the previous Baldwin government as 'a rake's progress', including its provision of more generous war widows' pensions. He even accepted the Tory argument that spending on unemployment benefit was 'appallingly high', adding for good measure: 'I admit that it cannot go on in the form in which it is being raised and expended at the present time.' Lest his arch conservatism be misunderstood, he went on:

> There is no Member who would welcome suggestions for economy more than I should; and no proposal submitted to me would fail to receive the closest and most sympathetic investigation. But I must have something tangible ... I say with all the seriousness I can command that the national position is so grave that drastic and disagreeable measures will have to be taken if Budget equilibrium and if industrial progress is to be maintained.[24]

So, the majority report of the May Committee, arguing for big welfare and other spending cuts, was just what Snowden wanted. Likewise, it was just what Keynes and Bevin had for months been arguing against, right up to the publication of the Macmillan Report two weeks before publication of the May Report. In parallel, all through 1931, Bevin had been resisting – generally successfully – the wage cuts proposed by employers. At the T&G conference in early July he made a big argument for 'national stimulus not national austerity'.

The May Committee's report – 'The most foolish document I have ever had the misfortune to read,' said Keynes – came out a day after Parliament rose for its summer recess on 30 July.[25] The government did not have to face Parliament again until October, so Snowden had no need to act precipitately, particularly since the two pro-labour members of the committee refused to sign the report but instead wrote a minority report arguing against cuts. Snowden ignored them and deliberately forced the pace towards big government spending cuts. He immediately and publicly accepted the majority report, including May's alarmist picture of the public finances and his recommendations for an immediate balanced budget, mainly financed by spending cuts of £96 million (two-thirds from cutting support for the unemployed), against £24 million to be raised in new taxes.

Snowden and MacDonald, who went along with his Chancellor unquestioningly, claimed to be acting to avert a banking crisis. It is true that they were acting on the strong advice of the Bank of England after a run on sterling in the second week of August. But other options were clearly available, notably to go off the Gold Standard and devalue, as was done by MacDonald's coalition government with the Tories only five weeks later on 21 September, and as Bevin had urged in his minority report to the Macmillan Committee. Coming off the Gold Standard could have been done by the government alone and did not require parliamentary approval, so the lack of a Commons majority did not matter. There would then probably have been an election in the autumn, but that happened anyway under the National Government. The difference was that, if the Labour government had acted boldly on these lines, the election would have been held by a united Labour Party putting its case for crisis action, whereas MacDonald's course of action, in coalition with the Conservatives, was to destroy a divided Labour Party in a national panic.

Between 11 and 23 August, amid a media circus in Downing

Street after MacDonald's dramatic unexpected return from holiday in Lossiemouth, the Labour Prime Minister and Chancellor sought to force their austerity package on a reluctant Cabinet. They deliberately intensified the crisis, and indicated its possible outcome, by briefing the opposition parties and negotiating with them and the Bank of England semi-publicly alongside the Cabinet. Baldwin and his shadow Chancellor Neville Chamberlain of course urged MacDonald to stand firm and carry out the cuts. The Cabinet moved a long way towards MacDonald, accepting cuts of £56 million, but it split on Snowden's demand that in order to carry Tory support this figure had to be increased to £78 million, including a 10 per cent cut in unemployment benefits. It was this that caused eight or nine ministers to threaten to resign, including Arthur Henderson as Foreign Secretary.

On the evening of Sunday 23 August, the Cabinet agreed to MacDonald's proposal that the Labour government should resign as they could no longer unite on an economic policy. Then, after talks with King George V and Baldwin, MacDonald the following day formed a new government in coalition with the Conservatives and the Liberals, minus Lloyd George. This astonishing manoeuvre was announced as a temporary emergency 'National Government' to enforce the spending cuts, but MacDonald soon decided to lead the coalition into an 'emergency' election and he ended up serving for another four years as a puppet at the head of a de facto Tory government.

In the 'emergency' election, on 27 October, MacDonald, Baldwin and their allies won 67 per cent of the vote and 554 of the 614 seats in the House of Commons. It was one of the bitterest elections in modern history. Most constituencies were a straight fight between

'National' and 'Labour', the party labels summing up Labour's predicament as the 'unpatriotic' party. Just fifty-two Labour MPs were returned, although the party polled 31 per cent of the vote. The Tory triumph was complete. MacDonald's 'National Labour' party secured just thirteen seats, including himself and his son Malcolm, against 470 'National Conservatives'.

Throughout the crisis, Bevin stood solidly behind Arthur Henderson, who led the anti-cuts minority in the Labour Cabinet and took over the leadership of the party when MacDonald formed his coalition with Baldwin. 'The crisis has not arisen as the result of anything that the Labour Government has done,' Bevin told the T&G executive on 17 August, having met MacDonald and Snowden with TUC General Council members on the 13th. 'It has arisen as a result of the manipulation of finance by the City ... The City must not be saved at the expense of the working class and the poverty of our people,' he urged.[26] In a sign of how well known MacDonald's intentions were by this point, Bevin added, 'There is talk of a National Government and interviews and intrigues are going on.' But, he emphasised, 'Whatever happens, it is essential that the trade unions should take a very firm line: there is a danger of a complete debacle unless this Movement of ours remains steady.'

A joint meeting of Labour's NEC and the TUC General Council, held on 20 August in the Council Chamber of Transport House, listened to MacDonald and Snowden talk of 'dread realities' but it rejected their campaign for cuts. Their presentation was 'not worthy of an ordinary shop steward reporting the settlement of a local wage problem', said Bevin. An angry confrontation took place between Bevin and Snowden later the same day. According to a minute, Snowden said, 'If sterling went, the whole international financial structure would collapse. There would be millions more unemployed and complete industrial collapse. Mr Bevin disputed this statement, but Mr Snowden insisted that his own view was correct.'[27] MacDonald's loathing of Bevin and the unions is laid bare in his diary entry after their meeting: 'It was practically a declaration of war. If we yield now to the TUC we shall never be able to call our bodies or souls or intelligences our own.'[28] For MacDonald, the aristocratic embrace had become far stronger than the labour movement. 'Tomorrow every duchess in London will be wanting to kiss me,' he said to Snowden the day he pulled the plug on the Labour government.[29]

Bevin was cool, decisive and ruthless, even as the pro-Labour media wavered. 'It is one thing to lead a revolt like that of the nine Ministers, it is another to develop that revolt into a challenge to a National Government,' the *Manchester Guardian* declared when MacDonald announced his coalition with Baldwin. Bevin, on the contrary, saw the one as leading necessarily to the other. As in the General Strike, he took charge. Hugh Dalton, a Labour rising star of the 1930s who was to play a central role in the post-war Attlee government alongside Bevin, records of the afternoon of 24 August:

> Straight round to Transport House, where in Uncle's [Henderson's] room is a council of war. With him are George Lansbury, Bevin, Citrine, Stanley Hirst [chairman of the NEC and financial secretary of the T&G], Middleton [assistant secretary of the Labour Party]. The Trade Union leaders are full of fight. They speak of financial assistance. 'This is like the General Strike,' says Bevin. 'I'm prepared to put everything in.' They send for X of the *Herald* to settle the line of tomorrow's leader. X – still under the influence of J.R.M. [MacDonald] and P.S. [Snowden] who

had been working on him very hard – had proposed to begin by paying tribute to the courage of those who are staying in. 'And what about the courage of those who are coming out,' asks Uncle. So the whole emphasis is changed. The *Herald*, in the days that followed, under Bevin's influence, gave a fine lead.[30]

Note that both of the institutions here, the *Herald* and Transport House, were Bevin's creation, and most of the people mentioned were his close associates. It is also striking to note what was *not* discussed: another general strike. Bevin wasn't going there again.

Dalton records an equally telling exchange when he and Bevin were heading north in early October, on the train to the constituencies they were fighting in the general election. MacDonald, Dalton said, had remarked to him and other members of his Economic Advisory Council: 'You must remember the low mental calibre of those I have to work with.' Bevin had replied, 'Mr Prime Minister, you shouldn't say that sort of thing in front of me.'[31]

Bevin rallied the TUC at its conference in Bristol in early September, setting the crisis in the context of the expansionary policies needed in place of *laissez-faire*. While 'in some ways confused and vague', it had 'the prophetic touch of imagination, that sense of historical change which mark Bevin's speeches off from the pedestrian oratory of most trade union conferences with their stock perorations and appeals to emotion'.[32] He did the same at the Labour conference in Scarborough, which met on the day (5 October) that MacDonald announced he would lead his coalition with the Conservatives into the election.

Bevin was initially reluctant to stand in the 1931 election. But needs must and he stood in Gateshead. He was attracted to Gateshead because it was in County Durham, close to MacDonald's seat of Seaham. 'Vote for Bevin and Public Control of Banking in the interests of Trade, Commerce and the People', ran the over-wordy slogan on the side of his campaign bus (see the picture in the plate section). The other side was even more wordy, but it encapsulated his new Keynesianism: 'Abundance Yet Unemployment, Want, Poverty, High Taxation and Bankruptcy! WHY? Banker's dictatorship and financial manipulation.'

For Bevin, like Churchill, the 1930s were wilderness years, but they were not fallow.

Bevin didn't save Gateshead for Labour. The 1929 Labour majority of 16,700 became a National majority of 12,938 in 1931. It was a bitter campaign. Bevin went to Seaham and roared, 'If any of you vote for MacDonald next week go afterwards to the Employment Exchange and apologise to the working men there because they are going to lose two shillings and ninepence. MacDonald can't cut your money without your help.'[33] It was hardly Walt Whitman's 'barbaric yawp', but the 1931 result could easily have been worse for Labour had MacDonald taken with him more of the ministers who initially backed Snowden's cuts in the Cabinet in August, including Herbert Morrison, but who nonetheless stayed loyal to the party. Bevin's role was crucial in quickly stabilising the Labour ship under Henderson's leadership after MacDonald's defection. In the event, although a rout, Henderson's 31 per cent share of the vote in 1931 was better than Michael Foot's 28 per cent in 1983 and only fractionally worse than Jeremy Corbyn's 32 per cent in 2019. Henderson lost his own seat but, crucially, Labour held on to its status as the official opposition. One of the survivors was Clement Attlee, then an obscure and unprepossessing junior minister in the former government.

For Bevin, like Churchill, the 1930s were wilderness years. But they were not fallow. In increasingly close and productive partnership with Attlee he led the rebuilding, re-energising and repurposing of the Labour Party. And the T&G grew stronger.

The epilogue to 1931 is poignant. MacDonald and Snowden painfully recanted. In his anguished diary over the following months, MacDonald talked of 'the desolation of loneliness' in No. 10 leading his Tory-dominated government. 'Was I wise? Perhaps not, but it seemed as though anything else was impossible.'[34] As for Snowden, by the mid-1930s this apostle of Treasury orthodoxy was advocating an expansionary policy as bold as Keynes himself, and using Bevin's arguments. MacDonald and Snowden died within six months of each other in 1937.

Bevin, as ever, sought to build institutions to house his ideas. He became chairman of the Society for Socialist Inquiry and Propaganda to generate ideas and policies for 'an economic policy based on planning'. It was particularly aimed at younger Labour and trade union activists. 'The young men who came out for the Tories were far in advance of our own,' he told the socialist academic G. D. H. Cole after the election: young men like Harold Macmillan who won Stockton-on-Tees in the North East near Gateshead in 1931. The Great Depression had persuaded Bevin that planning and nationalisation were the efficient, modern way to run industry. Planning, he argued, was 'the good side of the Soviet experiment – a new motive for industry. That new economy involves planning ... it is planning against the old world of economy of scramble and individualism and profit.' But he warned this would be harder to achieve in an 'old' country like Britain than a 'new' one like Russia.[35] We have already discussed that particular conceit.

As for Keynes, he supported Labour in the 1935 election, noting that there was 'little divergence between the political implications of my ideas and the policy of the Labour party'. Nine years later these ideas became national policy in the Churchill coalition's 1944 Employment White Paper, which included maybe the most important single sentence of any twentieth-century state paper: 'The Government accept as one of their prime aims and responsibilities the maintenance of a high and stable level of employment after the war.'[36] In 1945, Keynes became chief negotiator for the Labour government in its quest for financial support from Washington to maintain the new welfare state. He died a year later, having secured the loan and saved Attlee and Bevin.

Under Bevin and Attlee, thanks to Keynes, there was to be no repeat of 1931 after 1945.

THE "RED DANUBE";
OR, THE TWO LISTENERS.

Bevin evicted Lansbury and supported Attlee because he sized up the threat from
Hitler and Mussolini earlier and better even than Churchill, who had
a soft spot for the Italian fascist dictator. © *Punch Magazine*

CHAPTER 5

ATTLEE

B evin's creation of the Transport and General Workers' Union in
the 1920s was improvisation as much as creativity. The same was
to happen in the 1930s in the forging of his partnership with Clement Attlee, which propelled them both to the pinnacle of the British
state. Bevin created Attlee as leader of the Labour Party in 1935 by
chance as much as design. But he kept him in situ thereafter with
ruthless determination.

It was Bevin's decisive intervention to remove Lansbury in 1935
and to stop Morrison in 1945 that promoted Attlee both times.
He stopped at least four other attempts to remove Attlee and
never sought the Labour leadership himself, although he could
probably have secured it. This set the scene for the close and respectful eleven-year partnership between Ernie and Clem at the
top of the two transformational governments of the 1940s. It only
ended with Bevin's death in April 1951, which severely weakened
Attlee and possibly sealed his defeat in the very close October
1951 election.

It all started with scorched earth. Labour was eviscerated at the
polls in October 1931, reduced to just fifty-two seats against 554 for

the MacDonald–Baldwin National Government. George Lansbury became party leader after the election as almost the last man standing. Henderson, thrust into the leadership by MacDonald's defection in August, had lost his seat in Burnley by 8,200 votes and Lansbury was the only member of the outgoing Labour Cabinet to survive. Attlee became deputy leader for the same reason, as one of only two junior ministers to hold on; the other, Sir Stafford Cripps, had only entered the Commons a few months previously in a by-election. Attlee had been re-elected by just 551 votes in Limehouse. Such is the wheel of fortune.

'We were completely out-generalled,' Bevin wrote after the rout.

What I learned in my constituency [Gateshead] was that we had lost, almost completely, the better artisan class, the better type of railwayman and craftsman and most of those who used to finance the old Labour electoral associations. In their place we had a great mass of poor people on whose behalf the Labour agent had been acting more or less as a relieving officer.

Emphasising that Labour lost the argument, not just the vote, he said he was 'going to devote my attention to some educational work of a practical kind'.[1]

Actually his first priority, as ever, was the T&G and protecting his membership from employer demands for wage cuts in the wake of the 1931 crisis. He did pretty well. The dock employers sought a wage reduction of two shillings a day; he got it down to under a shilling. He also faced the usual barrage of disputes within the union. A communist faction of the London busmen constantly provoked unofficial strikes and attacks on Bevin from Holloway garage in Islington, but he kept them isolated within the wider union until the 1937 busmen strike.

Bevin travelled abroad on union business constantly in the 1930s, generating a steady flow of ideas, contacts and information. He was at the International Labour Organisation (ILO) in Geneva almost every year, sometimes more than once. He successfully negotiated its convention on the forty-hour week in 1935 and another on conditions for seamen in 1936. He became so central to the ILO that had Labour not won the 1945 election he might have become its post-war secretary general. But his travel was not limited to the ILO. He was also in Prague and Antwerp in 1932, Australia, New Zealand and Canada in 1938 and New York in 1939.

The TUC was another preoccupation, particularly its new Economic Committee, which, largely due to him, became the TUC's most important committee in the 1930s, strongly advancing Labour's new ideas on unemployment and nationalisation.

A key piece of radical thinking started by the 1929 Labour government – one of the few – was Herbert Morrison's London Passenger Transport Bill, which proposed public control and integration of London's buses, trams and Underground by means of a dedicated public corporation. This led to sharp disagreement between Bevin and Morrison on the issue of representation of workers on the corporation board. Bevin wanted worker representation but Morrison resisted – and carried the day – with the argument that the board should be composed of technocrats. This was fuel on the already substantial fire of animosity between the two men dating back to earlier slights which Bevin conceived Morrison to have made to the trade unions and himself, deepened by Morrison's prevarication on whether or not to stick with MacDonald in August 1931. It was a substantial policy dispute that went to the heart of the role of trade unions in the management of nationalised industries, and it is still alive today in the continuing debate about employee representation on boards of public and private companies.

Morrison was not Bevin's only *bête noire* in the 1930s. Stafford Cripps and Aneurin Bevan wound him up almost as much. He saw the austere and moralising Cripps, who in the mid-1930s cut an improbable double-breasted Robespierre figure, as another upper-crust Mosley on the make. As so often with Bevin, personal animosity and policy disagreement went hand in hand. 'We are not going to jump out of the frying pan into the fire,' he told the 1933 Labour conference in Hastings, opposing Cripps's motion that the next Labour government should take emergency powers to rule by decree. And that was before they got on to disarmament and appeasement.

An economic revival from early 1933, although halting and partial, reduced unemployment and took the edge off bitter discontent at home. Instead political attention moved remorselessly to events abroad and to one seismic event of 30 January 1933 in particular: Hitler's assumption of power in Germany.

It was the trade union dimension of the Hitler revolution that immediately alarmed Bevin. Germany's trade unions were the strongest in Europe and Bevin knew its leaders well. Within weeks many were arrested, their offices seized, their unions dissolved and collective bargaining and the right to strike banned.

Having seen both communists and fascists close up, Bevin never fell for the left delusion, harboured by Cripps and Bevan, that a common front with communists was the way to deal with the fascists. In his view they were as bad as each other and fundamentally the same in their threat to democracy and trade unionism. A

TUC/Labour statement of 24 March 1933 sums up his rock-like view: 'If the British working class hesitate now between majority and minority rule and toy with the idea of dictatorship, Fascist or Communist, they will go down to servitude such as they have never suffered.'[2] But the implications were still a long way from being appreciated. At Labour's 1933 conference in Hastings a resolution was carried unanimously calling for a general strike in the event of war against the fascist dictators being threatened.

The next three years, 1933 to 1936, saw Hitler and Mussolini move from domestic oppression to international aggression. Labour, and Britain at large, split in response. The majority wanted peace at almost any price, either from pacifism like Lansbury or by recoiling from the prospect of another major war. This led to the appeasement position embracing not just most of the Labour Party but also Baldwin, Chamberlain, Halifax and most of the Conservative Party until 1939. One 'war to end all wars', wiping out the cream of the nation's male youth, was quite enough for most Tories. Even as late as the summer of 1940, as Prime Minister at the start of the national struggle for survival, Churchill had to battle over appeasement with Lord Halifax, his Foreign Secretary. Halifax, who had almost become war leader instead of Churchill in May 1940, wanted to follow France and negotiate an armistice with Hitler through the 'good offices' of Mussolini. Roy Jenkins describes the aristocratic Halifax's world view:

He had a resigned desire to preserve as much as he could of the England that he knew and loved. There is a story, maybe only *ben trovato*, that he went to Garrowby, the lesser of his two Yorkshire houses, on one of the perfect spring weekends of 1940. On the Saturday evening he sat on the terrace looking out over the smiling Vale of York and decided that his primary duty was to preserve as much of that as was humanly possible: the landscape, the ordered hierarchical society, the freedom from oppression and vulgar ostentation.[3]

All these various sentiments attracted Halifax to the possibility of a negotiated peace.

Few political leaders were consistently anti-pacifist and anti-appeasement throughout the 1930s. Churchill was the most famous, Bevin the next. Indeed, cajoling the labour movement to resist the dictators of Europe – Hitler and Mussolini before 1945, Stalin thereafter – was to be the prime mission of the rest of his life. It would have astonished him to know this in the 1930s, given his exclusively trade union career. But the two came to be closely related, for Bevin's appreciation of the existential dangers posed by fascism and communism to Europe's freedom and stability grew directly out of his T&G and international trade union experience, a world about as far apart from Viscount Halifax's Garrowby and Vale of York as it is possible to imagine.

By the mid-1930s Bevin had spent a quarter of a century fighting communists in the T&G and was doing so in real time as the dramatic events unfurled across Europe in the 1930s. In 1932 he sued the *Daily Worker*, a communist paper, which had accused him of 'treachery' for settling a London bus dispute without a strike. Bevin won the then huge sum of £7,000 in damages. The same communists ultimately precipitated the 1937 London bus strike and tried to do the same in the docks. Bevin and Citrine were behind the 1935 General Council circular to unions, advising them to ban communists from holding offices. 'There is an organism at work,' Bevin told that year's TUC conference, defending what the communists dubbed the 'black circular' by invoking the thuggish tactics and organisation of communist cells:

> If you had my job in the last five years you would say there is an organism. But the communists are not going to get us down. I had admissions from my own executive at their last meeting that money was handed over to representatives of my union to get me and certain other officials in my union down. Vote for the reference back and you give the stamp of approval to the most nefarious practices this movement has ever had to face.

He only narrowly carried the motion, after a heated debate about whether communists were a fundamental danger or, as one delegate insisted, just 'a lively leavening to any meeting'.[4]

Just as Bevin harboured no left-wing sentimentality that communism was on a spectrum with democratic socialism, so he understood that fascism was radically different to conservative nationalism. Endemic revolutionary violence and totalitarianism made communism and fascism fundamentally similar and equally dangerous.

The equation of fascism and communism, and the imperative to resist both, was Bevin's most fundamental and consequential insight as a national leader. Surprisingly few others saw it this way. Most on the democratic left saw communism as better than fascism, both morally preferable and less threatening, even where they were themselves anti-communist and not fellow travellers akin to Beatrice and Sidney Webb who, amid Stalin's purges, brought out their infamous book *Soviet Communism: A New Civilisation*. On the right, particularly in Christian movements and political parties, it was *vice versa*: communism was morally far worse and more threatening than fascism because of its atheism and hostility to private property. Moral relativism was indeed deeper and broader on the right than on the left. Supposedly moderate nationalist and Christian parties promoted the fascist right to an extent that social democratic parties refused to support the communists, most starkly the Catholic Centre Party in Germany, which endorsed Hitler's Enabling Act. This was true even when social democrats were in 'popular front' coalitions with communists to keep out the right, as in France in 1936 with Leon Blum's government. Among truly 'nefarious practices', high on the list must be popes Pius XI and Pius XII's deals, as heads of the Catholic church, with virtually all Europe's fascist dictators in the 1930s. Not that this was unique to Catholics among the Christian churches: a quarter of Germany's protestant clergy had joined the Nazi Party before 1933.

None of this relativism clouded Bevin's judgement, least of all religion. He saw communism and fascism through the same prism of totalitarianism. 'If you do not keep down the communists you cannot keep down the fascists,' he told the 1934 Labour conference in Southport, opposing an attempt by Bevan and Cripps to restore Labour membership to members of communist front organisations. 'Our friends on the Continent failed at the critical moment to maintain discipline as we propose to do now. This is where they went wrong and they got eaten out and undermined. When they had to take action, half of their members were in one party, half in the other.'[5]

This provoked a celebrated exchange with Bevan, who appealed to the chairman to stop Bevin attacking him. 'Apparently my namesake can get on this platform and denounce the Executive and he is so thin-skinned that he cannot take his own medicine,' Bevin retorted. 'No, in this conference, Aneurin Bevan, you are not going to get the flattery of the gossip columns that you get in London. You are going to get facts.'

Bevin had witnessed revolutionary fascism at first hand. Travelling through Germany in 1932, *en route* to the International Transport Workers' Federation conference in Prague, this is what he saw:

> The position in Germany is rapidly approaching one of civil war. Outside the *Volkhaus* in one of the towns we saw armed Social Democrats acting as pickets with other members of the Party inside also fully armed protecting their property against the Hitlerites and the Communists. What is even more alarming is the war fever which is developing in Middle Europe. I sat in a middle-class café, the kind which in this country would cater for the civil servant and the small shopkeeper, and when the band played a military march, the way the people rose and cheered, one could have imagined that war was being declared that night. This indicates the development of a very dangerous spirit. As far as I would see, the workers of the European countries have little opposition left in them.[6]

Bevin was more strong-minded and consistent even than Churchill, for he never suffered Churchill's fondness for Mussolini. Churchill, in his own words on returning from Rome in 1927, 'could not help being charmed by Signor Mussolini's gentle and simple bearing and his detached poise. Anyone could see that he thought of nothing but the lasting good, as he understands it, of the Italian people, and that no lesser interest was of the slightest consequence to him.'[7] Churchill was impressed by all dictators that he met, including Stalin. Fatefully and fortunately, he never met Hitler: a meeting planned in Munich in August 1932, while Churchill was inspecting the Blenheim battlefields for his biography of his ancestor the Duke of Marlborough, was cancelled by Hitler. By contrast, Bevin was never overly impressed by meeting dictators, including Stalin when he confronted the communist monster at Potsdam in 1945 and in Moscow thereafter.

This is significant because it was Mussolini, not Hitler, who initiated the foreign aggression crises of the 1930s and got away with it. Churchill prevaricated but Bevin saw the Italian fascist dictator for what he was. And it was this that led him to topple Lansbury, install Attlee and prevent Labour becoming virtually pacifist.

Mussolini's chosen target was North Africa, which made it seem less immediately threatening to the European balance of power. Inter-war Italy was the North African colonial power in Eritrea and part of Somaliland. Seeking glory abroad, the 'gentle and simple' Mussolini lighted on neighbouring Ethiopia (then called Abyssinia) as a suitably weak but prestigious target to conquer and enlarge his empire and glory. After frantic diplomatic activity in early 1935, in which French Foreign Minister Pierre Laval effectively gave Mussolini the green light, an Italian invasion was imminent. Then Emperor Haile Selassie of Ethiopia staged a successful media campaign, including in Britain, presenting his country as the little nation about to brutalised by its big neighbour. Italy was pressured to agree to arbitration by the League of Nations.

However, as international attention lessened over the summer, Mussolini prepared to invade, and apart from weak economic sanctions, the other European powers, including Britain, did little. Mussolini invaded on 3 October. There were more protests and ineffectual sanctions by the league, but Mussolini pressed on regardless. Addis Ababa fell on 5 May 1936 and Haile Selassie was forced into exile. By then, taking his cue from Mussolini's success, Hitler had occupied the Rhineland in defiance of the Treaty of Versailles, also meeting only token international reaction. The path to Munich and the Second World War was set.

At the beginning of the Ethiopia crisis the stark choice between force and appeasement was not clear because the League of Nations, in its first serious trial of strength as international policeman since its creation in 1920, had not yet failed. The Peace Ballot of 1935, in which 11.6 million people voted, showed overwhelming support for the league and non-military sanctions. At this stage, the dominant view wasn't 'peace at any price'. But Bevin had little doubt the league would fail unless it was backed up by the threat of force, and it was this that brought him into conflict with Lansbury. The division between them went to the heart of the division in the country at large, with Baldwin and his supine Foreign Secretary, Sir Samuel Hoare, trying to straddle both sides.

If the sanctions against Mussolini failed, was the next step to do nothing or to intervene militarily? This was the defining question.

At the beginning of the crisis, Lansbury supported the league, including a resolution at the TUC conference in Margate in early September 1935 that pledged 'firm support of any action consistent with the principles and status of the league to restrain the Italian government'. Walter Citrine, speaking for the General Council, argued robustly and presciently that Mussolini had to be stopped with force if necessary: 'It may mean war ... But I say this. If we fail now, if we go back now, war is absolutely certain. I ask you what will happen to Germany if Italy can treat with contempt the nations of the world who have plighted their word to preserve peace?'[8] Bevin supported him strongly.

However, over the next fortnight, as war appeared imminent and the pacifist left became increasingly vocal and critical of him person-ally, Lansbury regained the courage of his pacifist convictions. Just before the Labour conference in Brighton at the start of October, he made it known that he could not, after all, support military force to halt the invasion of Ethiopia, even at the behest of the League of Nations. Cripps, describing the league as 'nothing but the tool of the imperialist powers', had resigned from the NEC in protest at the Margate TUC resolution, and Lansbury could not bear to be outbid or unpopular on the pacifist left. He therefore intimated that he would not support the TUC resolution if it was tabled at Brighton.[9]

The debate on Ethiopia on 1 and 2 October 1935 was the longest in the history of the Labour Party conference. 'We had to spend one and a half days at Brighton on a debate demonstrating the division in the party on a matter of foreign policy, which if its leaders had sunk their personalities in the interests of the greater movement, need not have lasted two hours,' Bevin told his T&G executive afterwards.[10]

Everyone thought it was the eve of war and, as in the House of Commons debates before Munich in 1938 and before Iraq in 2003, emotions at the 1935 Brighton conference ran very high. Dalton moved the same resolution as passed by the TUC at Margate, noting that sanctions, including war, were the lawful policy of the league to maintain borders. He pointed out that this had been support-ed in Parliament by Labour MPs including Lansbury as recently as 1 August. Cripps followed with a speech in opposition to war. Sentiment swung back and forth in eager anticipation of Lansbury's intervention. As he was called towards the end of the first day there was a long ovation and singing of 'For He's a Jolly Good Fellow' from almost the entire hall, apart from the group of trade union delegates around Bevin.[11]

Lansbury was a 1930s Jeremy Corbyn, just a bit older and more so. He was Labour hero of East End battles against poverty and injustice dating back to the Edwardians, including jail sentences for supporting suffragette defiance in 1912 and for leading a 'rates revolt' against Tory/Liberal local authority cuts in 1921. His impassioned anti-war speech, making a virtue of recent inconsistency as an exercise in wrestling with his conscience, pulled all the Labour Party conference heartstrings. He was content to stand down if people thought his conscience was 'intolerable', he said, but he had carefully barbed words for Bevin in particular:

When I was sick and on my back, ideas came into my head, and one was that the only thing worthwhile for old men to do is at least to say the thing they believe and at least try to warn the young...

It is said that people like me are irresponsible. I am no more irresponsible a leader than the greatest trade union leader in the country. If mine was the only voice in the conference, I would say in the name of the faith I hold, that belief I have that God intended us to live peacefully and quietly with one another. And if some do not allow us to do so, I am ready to stand as the early Christians did and say 'This is our faith. This is where we stand and if necessary, this is where we will die.'

Down to the final echo of Martin Luther ('Here I stand, I can do no other') it was a virtuoso claim to sainthood and martyrdom, and it got warm applause.

Lansbury's policy was now contradictory and it looked as if Labour would simply drift chaotically and discredited into the coming general election, a situation far from unusual in the party before and since. But 'as the applause died away and the wave of emotion subsided Bevin was seen to rise to his feet and without hurrying make his way to the platform. The moment for which he had been waiting had come.'[12]

With no grace words whatever, Bevin went straight for Lansbury, not just for his arguments but for his integrity too. There was initial barracking from parts of the hall, but Bevin went on, giving clinical chapter and verse as to what Lansbury had agreed and said up to and beyond the TUC Margate conference only a month before. Blow by blow, the hall became quieter, then silent, then attentive. These were the killer lines:

> I hope this conference will not be influenced either by sentiment or personal attachment. If George Lansbury finds that he ought to take a certain course then his conscience should direct him to the course he should take. But it is placing the Executive and the Movement in an absolutely wrong position to be hawking your conscience round from body to body to be told what you ought to do with it...
>
> I feel bitter in my very soul about it, because if this movement is going to win the country, when it is faced with a crisis, it has got to have confidence that it is capable of coming to a decision. I feel we have been let down, everyone of us on the General Council feels we have been let down.[13]

Bevin also dealt with Cripps, an easier target. 'People have been on this platform today talking about the destruction of capitalism. The thing that is being wiped out is the trade union movement.' Then he made the decisive point that carried the conference. 'The people who oppose this resolution ought to have the courage of their convictions and table a resolution to the effect that we should withdraw from the League of Nations. You cannot be in and out at the same time, not if we are honest.'

'Bevin hammered Lansbury to death,' said Dalton.[14] By the time he sat down he had turned the conference around. Head trumped heart. When Lansbury tried to reply, 'The conference would not listen to him and not a man rose in his defence.' (There were barely any women in the hall).

Lansbury resigned six days later on 8 October. 'Lansbury had been going about dressed in saint's clothes for years waiting for martyrdom: I set fire to the faggots,' Bevin replied to those who reproached him for brutality.[15] Without Bevin, Lansbury's saintly progress would probably have lasted for at least the week longer necessary for Lansbury to lead Labour into the election called by Baldwin just ten days later. There was no obvious alternative leader and most Labour MPs wanted Lansbury to continue even after the Brighton conference: they even voted for a resolution to this effect at the Parliamentary Labour Party meeting before his resignation left them no choice but to replace him – temporarily for the election – by Attlee.

Collective security in support of the League of Nations was Baldwin's characteristically ambivalent policy at the November 1935 election. For the duration of the three-week election campaign, he rallied both hawks, who wanted rearmament and military action against Mussolini, and doves, who would only support rearmament and the use of arms if authorised by the league. However, his policy was shown to be futile within weeks of the election as the league collapsed in inertia, largely due to Baldwin's own refusal to push hard within the league for military force against Mussolini.

Labour won a net 106 seats in the November 1935 election, taking its tally to 154. The party had got off the 1931 floor but it was still a pitiful showing against 386 Tories. Labour had now lost five of the seven elections since the advent of full democracy at the end of the First World War, and it had not won an overall majority in any of the seven. The only consolation was that 1935 could have been far worse but for the removal of Lansbury, who after the election went on a personal peace mission to Hitler and Mussolini. 'Hitler was free of personal ambition and wasn't ashamed of his humble start in life,' he declared on his return.

> He lived in the country rather than the town, was a bachelor who liked children and old people and was obviously lonely. I wished that I could have gone to Berchtesgaden and stayed with him for a little while. I felt that Christianity in its purest sense might have had a chance with him.[16]

Amen.

Had Bevin not displaced Lansbury immediately before the 1935 election, Attlee would probably never have become Labour leader. Attlee was only designated as 'interim' leader to fight the election. He was the sitting deputy leader and, as with Lansbury himself in 1931, there was no one else even half suitable to take over. The general view among Labour MPs was that after the election – a certain loss – Herbert Morrison, now Leader of London County Council and the dynamic force on Labour's National Executive Committee, would be back in the House of Commons and would become leader. This was certainly Morrison's expectation.

But it was not Bevin's – nor Attlee's, who had enough ambition and self-confidence to think he should stay in the job once he had fought a respectable election campaign. When Labour MPs met after the election, Attlee put himself forward against both Morrison and Arthur Greenwood, who had been Minister of Health in the 1929 government and was now back in the Commons too.

Bevin's main concern was to stop Morrison, whom he almost pathologically distrusted, both personally and politically. He branded Morrison anti-union after their battles over London Transport in the 1920s and doubted his loyalty to Labour or to anything but himself. There was also a lack of deference to Bevin personally, which coloured everything. Suspicious also of Attlee, who at the Brighton conference had muted his criticism of Lansbury and the left, Bevin initially swung his T&G-sponsored MPs behind Greenwood, who took enough votes from Morrison for Attlee to lead narrowly on the first round. This cleared the way for Attlee to win the run-off against Morrison by eighty-eight votes to forty-eight. Attlee topped the first round, partly because of his steady hand in the election; partly because Labour MPs 'who saw more of Greenwood than did the union leaders, reckoned either that he was past it or that he drank too much'; and partly because, despite Bevin, he had some trade union support, particularly among the miners. The momentum gained from topping the first ballot, and Bevin's support, delivered the second-round victory to Attlee.[17]

Attlee thought he got elected because 'the party did not want another charismatic leader who might "do another MacDonald". They wanted a leader who would lead as a good chairman leads committees.'[18] This is certainly what Bevin wanted, and he was soon comparing Attlee to his favourite Prime Minister Sir Henry Campbell-Bannerman, the bluff Liberal leader who won the 1906 election. 'CB' was sound yet undominating and had managed a government of big beasts including Lloyd George, Asquith and Churchill.

Attlee was elected Labour leader just one month and one day after he became interim leader. He was to go on to hold the leadership for the next twenty years, the longest tenure of any major party leader in the twentieth century and longer than any in modern times apart from Gladstone. His leadership was sustained by Bevin for the first sixteen of those years, until his death, and it proved to be career-changing for Bevin too. There would not have been much role for the T&G leader in a Morrison Labour Party. It is virtually inconceivable that Morrison, as Labour leader, would have brought Bevin into government from outside Parliament in 1940 and installed him at Churchill's right hand, still less that he would have made him Foreign Secretary in 1945. Such is the wheel of fortune.

It took time for Bevin's relationship with Attlee to develop, and the way Attlee was elected qualifies the historian Henry Pelling's view that Labour in the 1930s was 'the General Council's party'. Attlee recalled, 'I did not know Bevin well until 1940. After 1931 he had a great suspicion of politicians, and indeed failed to understand the conditions in which they worked.'[19]

By the late 1930s Bevin was leading the largest trade union not only in Britain but in the entire free world, with more than 650,000 members. He was president of the TUC in 1936, chairing the General Council for the year. Now in his late fifties, he thought these

would be his last posts of responsibility in the British labour movement and he was contemplating retirement at the age of sixty in
1941, possibly hoping for a leadership role thereafter at the International Labour Organisation (ILO) in Geneva. His non-T&G work
in the period had been focused on the ILO and workers' rights. He
served on a government committee in 1937 concerning annual holiday pay. He wanted a fortnight but compromised on a week, which
was implemented, also increasing the number of workers entitled
to paid holiday from 3 million to over 11 million in one go. This
was Bevinist pragmatism in action, even under a Tory government.
The first Butlin's holiday camp opened in Skegness the same year,
strongly encouraged by Bevin. He was also president of the Workers'
Travel Association, and he took Flo and Q on one of its cruises on
the *Esperance Bay*, which the WTA had organised at his suggestion.
In a typically aspirational Bevinist speech to the British Health Re-
sorts Association conference in Skegness in 1937, he urged them 'to
realise that in future they would have to cater for large numbers of
working-class families and to abandon the idea that anything was
good enough for working folk'.[20]

A key T&G success of Bevin's in the late 1930s was the introduction of statutory wage conciliation in the huge road haulage
industry. 'I have worked so long to try and get this trade put right
that I would not sacrifice it now for anything,' he told Frederick
Leggett of the Ministry of Labour, with whom he had worked
closely since before the General Strike.[21]

It was not all plain sailing, though. The 1937 London busmen
strike, the last major strike Bevin led, went badly wrong. Accounts
conflict as to how far this was Bevin's fault for ceding initial control of the dispute to the far left and communist Central Bus

Committee, and how far this was beyond his control, given their determination to strike. For their part, the communists claimed that Bevin undermined them by not enlarging the strike to include trolleymen, tramwaymen and provincial busmen, although these workers had no dispute. In any case, Bevin's strategy to conclude the strike by the coronation of George VI in late May, securing a seven-and-a-half hour working day, went awry. After twenty-seven days, Bevin asserted control and ended the strike, but without securing the reduction in hours. There was serious bloodletting, including the expulsion of several of the London busmen's leaders from the union, who also lost their jobs because of the closed-shop agreement with London Transport. The ever-defensive Bevin blamed the media for hounding him, to the extent of banning them from the union's bi-ennial conference that August. The strain was telling. At the TUC conference in Norwich the following month, 'Many delegates were shocked by his appearance. The strain of the past year had obviously affected his health. There was a tell-tale twitching of his facial muscles as he spoke.'[22]

Bevin was not much more successful with another aspirational cause dear to his heart: the introduction of occupational pensions. He negotiated a scheme in 1937 for the tinplate industry, but it failed because too few workers would join. 'I think it is a tragedy,' he told the T&G executive. 'A large number of the men take the view that if they become party to a superannuation they are merely saving the Unemployment Assistance Board expenditure.' His regret wasn't just about their welfare but also his concern to foster a something-for-something culture. In this, he was looking forward to the Beveridge Report of 1942 and a step change in the benefits of social insurance. 'When a large community develops a relief complex of this character it is not good for democracy,' he said, presaging a key part of the post-war debate about the welfare state that continues today.[23]

On the escalating European crisis, Bevin's leadership continued to be clear and sure-footed and it paved the way for his entry into government in 1940.

Stanley Baldwin's astuteness in handling the General Strike and the abdication crisis of 1936 did not extend to foreign affairs, his Achilles heel, not helped by the fact that 'he did not like foreigners of any kind'. Appeasement, an impulse of disengagement from mainland Europe as much as the making of positive concessions to the dictators, became Baldwin's overt policy in December 1935 with the Hoare–Laval pact between his Foreign Secretary Sir Samuel Hoare and the French Foreign Minister Pierre Laval, who went on to become Pétain's Prime Minister in the Vichy government of 1940. Hoare–Laval gave *carte blanche* to Mussolini to complete his conquest of Ethiopia. The outcry against the pact forced Hoare's resignation, but Baldwin's policy remained unchanged. Indeed, his decision to call a snap election in October 1935 was partly made because by then he already knew, secretly, that France would not support Britain in any military action against Mussolini by the League of Nations, and he was keen to hold the election before his foreign policy publicly imploded.[24] Baldwin's public stance, supported by Bevin and the responsible left, that league sanctions to stop Mussolini, including war, would be supported by Britain, was a sham. Within months, Ethiopia was conquered, the Rhineland was occupied and Franco's rebellion was underway, all three meeting no British or French resistance whatever.

Throughout these events, despite the unpopularity of rearmament and military action in labour circles, Bevin insisted that unless the fascist dictators were met with a credible threat of force, they would prevail. He argued this from his first-hand experience of the Continent. To Bevin, Czechoslovakia was never Chamberlain's 'far away country ... of whom we know nothing'. He had been to Prague, had socialised and debated with Czech, German and Polish trade union leaders, and he saw their cause as Britain's cause. Few other British political leaders of the 1930s were so well travelled – Churchill was another exception – and none knew Europe's labour movements so well.[25]

At the Plymouth TUC conference in 1936 Bevin pronounced the League of Nations and collective security to be effectively dead. 'The question of collective security is in danger of becoming a shibboleth rather than a practical operative fact,' he warned. 'We are not going to meet it by pure pacifism. If in certain respects it means uprooting some of our cherished ideas and facing the issues in the light of the development of Fascism, we must do it for the Movement and for the sake of posterity.'[26]

Bevin gave no quarter to Cripps and the left. Cripps argued that even if fascism was beaten by the 'imperialist powers ... the world situation would be no better. Another Versailles peace, another period of acute suffering from the workers, and then the next war. That's all.' Bevin gave his response at the 1936 Labour conference in Edinburgh:

I say this to Sir Stafford Cripps. If I am asked to face the question of arming this country, I am prepared to face it. Which is the first institution that victorious fascism wipes out? It is the trade union movement. We saw our movement go in Germany. Our men shed their blood in Austria, and nearly every one of them was a trade unionist.[27]

Prophetically, two years before Munich he went on:

> If ever there was a time when, whether it is popular or unpopular, we have got to tell our own people the truth, it is now and we must do it fearlessly whatever the consequences may be.
>
> The International Movement are wondering what we are going to do in Britain. Czechoslovakia, one of the most glorious little democratic countries, hedged in all round, is in danger of being sacrificed tomorrow. They are our trade union brothers ... You cannot save Czechoslovakia with speeches. We are not in office but I want to drive this government to defend democracy against its will, if I can. I want to say to Mussolini and Hitler: 'If you are banking on being able to attack in the East or the West, and you are going to treat the British Socialist Movement as being weak and are going to rely on that at the critical moment, you are taking us too cheaply.'[28]

In the same Edinburgh 1936 debate, he made an insightful observation on why the First World War had erupted after months of diplomatic weakness and fumbling by Sir Edward Grey and Asquith: 'I look back to 1914 ... The Liberals of that day never made themselves clear. They let this country drift on until we were in it and then they used propaganda to prove it was a righteous cause.'

The Spanish Civil War, which started with General Franco's revolt of 17 July 1936 against the Republican government, shifted Labour opinion in favour of rearmament. This was the one early anti-fascist war that most of the left supported, even militarily, with George Orwell and Jack Jones, both young admirers of Bevin, among those enlisted in the Republican cause. By contrast, Bevin himself was notably ambivalent about the Spanish Republicans because of the central role of the communists. He wrote bluntly to G. D. H. Cole in January 1937: 'Joining up with the Communists who are to destroy the trade unions ... [is] asking too much.'[29] In a war between fascists and communists, Bevin just wanted both to lose.

Bevin was in Australia during the Munich crisis of September 1938 on a union-related tour of the dominions. This gave him a keen and timely awareness that Britain's resources to resist Hitler extended far beyond Britain itself. On his return he installed a large globe on his desk in Transport House and talked to all comers about the Commonwealth and its potential as a bloc.[30] Fortuitously, he was then in New York at the end of August 1939, when news came through of the Nazi–Soviet pact, giving him an equally vivid sense of the pivotal role America could play in the coming conflict, to Britain's advantage. He docked in Southampton just days before the outbreak of the Second World War on 3 September. It was his last journey abroad until he attended the Potsdam summit of July 1945 as Foreign Secretary.

Meeting Chamberlain in the early weeks of the war, Bevin offered support in fighting Germany but was typically quick to raise concerns about excessive profits being made out of rearmament, and about the suppression of trade union rights in the expanding defence industries, as well as the government's failure to consult the unions properly. The ostracising of Labour was a constant Bevin theme of the 1930s. 'Since 1931 Labour has been treated like a class apart,' he told a business leader who asked him to support an army recruitment drive in 1936. As for Chamberlain and the Tory elite: 'It was not for us to appeal or be supplicants: it was for them to come to us and for the first time to recognise Labour as equals.'

Bevin's relationship with Attlee steadily strengthened in the late 1930s. This wasn't because of any great shared campaigns; there are no barnstorming pre-war foreign policy speeches by Attlee to set alongside Bevin's, let alone Churchill's. But the two men interacted constantly on Labour/TUC leadership committees and got along well. Bevin was not looking for a Labour leader who was adventurous or inspirational. He had had two of them in MacDonald and Lansbury, and both ended in disaster. What he sought was a leader who could and would hold the party together behind its agreed line. He also wanted a leader he could trust – and who was not Morrison. At the end of his TUC presidency in 1937, he disavowed speculation that he might seek to enter Parliament and supplant Attlee. When the *Sunday Dispatch* ran such a story, Bevin's response to the editor was categoric: 'Your correspondent must have known he was lying when he wrote it.'[31]

For his part, Attlee respected Bevin's judgement, his strength of leadership, and the trade union credentials Attlee himself so obviously lacked. There is a revealing letter from Attlee, as laconic as it is effusive, written after the abdication crisis in 1936. During the crisis Bevin had kept the *Daily Herald* – 'my paper' – behind the constitutional course that Edward VIII had to obey the advice of his ministers:

My Dear Ernie,

I think you would like to know ... everyone says that the *Herald* was among the two or three papers that kept its head and dealt with the matter in a statesmanlike, not merely a sensational, manner. I know this was largely due to you. Hence this letter.

With all good wishes,

Yours,

Clem[32]

A good sidelight on Bevin's developing relationship with Attlee is his twenty-year partnership with Walter Citrine. Citrine was the Attlee of the TUC: calm, factual, shrewd, competent, reliable, un-demonstrative. His minor classic, *ABC of Chairmanship*, produced Aneurin Bevan's jibe: 'Poor fellow, he suffers from files.' But that's just what Bevin wanted: a good administrator. Bevin–Citrine 'was one of the most successful involuntary partnerships in modern poli-tics', writes Alan Bullock.[33]

However, there was a crucial class difference between Citrine and Attlee. Like Bevin, Citrine was a working-class autodidact, son of a Mersey ship rigger father and nurse mother who left school at twelve. His early career as an electrician trade unionist in the Birk-enhead docks was also not dissimilar to Bevin's in the Avonmouth docks; they even engaged in their first dock strike at about the same time, a few years before the First World War. Attlee, by contrast, was about two classes upwards, son of a solicitor, public school (Haileybury), Oxford University and the Bar. He wore all this lightly as the radical ex-Mayor of Stepney, but it was the stronger for being understated, like his First World War service as a major in the South Lancashire Regiment. Bevin–Attlee was more than a political partnership; it was a social coalition that symbolised the electoral coalition they both aspired to forge, and which they did so brilliantly in 1945. As Roy Jenkins put it, Bevin's support in the trade unions provided Attlee with 'a working class sheet anchor'.[34]

Michael Foot later portrayed Bevin and Attlee as a composite. 'Often enough, Bevin was Attlee,' he remarked in his Nye Bevan biography. 'It would be folly to overlook the powerful authority of this composite figure.'[35]

Attlee did not dissent. 'My relationship with Ernest Bevin was the deepest of my political life,'[36] he wrote in retirement. 'Ernest looked, and indeed was, the embodiment of common sense. Yet I have never met a man in politics with as much imagination as he had, with the exception of Winston.'[37]

All those qualities were to be needed in the war ahead.

'By far the most distinguished man that the Labour Party have thrown up in my time,' said Churchill. Arthur Boughey's portrait of Bevin, commissioned by the Ministry of Information during the war. © The National Archives INF3/61

CHAPTER 6

ERNIE

'In Britain we have grown up with Bevin,' a journalist remarked at his zenith as Foreign Secretary in 1946. 'Today he is not so much a man as a phenomenon. Maybe he is both.'[1] By the time of Bevin's political power in the 1940s, what was the man and what was the phenomenon – and how did they relate?

ALL BEHIND YOU, WINSTON

'All behind you, Winston', David Low's famous cartoon, has Churchill and Bevin leading from the front, virtually the same person. © *Evening Standard*

The phenomenon can be described and dated precisely. Bevin became the working-class John Bull on 12 May 1940, the day he took office as Minister of Labour in Churchill's wartime coalition. It was an image of bulldog patriotism and defiance second in strength and authenticity only to Churchill himself. Two days later, David Low's famous cartoon 'All behind you, Winston', has Churchill and Bevin leading from the front, chins out, sleeves rolled up, virtually the same person. The bulldog image was authentic because it was true. And as with Churchill, it spoke to a lifetime of bruisingly tough independence.

With Bevin, there was an added element of menace. For inter-war Tory England he had been 'the enemy within', leading the barbarians at the gate. Everyone remembered or knew about the General Strike. His pragmatic and anti-communist streaks mattered little to the *Daily Express* and *Daily Mail*, which fed a conservative Middle England that had grown up to see strikes and trade unions as a huge monolithic threat facing the country. For many a solid citizen, not even Hitler was a greater danger than Labour and the trade unions until the outbreak of war in 1939.

Bevin's reincarnation as the 'working-class John Bull' was remarkable, and nothing but war and national emergency could have brought it to pass. Middle England sensed, because it was true, that although Bevin was – just about – a democrat in means, he was a revolutionary in goals. His indispensability to Churchill and the nation in 1940 did not lessen the radicalism of the social change he sought and wrought.

However, the 59-year-old bulldog of 1940 was not the 45-year-old Rottweiler of 1926, and this too explains why the man and the phenomenon exerted such political power in the 1940s. The Bevin of

Ernest's mother, Mercy Bevin. Her photograph was on Bevin's desk when he died.

Bevin aged three (*seated, front, centre*), at the start of his twenty-year nonconformist education. His teacher, Mrs Veysey, was also the village postmistress (*second from the left in a broad-banded hat*).
© Picture Post/Getty Images

Ernie aged fourteen: a big, smart, broad-shouldered boy with a square jaw, streetwise and, with his brothers, well able to look after himself; proudly working class but not remotely downtrodden.

The long and winding road led young Ernest from Somerset to Bristol High Street, where he delivered mineral water in a horse and cart in 1908.

ABOVE 'Labour owed more to Methodism than Marxism.' Ben Tillett, the dockers' leader (*inset left*), and Bevin (*inset right*) with a Labour brass band just like the Salvation Army, c. 1910.

LEFT Labour's first Prime Minister under Bevin's suspicious gaze in 1920. Bevin would accuse MacDonald of 'stabbing us in the back' during the General Strike, and much worse in 1931.

© London Illustrated News Group

LEFT A proud trade unionist aged twenty-nine: 'Ill fares the land, to hastening ills a prey / Where wealth accumulates and men decay.'

LEFT The Dockers' KC aged thirty-nine. The Shaw Inquiry of 1920 turned Bevin into a celebrity.

© Hulton Picture Library/Getty Images

LEFT 'These fellows quote statistics but they forget about human beings. I had to make 'em remember they were dealing with human lives.' Bevin preparing his 'docker's dinner' for the Shaw Inquiry.

BELOW A Baldwin-esque Bevin in the 1920s, now thoroughly middle class as well as working class.
© Hulton Picture Library/Getty Images

'I like to build, brothers.' Bevin in full flow.
© Pictoral Press Ltd/Alamy Stock Photo

A. J. Cook, the Arthur Scargill of the 1920s, inciting the miners to stay out after the General Strike.
© Print Collector/Getty Images

The greatest trade union leader in British history: 'A comparable understanding of the machinery of power to Stalin,' said Attlee's spokesman.
© Worger/Topical Press Agency/Getty Images

Transport House, Bevin's citadel: the Transport and General Workers' Union, the Labour Party and the TUC were all under one roof from 1928.
© Hulton Picture Library/Getty Images

On the roof of Transport House at its opening in 1928, the Houses of Parliament behind. Bevin (*left*), is pictured here with Margaret Bondfield and Ben Tillett, his sights set on power. © London Express/Getty Images

LEFT With factory workers, turning on the charm.
© Daily Herald Archive/SSPL/Getty Images

LEFT A coal deliverer with a horse and cart like Bevin's twenty years before.
© Daily Herald Archive/SSPL/Getty Images

BELOW Not the snappiest election slogan on the side of a bus.

With Walter Citrine, TUC general secretary, 1937. 'Poor fellow, he suffers from files,' said Nye Bevan – but they were Bevin's files.

With Ben Tillett on the eve of war, 1939. 'Small, wizened, loquacious, with bright bird-like eyes, telling of triumphs long ago and of the way in which Bevin, the man he "found and made", had pushed him to one side.'

© Trinity Mirror/Mirrorpix/Alamy

Rembrandt's Night Watch of 1940, planning a better Britain.

© James Jarche/Popperfoto/Getty Images

Bevin invariably called the workers 'my people'.

© Fox Photos/Getty Images

No minister in the war was more visible than Bevin. Here visiting blitzed Humberside in 1941.
© Keystone/Getty Images

'Bevin's Bar', decreed by the minister who said he needed to steal to feed himself when young.
© Hulton-Deutsch Collection/CORBIS/ Corbis via Getty Images

'The working-class John Bull.'
© Picture Post/Hulton Archive/Getty Images

'Ernest Bevin says – "We must have Exports".'
© Northcliffe Collection/ANL/Shutterstock

Bevin, Attlee and Churchill in Downing Street. 'The light of history will shine on your helmets' – or on your bowler hats.
© AP/Shutterstock

The chancellor of Bristol University confers an honorary degree on the Bristol barrow boy, 1945.
© Hulton-Deutsch/CORBIS/ Corbis via Getty Images

VE Day: Bevin led the crowd in singing 'For He's a Jolly Good Fellow'.
© Imperial War Museum

Central Wandsworth, 1945: the election Labour thought it would lose.
© Daily Herald

1940, while as tough and Stakhanovite as the Bevin of old, was more nuanced, more accommodating, more respected, more mellow, and despite his image and his dropped aitches, now reassuringly middle class as well as working class. This was a key part of his unique appeal. Indeed, he would not have become Minister of Labour in 1940 had Churchill and Attlee not appreciated this nuance.

We saw earlier that Bevin the man was much more educated than Bevin the phenomenon – all those sermons, the university extension classes in Bristol, the personal tutorship of John Maynard Keynes on the Macmillan Committee on finance and industry in 1930–31. His lifestyle tells a similar story: from labourer's cottage in Winsford; to digs with his brothers in Bristol; to 39 Saxon Road in the artisan St Werburghs district of Bristol in his early thirties with wife Flo and newborn daughter Queenie; to a furnished apartment on Adam Street in Central London, just around the corner from the Royal Courts of Justice in the Strand, convenient for the 'Dockers' KC' to present to the Shaw Inquiry, in 1920, aged thirty-eight.

Following Adam Street Bevin lived in one middle-class district of London after another as leader of the T&G in the 1920s and 1930s: there was a flat in Gloucester Place by Regent's Park, then a decade in a suburban semi-detached – 30 The Vale – near Golders Green station on the newly extended Northern Line, with fields at the back and located close to his daughter Queenie's north London secondary school. There, Q remembered him 'telling her stories, playing whist and monopoly and listening to Caruso, Marie Lloyd or Clara Butt on the gramophone'. He loved driving out into the country at weekends and had a big yellow Talbot Darracq. An annual ritual was the Whitsun Horse Show in Regent's Park, where Bevin 'had as much confidence in picking a winning "Shire" as in knowing the moment to launch a new initiative on behalf of his members'.[2] The legacy of the Bristol drayman.

In the mid-1930s, Q having now left home and about to marry an up-and-coming *Daily Herald* journalist, Ernie and Flo moved back to Central London, first to a flat at fashionable 34 South Molton Street, off Oxford Street in the West End, then, for the latter part of the war, 20 Phillimore Court, a new Poirot-style Art Deco-fronted mansion block on High Street, Kensington. During the Blitz, they lived in the Strand Palace Hotel, so Flo would not be alone during air raids.

By 1940 there was little working class about the Bevin lifestyle, apart from football matches and some persisting habits and dropped aitches. And a huge fund of Ernie stories.

As Foreign Secretary he lived in the grandest location of all: 1 Carlton Gardens. This was off the Mall next to Marlborough House, residence of Queen Mary the Queen Mother, who liked Bevin and gave him a key to her large garden. Carlton Gardens was allocated to Bevin by Attlee, though maybe with some help from the King's private secretary Sir Tommy Lascelles, since it belonged to the Crown Estate. It is where Bevin died and it has been the Foreign Secretary's residence ever since.

However, despite the increasingly genteel locations, none of the properties until 1 Carlton Gardens, an official residence, were particularly grand. They were all flats or modest houses. Bevin never sought riches or grandeur and was never enveloped by the 'aristocratic embrace' that got Ramsay MacDonald. Beyond cigars, red wine and spirits for immediate consumption, he never developed expensive tastes – less expensive than Flo, who loved glitz and West End shops, would have liked. Of her shopping expeditions during one summit in Paris while Ernie was Foreign Secretary, a private secretary recalled,

> What usually happened was that Mrs Bevin would sit down in a chair and ask to see an assortment of wares until half the contents of the shop had been laid out on the counter for her inspection. She would then announce cheerfully that she did not think she would buy anything that day and walk out.

At his death, Ernest's net worth was £13,988. Flo's was just £9,234 on her death seventeen years later. By comparison, Churchill's was £304,044, plus his huge personal estate of Chartwell, held in a special trust. Another of Bevin's private secretaries recalled that Flo had been left 'almost penniless' after Ernie's death and was helped out by a timber merchant friend of her husband's.[3] Bevin became comfortably off as a union general secretary in the 1920s, but he didn't accumulate money and was never seduced by it. His currency was power not possessions.

His dress told a similar story. Bevin was no continuity Keir Hardie in cloth cap and shabby clothes. Always smart from chapel days in his Sunday best, by the 1920s his well-cut suit and bowler hat were positively Baldwin-esque. They told a story of power as much as class:

> A massive watch-chain across his waistcoat, a bowler hat cocked over his eyes in place of his one-time cloth cap and the stump of a cigar in his mouth he looked, at times, like a caricaturist's version of an American trade union boss than anyone in real life ought to do.

It worked. 'I saw Ernest Bevin dominate a near riotous assembly of busmen,' one of his T&G officials recalled. 'He was wearing a fur coat and smoking a cigar, and he dominated that meeting not in spite of the coat and the cigar but because of them.'[4]

Bevin the man and the phenomenon, 1947.
© National Portrait Gallery

Bevin the man was far more complex than Bevin the phenomenon who stood alongside Churchill in May 1940. It was the two combined that made him so formidable in his decade of power: the blunt, bluff, working-class paragon, yet also the more subtle, aware, networked, in many ways classless leader in the same skin.

A telling aspect of Bevin the man and phenomenon was his love of 'showbiz' in the 1930s and 1940s. In 1941 he became a member of the Garrick Club, apparently a refutation of his entire life, with its mahogany dining tables, fine wines and liveried servants. But this wasn't just a social statement and somewhere to lunch in clubland during the war, although it had elements of both. His proposer was Sir Seymour Hicks, star of the Victorian music hall and Edwardian silent films. His fellow sponsors were the actor and theatre impresario Basil Dean and the writer J. B. Priestley. This was the old Bevin, who went weekly to the music hall with Flo, morphed into a new Bevin who cultivated and was cultivated by the stars of the music halls and the film industry, and put them at the heart of the war effort and the quest for a new Britain.[5]

Before writing this book, the best story I knew of Bevin, and would tell whenever his name came up, was the quip: 'There were only two posts in the Foreign Office that Ernie Bevin could have held: Foreign Secretary and doorkeeper.' It is amusing and encapsulates Bevin the phenomenon. But I now realise it is quite untrue. If he weren't beyond retirement age, Bevin was equipped in the 1940s to undertake almost any senior post that did not involve foreign languages, and he would have been a far better ambassador to the United States than Lord Halifax in 1940. He certainly knew more about America and would have been a bigger hit with the American media and the Roosevelt White House.

Bevin's authenticity came from appearing untutored and 'ex tempor [sic]', as he dubbed his off-the-cuff speeches, while in reality being thoroughly tutored and prepared. His staff commented without exception on his work ethic. His last private secretary at the Foreign Office recalls that, even when seriously ill, he often started on his ministerial boxes at 4 a.m. and came into the office first thing

with marching orders and a clutch of left-field ideas on the problems of the day. He seldom wrote lengthy comments, but 'speak' and
'see me', where it was not 'yes' or 'no', would soon turn into a clear
instruction when explained orally. Saturday was a normal working
day in the Bevin office until at least lunchtime, though sometimes
the entire weekend was working. He may have held his pen like a
chisel, with shapeless writing like a child's, but he was in command
and made his meaning very clear. As a wag put it: 'He could neither
read, write nor speak, and he did all three triumphantly.'

His speeches were powerful and utterly authentic. 'No man alive
is so skilful at handling a working-class audience, mixing the brutal
hammer blow with sentimental appeal,' said Richard Crossman rue-
fully after Bevin routed the left with his dramatic 'stab-in-the-back'
speech in response to critics of his anti-Stalin foreign policy at the
1947 Labour conference. 'He did not merely smash his critics; he
pulverised them into applauding him.'

Francis Williams highlighted 'raw strength' as Bevin's essence.

> The very clumsiness of his sentences, his contempt for syntax and
> the niceties of pronunciation, the harshness of his voice and pow-
> erful emphasis of his gestures seemed when he was speaking to
> a mass audience to make him the embodiment of all natural and
> unlettered men drawing upon wells of experience unknown to the
> more literate.

Or as Michael Foot, Nye Bevan's disciple, put it more than a touch
condescendingly: 'A speech from Ernest Bevin on a major occasion
had all the horrific fascination of a public execution. If the mind was
left immune, eyes and ears and emotions were riveted.'[6]

Bevin the phenomenon and Bevin the man come together in this brilliantly recounted 'day in the life' of his youngest Foreign Office private secretary, Nicholas Henderson, published forty years after the event. It was Saturday 16 March 1946 and Bevin was receiving the freedom of the steel-making town of Port Talbot in South Wales. The previous day, after two bottles of sherry at lunch time to celebrate the signing of a financial agreement with the Swiss government, the Foreign Secretary asked Henderson if he would like to come along for the ride:

I said I would like to very much.

'Yes,' Bevin said with a big grin, 'and it's about time you saw something of the proletariat. You come down with me. We'll have the hell of a time wiv all those people and the football match.'

Bevin's capacity for enjoying himself was infectious; I began to feel exhilarated at the prospect of our day at Port Talbot.

'We'll have none of those darned boxes,' he said beaming.

The following day began with the 8.55 from Paddington:

We had a carriage to ourselves. Leaving the detectives in charge of the boxes – which had followed us despite Bevin's injunction – we went to the restaurant car for breakfast. Bevin, who in the drive to the station, had expressed annoyance with Churchill's Fulton speech ('He thinks he is Prime Minister of the world'), soon recovered his spirits. He tucked into a colossal meal telling me about all the other breakfasts he had eaten on railway trains. We read the morning papers.

'You know, I think this India business is a wonderful thing,' he said out of the blue. 'I don't believe any country but England could have made a gesture like Clem did in his speech in the House and grant freedom to 400 million people with a wave of the hand. Churchill couldn't have done it. He never understood India and wouldn't listen.'

I didn't say anything. By now we were travelling rhythmically through the Elysian water meadows of the Kennet valley. 'You know, Henderson, we're capturing the moral leadership of the world.'

We returned to the carriage and settled down to work at the boxes, which kept Bevin busy for about two hours. By the time we reached the other side of the Severn tunnel, he had finished all the papers and announced that he was going to sleep. But propped up against one end of the carriage like a porpoise basking on a rock, his eye suddenly caught sight of the countryside through which we were passing, and that meant it was all over with the sleeping and on again with the stories. The valleys, villages and factories outside evoked such memories – of early speeches, strikes and difficult situations triumphantly surmounted – that he had to tell the detectives and me all about them. He remembered the Christian and nicknames of all the Joneses, Davieses and Thomases with whom he had been connected in his adventures. Before we reached Port Talbot he sent me along to the restaurant car to get some whisky.

Immediately after our arrival we had lunch with the Mayor of Port Talbot, the Town Clerk, Councillor Richard Evans, who was also to receive the Freedom of the Borough, and their wives. This took place in a private parlour at the Grand Hotel, a room which was generously adorned with china ornaments, brass pots, fire-irons, and highly coloured gravures of sunsets. The tall, dark chimneys of the steelworks could be seen through the lace curtains of the windows. The wives seemed to be quite at home, but they said nothing. Nor did Councillor Richard Evans whose shining face exuded pride and happiness. Bevin made up for any lack of talk in others.

'How's everything?' he asked. 'How's business? Has the new strip mill started yet?'

He listened, as he always did, to the answers.

Preceded by an orderly column of Borough Councillors and pursued by a rabble of screaming children, Bevin walked through the streets to the Grand cinema where the ceremony of bestowing the Freedom was to be held. Either side of him were the Mayor and the Town Clerk in full regalia; and flanking them marched policemen bearing standards. There must have been close on 2,000 people in the cinema. Bevin was placed upon a minute, none-too-steady platform, blindingly floodlit. The ceremony began with a prayer, including a prayer 'For our industry'. This was followed by Welsh folksongs sung beautifully by a large choir of men in evening dress and women in black skirts and white satin blouses. 'Aren't the Welsh girls lovely?' Bevin whispered to me. Then there were speeches, a great many speeches by all the local dignitaries, until at last Bevin was called. He said that he had been associated with Port Talbot for forty years, since 1906. We were better off now than then, better fed and clothed. There had always been a fine spirit among the people of South Wales. This had been a great support to him as Minister of Labour. On foreign affairs he spoke little except to emphasise that he would go on striving and not be deterred 'by passing events' in his search for lasting peace. After his speech came the presentation of silver caskets and scrolls to Bevin and his co-freemen; then more singing to end up.

Everyone thereupon started surging towards the football ground where Aberavon were to play Swansea. We all went on foot. Prominent in Bevin's retinue was the grandly uniformed, hook-nosed figure of the Chief Constable of Glamorgan. I commented to him on the splendour of the day which was truly mild and sunny. 'Yes,' he said, 'it's always fine in South Wales.'

Bevin kicked off to tremendous applause from the large crowd. During half-time he signed autographs. Otherwise he was left alone and sat a bulky, brooding, silent figure, throughout the game. He told me afterwards that while watching he had assembled his thoughts for the speech he had to make in the evening.

The match over, we made our way back to the Grand Hotel for tea. Once again I found myself next to the Chief Constable.

'Well, that was a fine game,' I said.

'We always have good football in South Wales,' he replied.

The guests at tea were the same as at lunch, but there was a shifting population of old friends of Bevin's who also came to pay their respects – or rather to greet him on equal terms and exchange yarns.

'Hullo, Ernie, how yer keeping,' was a familiar welcome. They talked of the docks, the mines, the tin works. He listened, laughed and reminisced. I thought of a remark his daughter had once made to me: 'He is always himself.' They were all happy. The Foreign Secretary was one of them in their, and in his, eyes.

In his speech that night at the dinner, Bevin showed his remarkable skill at linking the particular with the general, and the local with the world-wide. Somehow Port Talbot was fitted into his dramatic account of the social, economic and political torments of the world. Their problems were his problems. If they produced more they would be doing more to aid Britain's foreign policy than any amount of oratory or diplomacy on his part. The range of his speech was kaleidoscopic; education, local government, production, famine, foreign trade, Russia, Greece, the USA, UNO [the United Nations], Vyshinsky [Stalin's deputy foreign minister] and the speech that Churchill had just made at Fulton.

It was convincing and moving and appropriate. He left the dinner to loud applause and was cheered by a big crowd as he got into his car to drive to Cardiff for the night. He was temporarily exhausted, but happy. In the car he said to me: 'You know, it's worth more to me than all the wealth or fame or anything in the world, to feel that all those people really love me. I suppose I'm sentimental at times.' Then he added, shifting his bulk a little: 'It's not like Winston with all that doing the V sign and standin' up in open cars. This is genuine.'

When we reached the Angel Hotel, Cardiff, the Chief Constable was there to usher us into a private sitting-room. I left them talking over a bottle of whisky and went to my room to go to bed. Just as I was getting into bed, I heard Bevin's familiar tread outside.

'Come on, lad,' he said, putting his head round the door, 'the Constable has gone. Let's have one more drink and a chat before we turn in.'

So I went back into the sitting-room. Bevin's deep well of stories was not yet dry. And so for another half-hour of this very long day we talked about pitch-cancer amongst coal workers, dermatitis amongst flour millers and gastritis amongst bus drivers. At last, at last, even Bevin's stamina was feeling the strain. I went with him to his room. Outside the door he kicked off his still-tied shoes, leaving them in the passage. He waddled barefoot into his room, saying 'Good night, lad.'[7]

It is all here: man and phenomenon; man of power, man of the people. The irritation and competition with and grudging admiration for Churchill. The unalloyed admiration for Attlee. A kaleidoscopic off-the-cuff speech. The whole thing undisciplined yet highly disciplined. The work ethic, the massive egoism but also the humanity and empathy. Aberavon vs Swansea and the Port Talbot strip mill: hail the new democratic politician for a new democratic era. He was probably the first Foreign Secretary to support a football team: Chelsea. 'If he and Flo happened to be at home on a Saturday,' according to one profile, 'he would get out his crystal wireless set and tune in to the match on a pair of headphones. Nobody dared interrupt if Chelsea were playing.'[8]

The 'Fulton speech' was Churchill's epochal 'Iron Curtain' speech of ten days previously. Bevin half-resented Churchill stealing the limelight but didn't actually disagree with a word of his excoriating attack on Stalin. 'This India business', of which he spoke to Henderson on the train, was Attlee's bold declaration that Britain would quit India unconditionally. This, as we shall see, Bevin opposed, because he wanted to keep imperial India, which makes the comments that it was 'a wonderful thing' a telling tribute to his ongoing loyalty to 'Clem'.

Henderson's account of the following day, a Sunday, paints Bevin in the same primary colours. Ernie and Flo were spending the day at the Buckinghamshire mansion of their newfound film-producer friend Filippo Del Giudice, who had made Noël Coward's *In Which We Serve* (1942) and Laurence Olivier's *Henry V* (1944):

The next morning we had a long car drive to a house near Bourne

End owned by Bevin's film-producer friend Del Giudice. Mrs Bevin had gone down there the previous day. She loved it there, he said. He was glad she had not come to Port Talbot with us: it would have been too long a day for her; she would only have caught a cold at the football match and he would have had her in bed for a fortnight.

Somehow during the car drive the conversation turned to a leading London political hostess of the time. 'She's an awfully silly person,' Bevin said. 'I had to sit next to her at a lunch the other day and do you know what darned silly thing she said to me?' I listened surprised because he was so rarely critical of people personally. He went on, mocking the hostess's affected way of talking. 'She said, "Mr Bevin, I'm very annoyed with you because I think you like Sir Stafford Cripps more than my husband." Now,' Bevin went on indignantly, 'did you ever hear such darned nonsense? So I said, "Do you really think we men go about workin' out which of the others we like best?"'

From there he went on to censure the whole world of London society, some of which still centred on the Dorchester Hotel where it had taken refuge from the air raids during the war. His heart sagged when he had to attend a lunch or dinner with them. 'They don't stand for nothing. But', he added a little dolefully, 'the trouble is the Mrs rather likes it.'

He spoke of Jimmy Thomas and Ramsay MacDonald, but without bitterness. 'When a man goes bad, like Jimmy Thomas or MacDonald, we just write him off. We don't go on talking about him or running him down. That's where the rest of the Labour Party is different from the intellectuals, who never stop criticising when a man has made an awful mistake.'

All this talk was particularly interesting to me at the time. There had been many suggestions in the Press recently that Bevin, exasperated by the extreme Left, would part company with the Labour Party one day and join forces with the left wing of the Tory Party either to form a coalition or a new party. Everything he had said and done that weekend confirmed me in my conviction that he would never take a step of that kind. It was not merely that the Labour Party was an integral part of his being, and that he himself could never change; but he believed, as a matter of pride, that Labour, and he himself in particular, could govern the country without the Tories, and even better than the Tories. It would have been quite out of keeping with his monolithic and dependable character for him to have renounced the habits of a lifetime.

After we had been driving for about an hour we turned off the main road and stopped outside a row of council houses. Bevin wanted to call on his brother who was eighty-seven. After he had been inside a few minutes he reappeared to fetch the silver casket from Port Talbot which he wanted to show his brother. He stayed with him about three-quarters of an hour, and when he eventually emerged he was met by a throng of children asking for his auto-graph. He signed, if not easily, at any rate willingly. I never knew him to refuse an autograph.

Bevin told me that his brother had been a butcher all his life. He had never seen much of him, or of his two other brothers who were also older ... As we drove over the Cotswolds Bevin revealed that he had been a keen walker in his youth. It was the only exercise he had taken for pleasure. At the age of twenty-one he had developed some glandular trouble which left him for life with a great roll of fat round his middle. When motoring for the Union he had often stopped the car on a fine morning and walked fast for eight or ten miles.

The doors of Del Giudice's stockbroker Tudor house, which we reached in time for lunch, were opened by two watery-eyed footmen. Del greeted us with soft, yet demonstrative handshakes, and a faint smell of perfume. He was wearing loud-check tweeds and thick-rimmed, dark tortoiseshell glasses. He exuded hospitality. He led us over deep-pile carpets and between enormous bowlfuls of mauve tulips to the drawing-room. The house party were already a little tight. They pressed cocktails on us and congratulated Bevin on his Freedom. Mrs Bevin shouted merrily to me through the ether: 'Hello, Henderson, we're having a lovely time'. Del, who had just returned from a visit to the USA, produced a box of a hundred cigars and a trousseau of ties, socks and coloured braces, all of which he gave to Bevin.

We drifted alcoholically into lunch. Del was most solicitous of everyone, particularly Bevin. He wanted to be sure he was enjoying every mouthful of food and drink. At one moment he jumped up from his chair and came hurrying round to Bevin's side to ask him if he would like him to clean his spectacles. Bevin removed them and Del slid from the dining-room in search of a special leather.

As the company tired of eating and drinking there was a murmur of a film to be shown in Del's barn. We staggered for our overcoats.

'You must stay, Henderson,' Bevin insisted. 'I want you to see Del's barn.'

'Yes, it's a lovely barn,' Mrs Bevin said.

She asked Del to take us in the car, but in the end we walked the hundred yards. The barn was certainly worth the detour. From the outside it did not make much pretence at age, but no Tudor effect was spared within: beams as numerous as zebra stripes, plenty of oak and iron-work, electric logs in the grate, and round the walls antlers and tiger skins. There was also a bar. The lights of the barn went out and cigars were handed round as the Dolly Sisters came on the screen.

After the film footmen served tea in the bar. Del and the Foreign Secretary talked about their insides and, at the former's request, I agreed to arrange for Bevin to see a certain Madame X in London the following day. 'It's only a lavage,' Del confided to me, 'but it'll cleanse the whole business. Royalty and lots of nice people go there. It's very clean.' Bevin duly went there the next evening; but I failed to ask him how the lavage had gone, and he never mentioned it.

By the time tea was over the house party were ready for another film. But Bevin and I went back to the house to do some work on the fresh consignment of boxes that had arrived from London. The day's activities had not provided the ideal prelude to the task of deciding about the future level of German industry. However, I got the gist of what Bevin wanted and returned to London by car. During the journey I reflected on the curious contrast for Bevin between his old pals in South Wales with their working-class solidarity and this new film-producer acquaintance with his neo-Tudor luxury. Del Giudice was not a British aristocrat trying to corrupt him – an overriding fear among Labour politicians since the debacle of MacDonald – he was a self-made man like himself and the fact that he was an Italian somehow made the relationship easier. It could not be denied that Bevin liked food and drink, and he said more than once that he would never have got where he did, had the good things of life been available to him when he was a young man. But more than anything, I think he mixed with people like Del to please Mrs Bevin. He was always most considerate towards her, as well as patient and understanding.[9]

Where does one start on that? Del Giudice, with his mock Tudor mansion on the Thames, was an Italian Jew who fled Mussolini in 1933 and was briefly interned as an enemy alien in 1940. With an outsider-artist fascination with English society, he clearly treated Ernie as encyclopedia as much as patron. As well as the Bevins, he cultivated Stafford Cripps, who gave big financial support to the post-war film industry ('Cripps, who was counting every penny for the welfare state, was ready to raid the tills for Del,' Harold Wilson noted cattily).[10] Ernie and Flo, especially Flo, appreciated the attention and the luxury – Del's film company had been bought by J. Arthur Rank, who also lived grandly in Buckinghamshire – but Ernie didn't do it just for Flo. He loved Del's social-realist films, particularly *The Guinea Pig* (1948) starring Richard Attenborough as Jack Read, the bright, roughish working-class boy sent to a public school under a short-lived post-war scheme to break down class barriers. Jack gets into fights and scrapes, but it works out. Jack could have been Bevin. Part of him wished it had been: he was proud of having spoken at both Eton and Harrow.

Then there is his brother – Jack, his first guardian as a teenager – on a council estate near Bristol: Ernie never lost touch with his roots. The still affectionate marriage to Flo, who loved the glitz. The routine dig at 'intellectuals'. The measured contempt for 'the Tories' and determination to prove that Labour could govern better. The celebrity. And, again, the work ethic, deciding on coal and steel production levels in the Ruhr on a Sunday afternoon, between screenings in a film mogul's private cinema hung with antlers and tigers.

Then there is Bevin's daughter Queenie, who in 1935 married Sydney Wynne, a *Daily Herald* journalist who went on to work for Rank. Maybe Bevin got him the job? All this shows the Bevins expanding well out of the working class long before Ernie left the T&G.

And then there is the 26-year-old 'Nico' Henderson himself: hailing from public school (Stowe) and Oxford, president of the Oxford Union, later ambassador to Poland, West Germany, France and finally the United States at the time of Margaret Thatcher and the Falklands War, and maybe the greatest ambassador of post-war Britain. Henderson likewise regarded Bevin as its greatest Foreign Secretary. Bevin became Nico's mentor not just because the young diplomat worked in his office: Nico's father was Sir Hubert Henderson, a Cambridge economist and prominent Liberal who had been on the Macmillan Committee with Bevin and Keynes. (Ernie's contempt for intellectuals only extended to the ones he disliked.) Nico hit the headlines in 1979 for his celebrated retirement dispatch to Callaghan from the Paris embassy – 'Britain's decline: its causes and consequences' – an elegant lament for Britain's post-war decay amid delusions of empire. He was by then a close friend of Roy Jenkins, who was initially to be Bevin's official biographer and whose father had been Attlee's parliamentary private secretary.

Why was Bevin so admired by most of his officials and close associates?

As Ambassador to Paris in 1977, Henderson was 'taken aback' when David Owen, Bevin's chippiest Labour successor, 'upon looking at the photograph of Ernie Bevin that stands in one of the rooms in the Embassy said, "I can't think why all you Foreign Office people were so keen on him, except for reasons of inverted snobbery."'[11]

It is certainly true that Ernie's public school and grammar school

officials – and the King and Queen – revelled in his dropped aitches and homespun wisdom. They competed with stories for decades
to come. Roddy Barclay, his last private secretary, even published a
catalogue of Bevinese. The best: 'If you open that Pandora's Box you
never know what Trojan 'orses will jump out.' Runner-up, about an
eloquent speech by Nye Bevan: 'It sounded as if he'd swallowed a
dictionary. 'E used a lot of words but 'e didn't know what they all
meant.' Another Bevan speech was 'nothing but clitch after clitch'
(i.e. cliché).[12]

Bevin folklore swirled around political and diplomatic circles for
decades. 'This jam tastes fishy,' on eating caviar for the first time.
Summoning 'another bottle of Newts' – aka *Nuits St George* – on an
ocean liner to New York. However, as often as not, he was playing
up to the audience, 'In the same way,' wrote one shrewd observer, 'as
he deliberately dropped his aitches for particularly posh audiences.'
As late as 1986, the then permanent secretary at the Foreign Office,
Sir Patrick Wright – educated at Marlborough and Oxford (clas-
sics) – sought to reassure an anxious junior minister that she would
do fine: 'I reminded her that by far the most popular and most
successful Foreign Secretary since the war had been Ernie Bevin,
who had commented on a marginal reference to the phrase *mutatis
mutandis*: "Please do not write in Greek: I have never learned it."'[13]

Another telling Roddy Barclay story, because of the coda, is about
a visitation to the Foreign Secretary from the Guatemalan ambassador, who came to protest about a frontier incident with British
Honduras, as it then was.

Ernie listened to him for a while and then became irritated. 'Where
was it you said you came from?' he asked the rather surprised

Ambassador, and when the latter said rather pompously that he was the Ambassador of Guatemala Ernie replied, 'Guatamelia, Guatmamelia? Why, I never 'eard of the place until this morning!'[14]

But, Barclay went on, it was 'quite untrue' that his boss had 'never 'eard' of Guatemala. 'It effectively crushed the Ambassador who withdrew as quickly as possible. Ernie Bevin was in reality remarkable well informed about Latin America, and one South American Ambassador in London commented with surprise that Ernie seemed to know more about his country than he did himself.'

Bevin's subordinates and associates thought he was good and often brilliant. This wasn't inverted snobbery; he inspired admiration because he inspired confidence. In another piece of Foreign Office folklore, the difference between Bevin and Morrison, his successor, was: 'Ernie can't pronounce the names either, but he does know where the places are.'[15]

There was no snobbery among the intellectuals who worked with Bevin. Keynes regarded him as the best practical politician he had encountered besides Lloyd George. A. L. Rowse, Fellow of All Souls College, Oxford, and budding Cornish Labour politician in the 1940s, who was taken with few politicians, recalled:

I never heard him speak without being intellectually convinced. Behind the rough, clumsy, ungrammatical sentences he was a match for anyone – lawyers or economists, let alone industrialists or politicians. I am astonished to realise how much he *knew*, the range of information he commanded. He had no inferiority complex, not a shadow of one – unlike MacDonald. He had a world of experience behind him – wider than any except Churchill's.[16]

By 1940 Bevin, like Churchill, had a reputation for being right, against received wisdom. But whereas Churchill was vindicated on one big issue, Bevin was vindicated on practically all the big issues, not only Hitler and appeasement but also Mussolini, unemployment, the Gold Standard, the economy, and what came to be called 'Keynesianism'. Looking back, Rowse thought it 'astonishing how right he was'.[17] Crucially, as we shall see, he was vindicated after 1945 on his handling of Stalin, his biggest foreign policy challenge by far. He got it badly wrong on Israel/Palestine – a sorry story told later – but to an unusual degree in political leaders, he had what Roy Jenkins considered one of the greatest of leadership qualities: a good sense of proportion.

Most of Bevin's key associates shared this confidence in Bevin's judgement, not least Attlee. 'He could lead and learn at the same time,' said Dean Acheson, the last of the three US Secretaries of State with whom he dealt. 'To work with him inevitably evoked deep affection, respect, and trust.' So too for King George VI. Barclay recalls that, on becoming Bevin's private secretary in 1949, the King's private secretary Sir Tommy Lascelles was 'the first to impress on me that my most important duty was to ensure that my new master did not work himself to death, since it was in the country's interest that he should carry on as Foreign Secretary for as long as possible'.[18] He was given the same advice by the chief of the Imperial General Staff, Lord Slim, and the then Foreign Office permanent under-secretary Lord Strang.

Memoir after memoir of those who worked for Bevin is the same: he was their best ever chief. He was generally right. He got things done. He was warm if not charming. He generated excitement and energy.

And the loyalty they gave, he repaid. In 1945 the Foreign Office feared Labour would fillet the diplomatic service: Dalton and Morrison said as much. But not Bevin, who never dismantled machines that worked. He even kept Lord Halifax as ambassador in Washington and Duff Cooper in Paris, to the disgust of Labour left-wingers including Laski, who had lobbied for Washington. 'In general we were treated rather as a benevolent uncle might treat some promising nephew who had talent but still had a good deal to learn about the ways of the world,' recalled Barclay. 'Indeed, Gladwyn Jebb [later Ambassador to the UN and Paris] and others used always to refer to him as Uncle Ernie.'[19]

Bevin invariably promoted subordinates on talent and loyalty; both were essential, but he never promoted incompetent loyalists. He had known Godfrey Ince, his manpower director at the Ministry of Labour, since Ince was secretary of the Shaw Inquiry where he became 'the Dockers' KC' twenty years before. Bevin and Frederick Leggett, his industrial relations director at the Ministry of Labour, went back to the General Strike as interlocutors, and travelled together on Bevin's post-strike industrial tour of the US, for which Leggett had nominated him as the best of the trade union leaders. They met constantly in the 1930s when Leggett was head of the British government delegation to the International Labour Organisation in Geneva.

Such long and close partnerships, both with equals and subordinates, were a hallmark of Bevin's career. The sixteen-year partnership with Attlee was the foundation of his ministerial career, just as his twenty-year partnership with Walter Citrine was the foundation of his leadership of the trade union movement after 1926. Even longer, and just as vital, was his thirty-year partnership with Arthur Deakin, his protégé, deputy and successor at the T&G. Deakin was strong and tough, yet totally subservient to Bevin. Even when he became general secretary himself after 1945, and the leading trade union player in the industrial politics of the late 1940s, he was content to take marching orders from his predecessor, calling at the Foreign Office when Bevin didn't himself drop into Transport House. His old office there was so unchanged that photos of Deakin show him next to the same globe that Ernie installed on returning from his Commonwealth tour of 1938. 'Deakin was essentially a Bevin creation and perhaps the most loyal supporter of a man upon whom he modelled himself to the extent of copying some of his public mannerisms,' writes his biographer.[20] He 'dressed flamboyantly, smoked large cigars and courted publicity', like the boss. He was even Bevin's executor on his death in 1951 and was so fiercely protective of his memory that he sought not merely to choose his 'official' biographer but to dictate what he wrote.

When people recalled Bevin, for every quirk they identified an essential strength. His humanity and lack of pomposity. His memory and recall. His work ethic and creativity. The brilliant negotiator. 'When you are negotiating with Boilermakers you want to speak very low – they're all a bit deaf,' was one of hundreds of his tricks of the trade, endlessly retold. Another: 'Patience in negotiation is essential: someone has to get worn out.' And it was rarely him, even against Molotov, Vyshinsky and Stalin. He was thought to have a sixth sense for the mood of a meeting and how to turn it round. Early in the Korean War, there was a sticky meeting of NATO ministers with Acheson. Bevin intervened to say: 'I know what is worrying all my European friends, though they daren't say so. They are afraid that the United States with its Pacific preoccupations is going to leave them in the lurch.' Acheson immediately responded that the United States would stand resolutely by Europe, and the cloud lifted. Alan Brooke, chief of the Imperial General Staff and acerbic diarist of all the fools he affected to see around him, including frequently Churchill, remarked of Bevin: 'The more I saw of him in later years the more I admired him. A very great man.'[21]

Bevin never professed false modesty and never doubted he was the best man for the job, and often that he could do other people's jobs too. In the 1929 election, he remarked in one speech attacking Tory incompetence: 'I am not given to boasting, but if I were asked to take on any job which Mr Baldwin has handled, I would take it on with perfect confidence.' He 'talked about himself non-stop', Churchill's doctor Lord Moran recalled. In 1945, he regarded himself as absolutely up to dealing with the future of the world. 'You see, I've had a good deal of experience with foreigners,' he told Nico Henderson on the plane back from Potsdam.

> Before the last war I had to do a good deal of negotiation with ships' captains of all nationalities. These people, Stalin and Truman, are just the same as all Russians and Americans; and dealing with them over foreign affairs is just the same as trying to come to a settlement about unloading a ship. Oh yes, I can handle them.[22]

In all three of his big jobs – leader of the T&G, Minister of Labour and Foreign Secretary – Bevin's staying power, self-confidence and sheer persistence were extraordinary, despite his increasingly poor health. He held these three offices for thirty-four years in total, being the entire last thirty-four years of his life bar six weeks. It was a longer career in top posts than any other politician of the twentieth century, including Churchill (twenty-six years), Lloyd George (seventeen), Thatcher (fifteen) and Attlee (eleven). Resignation was not a word in Bevin's dictionary: he never resigned from any leadership role and never seriously threatened to do so, either. In this respect too he was Churchill, who also never resigned from a big job and clung on following almost incapacitating illness after 1951, believing himself indispensable.

What followed both Bevin and Churchill respectively – Morrison and Eden – sort of made their point. For all their imperialism, it is inconceivable that Churchill or Bevin would have made Eden's catastrophic misjudgement over Suez, conducting covert diplomacy with France and Israel, lying to Parliament, breaking with the US and ignoring virtually all diplomatic advice. As for Morrison, Roddy Barclay, who handled the transition from Bevin at the Foreign Office as principal private secretary, recalled his new boss as cold, rude and incompetent, 'appalled by the amount of work he was expected to do'. There were also disastrous encounters, including with Acheson. Morrison 'seemed to lack not only the background knowledge but also the ability to comprehend the essentials of the problem before him', said Barclay.[23]

Bevin had plenty of weaknesses. The love of applause. The heavy drinking ('he used alcohol like a car uses petrol'). The grudges. The prima donna, so prima donna-ish by the end that, when told that Churchill was to be staying at the Washington embassy at the same time in 1949, 'This caused an explosion from Ernie, who said that he was not prepared to play second fiddle.' It was always 'my policy', 'my people' and 'I won't have it'. The only two wartime leaders who routinely referred to 'my people' were the King and Ernie Bevin.

Any of these weaknesses might have been his undoing had there not been such intense confidence in his leadership, pre-eminently from Churchill and Attlee. In particular, they set aside the biggest obstacle of all to Bevin holding office in the 1940s: his health. For the entire six years of his foreign secretaryship he was often ill, including recurrent incapacitating bouts of angina. In his last eighteen months in office, from the autumn of 1949, he was a semi-invalid; the Foreign Office had his doctor Sir Alec McCall in constant attendance, giving tablets and injections and logistical advice on avoiding stairs and walks of any but the shortest distances. He could fly only at very low altitudes. 'This is Alec,' Ernie would say. ''E treats me be'hind like a dartboard.'[24]

In the five months from March to August 1950, which saw the Schuman Plan and the outbreak of the Korean War, Bevin was in hospital (he had two operations) or convalescent for 85 out of 153 days. Angina, haemorrhoids, fistula: his body was closing down. Most of the time he was still chain-smoking. In the entire year from November 1949 to November 1950 he spoke only twice in the House of Commons and made only two speeches outside Parliament, at the United Nations in September and the Labour Party conference in October.

None of this was a secret — the absence from Parliament could hardly be so — and it was discussed virtually daily by his staff and periodically with Attlee. 'Alec told me that almost the only sound part of Ernie's body was his feet — and they had quite a heavy task for he weighed eighteen stone,' said Barclay. It was tolerated until a 'Bevin must go' campaign was got up by Churchill and Beaverbrook in early 1951, when an election was looming — but not before, when they could easily have made an issue of it. The reason for the tolerance, beyond a liking for the man, was the general belief that a sick Bevin was better than a well A. N. Other.

'Until he fell ill with pneumonia at the beginning of 1951 I had no hesitation in replying that I considered that from the point of view of the national interest the longer he could stay at the Foreign Office the better,' said Barclay. He continued,

I sometimes used to compare notes with William Strang [the permanent secretary], and we always came to the conclusion that Ernie Bevin, even if operating at something considerably less than full efficiency, was a more effective Foreign Secretary than any of the possible candidates for the succession was likely to be.

Barclay insists that even when in hospital Bevin's 'grip on affairs never really weakened', recalling that the only time he ever received a reprimand was when he didn't phone Bevin in hospital to tell him that hostilities had begun in Korea on 25 June 1950.

In meetings, as Barclay describes them, Bevin 'often appeared rambling and chaotic and the conclusions reached were not always clear, but the senior members of the FO had learnt the way the Secretary of State's mind worked and many of them were remarkably adept at producing at great speed a document which correctly represented his ideas'.[25]

'He was still all right as far down as the neck,' his doctor, Alec McCall, told Attlee, which was decisive in the decision to keep Bevin at the Foreign Office into 1951. When McCall advised against his last long overseas trip to the Commonwealth conference in Colombo, Sri Lanka, in January 1950, Bevin countered that he should go – and McCall should come with him. Which is what happened. When he got there, he was so immobile that he was carried up the stairs into the conference room in a richly decorated palanquin. Back in London in the spring of 1950 Kenneth Younger, his ministerial deputy, thought he was now 'only half alive' and the position was unsustainable, but added, 'I have to admit that when he pulls himself together he usually does pretty well for short periods. In Cabinet he appears to be asleep, but then suddenly weighs in with comments which show that he knows exactly what has been said.'[26] It is unlikely that the key decisions on the Korean War and the Schuman Plan would have been different had Bevin been fully mobile, although maybe shuttle diplomacy and physical presence would have made the rejection of Schuman more nuanced.

All this makes Bevin an interesting case for David Owen's thesis as to the importance of sickness in political decision-making, influenced by his experience as both a doctor and a senior minister.[27] Bevin in his last year in office is an extreme case of a decision-maker persisting through serious illness. Yet, he does not fit Owen's pattern, which applies to Eden, of severe illness leading to poor decisions. Of the big mistakes Bevin made, none are obviously attributable to illness, and he continued to make broadly sensible judgements from his hospital bed. And he does not remotely fit into Owen's other category of leaders whose cognitive faculties functioned well, but who developed a 'hubristic syndrome' that powerfully affected their performance. This never happened to Bevin. On the contrary, Bevin raises the opposite issue of how far serious illness in one who is cognitively sound and balanced, although performing well below par, should outweigh the benefits of someone less capable occupying their post.

Bevin's career ended not in failure but in pathos. For his seventieth birthday, on 9 March 1951, in an unprecedented act, every member of the foreign service, from doorkeepers to ambassadors, contributed sixpence – 'the docker's tanner' – towards a cake and

ERNIE

a dinner service. 'In that period of continuing shortages it was not easy to get hold of a good new dinner service but this was finally achieved,' recalled Barclay.[28] The party was in full swing when Attlee phoned to tell Bevin that he finally had to go ahead with his departure from the Foreign Office. 'I've got the sack,' Ernie said to Flo with real bitterness.[29] He wasn't being fair: Attlee had warned him of the change and kept him in the Cabinet in the sinecure post of Lord Privy Seal – leading to a good Bevin joke: 'I am neither a lord, nor a privy, nor a seal' – and insisted that he be left undisturbed at 1 Carlton Gardens, where he died six weeks later. The point is, Bevin simply could not bear letting go. Attlee believed his friend wanted to die in harness as Foreign Secretary, and all but let him do so.

Ernie went into the Foreign Office one last time, the morning after his resignation was announced. His very last visitor was young Nico Henderson, back from Washington where he had been posted on leaving Bevin's office. 'I asked the Private Office if I might see him for a minute to say goodbye':

He was sitting as usual behind the large desk looking straight ahead. He half turned and said 'Hullo, Nico.' He held out his hand limply and I took it but feared to shake it in case I should hurt him, so frail did he seem...

'I am so sorry you are going.'

'Yes, I know,' he said in a friendly way, but very quietly. 'Six years is a long time, and you know I don't know if I've succeeded.'

I was struck by his doubts. When I had seen a lot of him in earlier days he had never admitted to any failure or to qualms about the rightness of what he was doing. But now he was talking almost introspectively. I noticed how immovable his lower lip seemed; it jutted out, dark in colour, as if the blood was clotted inside. His face was much thinner, and the lines of his forehead more sharply delineated; the only thing the same was the streaked black and white hair that, I had always thought, made his head look from behind like a giant bull's eye.

'I think it has been successful, very successful,' I replied in a matter-of-fact way.

'Well, not altogether,' he said. 'If only I had had a bit longer. But then I don't know if you can ever settle with the Russians.'

'No, you can never settle,' I said, emphasising the last word. 'But I don't think there'll be war. Do you?'

'No, there won't be war,' Bevin replied slowly and stolidly. 'If only,' he went on, 'I'd had time to make the Atlantic Pac [he always said the word as though it was spelt without a 't'] into something large, into a wider organism, with a budget and other things for the whole area' – he was talking more in his old way now, great, vague but visionary ideas...

He began rubbing his chest over his heart just as he had always done. I might have been back four years, so vividly did I recall the many times I had stood there watching him overcome pain and frailty to tackle some foreign visitor or go over to the House of Commons for a speech...

He began denouncing Churchill in a way that suggested to me that the widespread call for his resignation had been heightened by something that Churchill had said.

As he mentioned Churchill there was a flash of the old indignation, but you felt there was no longer the power behind it. I noticed he no longer chewed the inside of his left cheek, a tic that used to be a favourite accompaniment to wrath or rumination...

Bevin seemed to be getting very tired. He got up gingerly from his chair. I noticed he had been sitting on an air cushion. He held out his hand for me to shake it. I did so and he moved slowly towards the cloakroom.

'Give my wishes to your father,' he said...

He managed to inspire affection without being sentimental. I thought how completely without self-pity he was – in spite of his stab-in-the-back speeches – and how, although egotistical, he was not vain. ...

I never saw him again, but such was the pull of his personality that when, a few weeks later, I read of his death on the Reuters tape, I hurried, without thinking, to his flat at No. 1 Carlton Gardens. I asked for Bevin's detective, Ben Macey, and was told, 'Oh, he's gone off, of course, now.' That certainly seemed to sum up the finality of Bevin's death, and thinking of him I walked away disconsolately. His capacity for winning loyalty and affection from those who worked most closely with him – singled out by Attlee as his outstanding characteristic – made his loss the greater as it also heightened the gain of those who had had the chance of knowing and serving him.[30]

Of Britain's twentieth-century leaders, perhaps only Churchill was so highly rated by his associates and so universally mourned on his death. There was a touch of genius about Ernie, and not just in his own estimation. However, circumstance played a key role. For both Churchill and Bevin, transfiguration followed heroic victory in the Second World War.

HIS WINNING WAY

"I want you, I need you,
There's such a lot to do,
I gonna make you help me
Weekdays and Sundays too—oo—oo."

Bevin's wartime leadership was inspirational. He masterminded the home
front while Churchill commanded the battle front. © *Punch Magazine*

CHAPTER 7

WAR

'The British working class want this war won. They know what is at stake. It is their liberty,' Bevin said in a speech in Stoke-on-Trent on May Day 1940.

> But they want a government that is going to please the nation before its friends and private interests … I am afraid that the kind of middle-class mind which accentuates those responsible for strategy and government has little knowledge of the psychology and organising ability of the people in charge of the totalitarian states.

This was a declaration of no confidence, not only in Neville Chamberlain but in the whole management of the Second World War and the failure to engage the trade unions and the working class. He rammed the point home brutally just as in his 1935 speech against George Lansbury: 'The time has come when there must be no mincing of words. It is no use disguising the fact that those like myself are intensely dissatisfied with the kind of obstruction, lack of drive, absence of imagination and complacency which exists.'[1]

Chamberlain had foolishly kept Labour and the unions at arm's length in the early months of the war. He met Bevin only a couple of times and his engagement with Attlee was little better.

By May 1940, Britain's situation was desperate. In what Churchill called the 'white-hot weeks' after 9 April, Hitler overran most of Western Europe, defeated and occupied France, and drove Britain into the sea, first in Norway then at Dunkirk. Defeat seemed imminent. Meanwhile, Chamberlain told the Conservative National Union, only five days before the Blitzkrieg in April, 'Hitler has missed the bus.'[2]

Ten days after the May Day speech, Churchill was Prime Minister with Bevin at his right hand – the 'proletarian patriot' famously marching alongside Churchill in Low's 'All behind you, Winston' cartoon of 14 May, with an emaciated Attlee squeezed in between.

Attlee played a decisive part in bringing Chamberlain down by deciding to force a vote at the end of the impassioned and acrimonious Norway debate in the House of Commons on 7 and 8 May. The scale of the Tory rebellion, and the hostility of Labour, made Chamberlain's position untenable. He was gone within two days. Churchill's wind-up speech immediately before the vote included a signal tribute to Bevin, although he was not even an MP:

> Well then, the question was asked by a very influential person, not a member of the House, Mr Bevin – who is a friend of mine, working hard for the public cause, and a man who has much gift to help and who asked in a public speech – 'Why, when you went into Narvik on the first occasion, did you not send a big ship in with the destroyers and Captain Warburton-Lee?' I think that it should have its answer, and I will give it.[3]

The respect was now mutual. Setting aside decades of antipathy – the exception proving the rule in Bevin's case – they developed a good relationship after a first wartime meeting on 19 October 1939. Churchill had set out the big strategic picture while Bevin made a host of practical suggestions, including how the fishing industry could better co-exist with the navy, which the admiralty immediately implemented. Wary courtship turned into a firm alliance. 'ACTION THIS DAY' headed Churchill's wartime instructions: it was Bevin's motto too.

Bevin's rapport with Churchill was vital to the two key decisions that Labour took in May 1940, neither of which was inevitable: first, to join a Tory-led coalition, and second, to support Churchill becoming Prime Minister.

When Attlee phoned Bevin about the formation of a coalition after meeting Churchill on the morning of 11 May, Bevin backed him without caveats. 'You helped to bring the other fellow [Chamberlain] down; if the party did not take its share of responsibility, they would say we were not great citizens but cowards.'4 Attlee then said that he and Churchill wanted Bevin to be Minister of Labour. 'You have sprung it on me,' was Bevin's immediate response. When they met in Attlee's office a few hours later, Bevin said his fear was that the Ministry of Labour would remain 'a glorified conciliation board'. Attlee reassured him that it would be central to the war effort with extra powers. Bevin then accepted, subject to agreement by the TUC General Council, which met shortly afterwards at the Labour Party conference in Bournemouth. This was a formality, although symbolically important after the experience of MacDonald and 1931.

The striking point is that both Churchill and Attlee wanted Bevin in the new government: they both saw him as indispensable to mobilising the working class for war, reaching parts neither of them could reach. 'He was the Labour man I wanted most,' Churchill said.[5]

Still, Bevin wasn't immediately included in the five-member War Cabinet. Arthur Greenwood, Labour's deputy leader, who made a good speech in the Norway debate but was ineffectual in government, took the second Labour slot until he was replaced by Bevin in October. By then, the T&G leader's indispensability was universally acknowledged.

Bevin was a key play by Attlee and Churchill. Above all, Churchill trusted Bevin to fight and not surrender, unlike Halifax and the appeasers whose influence was still strong, particularly in the days surrounding the Dunkirk evacuation. 'He said Bevin was a good old thing and had "the right stuff in him" – no defeatist tendencies,' Churchill's private secretary Jock Colville recorded. Bevin did not participate in the 'five days in London' War Cabinet discussions about Halifax's proposed armistice at the end of May, but his views could not have been clearer and Attlee held the line with Churchill. According to Beaverbrook, Churchill said that, if the Germans landed in Britain, he would set up a Committee of Public Safety composed of himself, Bevin and Beaverbrook to lead the British resistance.[6]

It is striking how much wartime commentary and cartoonery paired Churchill and Bevin, particularly in the desperate early months. 'A great hulk of a man,' recalled the American ambassador John Winant on meeting the Minister of Labour in the dark days of May 1940. 'He called out to me as I passed through the door, before I had a chance to speak, explaining the pressures and problems that were piling up because of the fall of France ... Both he and Churchill had the same fighting stamina for meeting reverses head on.'[7]

Bevin's formal title was Minister of Labour and National Service. But his real job was 'minister for my people', as he now invariably called the working class. Indeed, wartime Bevin was a continuation of pre-war Bevin. He did not stop being a working-class leader because he became a minister. On the contrary, his whole persona as Minister of Labour was of the trade union leader who was also a national leader. Alan Bullock compartmentalised his official biography of Bevin into three volumes: 'Trade Union Leader', 'Minister of Labour' and 'Foreign Secretary'. To be fair, Bullock wrote more than 2,000 pages and had to divide his material somehow. But in a fundamental sense all three volumes should have been entitled 'Trade Union Leader'. Volume One ends with Bevin entering the Ministry of Labour on 14 May 1940, as German troops poured through the Ardennes towards Paris: 'One career had ended, another was about to begin.'[8] But actually, it was the same career, just in a grander setting.

This duality – trade union leader and national leader – continued after the war too, when Bevin was Foreign Secretary. In February 1946, he rushed back from the United Nations General Assembly in New York to speak in the House of Commons on the repeal of the penal anti-union legislation imposed by Baldwin and Churchill after the General Strike. He laid into the Tories, particularly Churchill. After the 1924 election, he said with heavy sarcasm, 'Mr Baldwin put the greatest financial expert in the world in charge of the Treasury, the right hon. member for Woodford [Mr Churchill].' This led to the 'complete upset' and 'bolt from the blue' of the reintroduction of the Gold Standard in 1925, undermining 'our whole wage structure in this country'. The only saving grace of the General Strike, Bevin quipped, was that Baldwin took the 'wisest decision of his life' to put

Churchill in charge of the *British Gazette* – the government's anti-union newspaper – 'because if he had not, that gentleman would have landed the whole country in a series of Sidney Streets [where Churchill famously, as Home Secretary, directed the police against a barricaded hostage taker] instead of the strikers and the police playing football together as they did'.

'You cast the trade unions for the role of enemies of the State,' he rounded on the Tories opposite him, continuing:

I have never been an enemy of the State. I have been as big a constitutionalist as any member on the other side of the House, and I am fighting to remove the stigma which the Tory party put upon me as the leader of a trade union…

We are subjects of the King as much as anybody else. We are part of the State. Disraeli said that we are two nations. At any rate, we have done our best to make this country into a classless society where, at least, we are equal.[9]

As both Minister of Labour and Foreign Secretary, Bevin championed trade unions and a 'classless society': it was his essence. Everything he did in his career, including his eleven years in the Cabinet, was a continuation of his mission to make the trade unions an 'equal part of the state'.

Bevin deliberately did not resign the general secretaryship of the T&G on becoming Minister of Labour but took a leave of absence while Arthur Deakin did the job day to day. He was regularly in Transport House throughout the war. On at least one occasion he even turned up at the TUC General Council to argue the government's case. And his grip did not weaken after the war, which is largely why the 1945 Labour government had few of the problems with the unions that the Wilson and Callaghan governments experienced in the 1960s and 1970s. Even in the depths of post-war austerity in the late 1940s, the unions, led by Deakin at the T&G, moderated their wage demands in return for social partnership, and came down on unofficial strikes and communist disruption with an iron fist.

Gladstone is often quoted as saying that 'a man might as well start training for the ballet as for the Cabinet at the age of forty-five'. Bevin was fifty-nine in May 1940. Actually, Gladstone's full remark begins: 'There have been honourable and distinguished exceptions, but, as a rule…' However, Bevin was only a distinguished exception up to a point, because, apart from performing in Parliament, there was virtually no aspect of being a minister that was new to him in 1940, and few that he had not been practising day-in day-out as leader of the largest trade union in the free world for the previous eighteen years. On the contrary, he made a point of being a minister in much the same way he had been a trade union leader. He was just as blunt, just as egocentric, just as 'working class', just as bold, just as decisive, just as pragmatic. He didn't change: he gloried in not changing, except when it periodically suited him to become even more assertive in his self-promotion and his dealings with colleagues.

This helps explain why Bevin succeeded where other ex-trade union leaders failed as politicians. Arthur Henderson and George Barnes, Labour's members of the Lloyd George coalition of the First World War, acted as conventional ministers in the classic parliamentary and Whitehall mould. They vanished without trace after the 'doormat incident', where they were kept waiting outside a key meeting in No. 10, the title summing up their ministerial status. Frank Cousins, a successor of Bevin's as leader of the T&G, suffered a similar fate as Minister of Technology under Harold Wilson. Alan Johnson, a former leader of the Communication Workers Union, was a popular Home Secretary for a year under Gordon Brown, but by then he had essentially lost his union lineage and he left politics soon afterwards. Bevin, by contrast, kept his union heft and then acquired more as a minister.

Fittingly, Bevin's first big speech as Minister of Labour wasn't in Parliament but to a conference of 2,000 trade union officials. 'I have to ask you virtually to place yourselves at the disposal of the state,' he told them as no one else could. 'We are socialists and this is the test of our socialism. It is the test of whether we have meant the resolutions which we have so often passed.' He also said presciently: 'If our movement and our class rise with all their energy now and save the people of this country from disaster, the country will always turn with confidence to the people who saved them.'[10]

While Churchill travelled the world, Bevin travelled the country, just as he had done at the T&G. The difference was that this time, as well as doing meetings of trade unionists, he did meetings with industrialists and civil servants too, often bringing them all together to thrash out common challenges. There were also lots of public meetings, and more than three hundred reported speeches outside Parliament as Minister of Labour. A typical two-day tour of the north-east, in March 1941, took him to several factories, giving a speech to local staff of the Ministry of Labour, a speech at a Durham miners' conference, a speech at a civic dinner in Newcastle, and speeches to crowded public meetings in Newcastle City Hall and in a cinema at Ashington.

Six weeks after taking office, Bevin was parachuted into the House of Commons for the inner London constituency of Central Wandsworth, whose sitting Labour MP was given a peerage to vacate the seat. Under the coalition agreement on by-elections, there was no Tory candidate and Bevin had the rare privilege of being returned unopposed. There weren't even any fringe or protest candidates, unlike later wartime by-elections, many of which the government lost. It was a sign of Bevin's standing and the public's desperate yearning for leadership.

Bevin never became a classic parliamentarian. He never learned the names of more than a few dozen backbench MPs, was rarely in the bars or tea rooms of the Commons and 'never bothered to learn the rules of parliamentary procedure', recalled Christopher Mayhew, later his junior minister at the Foreign Office. 'Tell me when to get up – I'll know when to get down,' he used to say.[11] But he did okay in the House. At times he was too leaden, at others too combative, although the first didn't stop Attlee and the second was Church- ill's trademark. He survived because he was not remotely afraid of the chamber, even when under sustained attack for war production shortages in 1941. He always had a big argument with supporting facts and was never intimidated. This, more than flowery oratory, is what matters in Parliament, and he held his own.

On occasion, he could carry the House like the greats. Presenting the Employment White Paper in June 1944, he scored a notable par- liamentary success, yoking war and post-war together into a national plan to eradicate unemployment. He even got away with a character- istically self-regarding flourish ('They call me Ernie'), which was quite a feat, since there is nothing MPs like more than deflating big egos. It comes alive even in the dry verbatim report of Hansard:

MR BEVIN: We are grappling with the problem which is uppermost in the minds of those who are defending the country today ...

With the Prime Minister, I had an opportunity of visiting one of our ports and seeing the men, of the 5th Division among others, gallant men, brave men with no complaint. They were going off to face this terrific battle, with great hearts and great courage. The one question they put to me when I went through their ranks was, 'Ernie, when we have done this job for you, are we going back to the dole?'

MR PICKTHORN (Cambridge University): For you?

MR BEVIN: Yes, it was put to me in that way because they knew me personally. They were members of my own union and I think the sense in which the word 'Ernie' was used can be understood. Both the Prime Minister and I answered, 'No, you are not.'[12]

The Tory MP who followed, Henry Brooke, a future Home Secretary, praised his 'lucidity and sincerity'. Even inveterate critic Manny Shinwell, sensing the mood of the House, extended 'cordial congratulations'. 'I feel that we were very glad to detect in my right honourable friend's speech a note of idealism, of passionate concern for the men now fighting on all the battle fronts for this nation.'[13]

Bevin's sheer drive and power impressed the Commons. 'No one in our Movement can ever accuse me of playing to the gallery,' he retorted to critics in a debate in May 1942.

I do not care whether I lose a seat in this House or whether I lose my place in the Government. I came into the government with my eyes open to try to win the war, and when that is done, let others go on and build the peace, if you like, but I knew what was at stake between fascism, Nazism and ourselves.[14]

Britain mobilised more of its population in the Second World War
than did totalitarian Germany or Italy. © *Daily Mail*

However, Bevin's claim to fame was never going to be for parliamentary lucidity. His reputation from the outset turned on his effectiveness at war mobilisation.

It was frequently stated, not least by Bevin himself, that Britain mobilised more of its population in the Second World War than did totalitarian Germany or Italy. It was certainly a vast mobilisation, longer and with greater public consent, and involving more women, than during the First World War. By September 1943 more than 22 million men and women out of a population of 33 million between the ages of fourteen and sixty-four were serving in the armed forces, civil defence or industry, an increase of nearly 3.75 million in four years. The armed forces had increased by nearly 4 million, munitions industries by nearly 2 million and less essential occupations reduced by more than 3 million.[15]

Much of this had little to do with Bevin. The cause of the war was less contentious than in 1914, particularly among the working classes and on the left. This time, the critical issue of male conscription was resolved by conscripting at the outset of the war in 1939, rather than midway as in 1915–16. And mercifully, free of trench warfare, the day-by-day military horror was less than in the earlier conflict, although from Borneo to bomber command, from V1s to V2s, it was still horrific.

However, Bevin's leadership was inspirational and his strategy and decisions undoubtedly contributed to victory. 'He came out of the war second only to Churchill in courage and insight,' declared the *Manchester Guardian* as the coalition ended in May 1945.[16] Churchill shared this view, about both the first and the second place. Bevin was the only minister besides himself to serve in the same post for the full five years to 1945. At the end of the war, having failed to persuade Attlee to continue the coalition beyond the conflict, Churchill tried to detach Bevin from Labour, so valuable did he regard him.

The Emergency Powers Act vested in the Minister of Labour and National Service 'the control and use of all labour by giving him power to direct any person in Great Britain'. © *Evening Standard*

But it didn't start that way. In the early months Bevin was attacked fiercely by Conservatives for not supporting industrial conscription alongside military conscription. Bevin insisted on maintaining what he called 'voluntaryism' on the home front: the right of non-conscripted adults to work wherever they could get jobs. He also argued for a continuation of collective bargaining by unions and employers for wages and conditions.

The 'voluntaryism' against 'compulsion' debate, which raged in the early months of Bevin's tenure, wasn't remotely that simple. Within days of taking office, he acquired draconian powers under the Emergency Powers Act, which

> vests in the Minister of Labour and National Service the control and use of all labour by giving him power to direct any person in Great Britain to perform such services as may be specified by directions issued by the Minister ... for regulating the engagement of workers by employers and the duration of their employment.

Bevin used this power of direction fairly regularly, in the most extreme case, as we shall see, to force the Bevin Boys down the mines to boost coal production at the end of the war. By May 1942, 6.5 million non-military staff were under Essential Work Orders, forbidding them from moving job, and the regime for the deferment of military service was radically recast to yield more conscripts without reducing war production.

Bevin also pushed through the conscription of women over the objection of many Tories, initially including Churchill. In December 1941, Bevin got the War Cabinet to agree to conscript unmarried women aged between twenty and thirty into auxiliary services, civil defence and public services. This was a careful compromise and was accepted as such with little public controversy. Bevin's labour exchanges did a good job implementing the policy, including with the provision of hostels and child support for working women. He also instructed labour exchanges to interview all women of working age to encourage them to take up war jobs. Eight million such interviews were conducted which, according to one study, 'contributed more perhaps than anything else to the successful mobilisation of women for work'. By the end of 1942, 8.5 million women aged between nineteen and forty-six were registered for national service, a remarkable organisational feat. Between 1939 and 1943 the female share of the labour force increased from 18 to 30 per cent and the number of women employed soared from 4.8 million to 7.3 million.[17] 'You must proceed with tact,' Bevin told MPs when moving towards partial female conscription. 'I have carried the confidence of the parents of this country. I think that is very vital.'

The bigger controversy and ill feeling about female employment came, ironically, in 1945, when married women were often barred from continuing in the very jobs and occupations, including the civil service and teaching, that they had entered during the war at Bevin's entreaty. For Bevin had no time for claims by women for equal treatment. One of his labour inspectors noted in 1941 that 'women workers had about as much say in agreements on their wages as Czechoslovakia had in the Munich Agreement'. Bevin opposed equal pay on the argument that 'industrial peace might be endangered'. And when, in 1944, the House of Commons passed an amendment to R. A. Butler's Education Bill granting equal pay for women teachers, Bevin was adamant that it had to be reversed.

'Any sign of weakness on the part of the Government would have the worst possible effect on industrial relations.' Maybe this wasn't just about equal pay: Bevin didn't much like teachers. They were 'a spoiled lot', he told the junior education minister Chuter Ede. 'They were the blue-eyed boys and girls of the family who had all the sacrifices made for them.'[18] Not his finest hour.

However, Bevin shrewdly refused to set himself up as a universal employment dictator, which he knew would end in tears. Nor was he prepared to play the Tory game of becoming a 'tsar', only to make the working class bear the brunt of the war. Wage freezes and wage cuts, much enamoured of employers and the Treasury throughout the war, were consistently refused by Bevin, as he boasted at the 1941 TUC conference. One of his first acts, over the objections of the Chancellor, Kingsley Wood, was a sharp increase in the wages of agricultural labourers before he 'would feel justified in stopping the drift from the country by administrative order'. Frederick Leggett, his industrial relations director, said that within Whitehall Bevin's 'word was law' and he sought to dictate large awards to arbitration and wage-setting bodies. Bevin even instructed Deakin privately to reject a wage agreement that the T&G had already accepted, because he felt the award wasn't high enough.[19]

Immediately Bevin became Minister of Labour, he insisted that responsibility for health and safety at work be moved from the Home Office to the Ministry of Labour. Within a month he had established a new Factory and Welfare Board – comprising representatives of trade unions, employers, voluntary organisations, health services and his own staff – to make recommendations for improved workplace welfare. He attended the board's first meeting and gave it a list of practical issues for 'speedy action' including works doctors, better working conditions, a workers' diet, day nurseries, communal facilities and communal feeding. New and better factory canteens were a perennial Bevin concern, including what he called 'wet canteens' which served beer. As he told a Liverpool shipowner: 'The Liverpool "Coalie", when he has a throat with some dust on it, wants a drink, and what is the good of pretending he does not. I do not mind if they have a pint of beer, or what they do, as long as they get on with the work.'[20]

A trademark Bevin initiative was his Factories (Canteen) Order 1943, giving the chief inspector of factories the power to serve notice on an employer whose canteens were being run unsatisfactorily. More than 5,000 work canteens were set up by 1944, 171 in the docks alone. 'Communal feeding will be one of the great services for the people of this country,' he proclaimed.[21]

Wartime popular entertainment was a big concern of Bevin's, an extension of his growing love of showbiz described earlier. On becoming Minister of Labour, Bevin asked Churchill 'to be allowed to be in charge of amusements, from philharmonic concerts to horseracing, in order that the public's entertainment might not be neglected in wartime'. He explained his perfect qualifications: 'There's nothing like singing to keep your spirits up. As you know I have organised more strikes than anybody in the country, and when we ran out of money I always got the men to sing.'[22] Churchill 'assented heartily', and Bevin was soon the wartime arbiter of popular culture and workplace morale.

In the process he struck up a firm friendship with Seymour Hicks, the 'king of music hall', and Basil Dean, the actor and

'Welcome to the welfare state.'
© Hulton-Deutsch Collection/Getty Images

Victory, 26 July 1945. Morrison had just failed to oust Attlee, again. 'Clem, you go to the Palace straightaway,' Bevin told him.
© Popperfoto/Getty Images

LEFT Potsdam – the Big Three, or Stalin and the two replacements, Foreign Ministers behind.
© AP/Shutterstock

BELOW Stalin holding court at the Potsdam conference. Bevin, opposite, challenged him aggressively while Attlee nodded.
© Shawshots/Alamy Stock Photo

Bevin in the ruins of Berlin while at the Potsdam conference, July 1945. 'I tries 'ard, but I 'ates them,' he said of the Germans, even as he helped rebuild their country.

'A speech from Ernest Bevin on a major occasion had all the horrific fascination of a public execution. If the mind was left immune, eyes and ears and emotions were riveted.' – Michael Foot

The most successful partnership at the top of British government in the twentieth century.

'Ernie Bevin was by a long way the most remarkable of my various chiefs,' said his last Foreign Office private secretary, Roddy Barclay. Note the pen held like a chisel.

Archbishop Damaskinos of Greece upstages the Foreign Secretary. Bevin's support for Churchill in preventing a communist coup in Athens in 1944 was a key power play.

© Ian Smith/The LIFE Picture Collection via Getty Images

Working the room: United Nations General Assembly, 1946.

© David E. Scherman/The LIFE Picture Collection via Getty Images

LEFT 39 Saxon Road, Bristol, Bevin's terraced house after his marriage to Flo. Here, John Prescott seeks inspiration for the 2005 election.
© Matt Cardy/Getty Images

BELOW 30 The Vale, Golders Green. Suburban respectability in the 1920s.
© Andrew Adonis

20 Phillimore Court, Kensington, a long way from Winsford.
© Andrew Adonis

1 Carlton Gardens, which Attlee gave Bevin as the Foreign Secretary's official residence, as it remains today. Marlborough House is beyond; Queen Mary gave him a key to the garden.
© Andrew Adonis

LEFT Mr and Mrs Bevin in New York, 1946.
© London Illustrated News Group

BELOW Bombed remains of the King David Hotel in Jerusalem, British headquarters in Palestine, destroyed by Zionist terrorists on 21 July 1946. Bevin reportedly said of such violence: 'What could you expect when people are brought up from the cradle on the Old Testament?'
© Fox Photos/Getty Images

Bidault and Bevin unite on the Marshall Plan, Quai d'Orsay, June 1947.
© KEYSTONE-FRANCE/Gamma-Rapho via Getty Images

Thanksgiving lunch, 1947. Giving thanks to George Marshall for Marshall Aid.
© Nat Farbman/The LIFE Picture Collection via Getty Images

Acheson, Bevin and Schuman, Paris, 1949.
'I doubt there has ever been a closer or more fruitful understanding between an American Secretary of State and a British Foreign Secretary.'
© Keystone/Getty Images

Tea and smiles: Bevin and King Abdullah of Jordan.
© Ron Burton/Keystone/Hulton Archive/Getty Images

ABOVE LEFT A royal favourite, here between George VI and Queen Juliana of the Netherlands. The King asked Bevin where he acquired so much knowledge: 'Sir, it was gathered in the 'edgerows of experience.'
© Topical Press Agency/Getty Images

ABOVE RIGHT In Berlin for the airlift, 1949. Stalin gambled; Bevin won.
© British Pathé News

LEFT The Sphinx and Ozymandias? End of Empire, 1950.

LEFT With Prince Philip and King Farouk at lunch in Cairo, January 1950. It was Bevin's last imperial voyage: very grand, very unproductive.

© Keystone Press/Alamy Stock Photo

LEFT With Flo on the *Queen Mary*, October 1950. She liked shopping on overseas visits, but not buying anything.

© Hulton Picture Library/Getty Images

BELOW Evening honours: nodding off at Colombo University, January 1950. Like Churchill, Bevin always travelled with his doctor.

© Dmitri Kessel/The LIFE Picture Collection via Getty Images

During the war Bevin always broadcast after the 1 p.m. news on Sunday, not after the 9 p.m. news like other ministers, so he could speak to 'his' people 'sitting down nice and comfortable to their Sunday dinner'.
© TUC Library Collections at London Metropolitan University

Addressing Labour members in his East Woolwich constituency days before he died. 'I don't think there is any need for me to apologise for being ill. If I have been ill, a lot of it has been brought on by hard work.'
© Illustrated London News Group

Last of the Victorians. Churchill and Attlee at Bevin's memorial service, Westminster Abbey.
© British Pathé News

'Today he is not so much a man as a phenomenon. Maybe he is both.' Bevin cast in bronze, 1930.
© Hulton Deutsch Collection/ CORBIS/Corbis via Getty Images

Ealing Studios impresario. 'Throughout the war I used to meet Bevin fairly regularly on Saturday afternoons in the hot room of the Turkish bath where it was difficult to observe formality,' recalled Dean. 'He soon put me on Christian names with himself. At these vaporised meetings I used to report progress and received much wise advice in exchange. It was during one of these first encounters that Ernie confided to me that he thought that CEMA's early efforts were 'too 'ighbrow'.[23] CEMA was the state-funded Council for the Encouragement of Music and the Arts, which produced a stream of wartime films and events. Keynes became its chairman in 1941.

With Bevin's support, Dean founded and managed a new vehicle for mass popular entertainment: the Entertainments National Service Association (ENSA), which took its troupes of performers to garrisons and factories nationwide, and many theatres of war internationally. Dean cut a deal with Bevin on the deferment of national service for ENSA performers. It started from a low base, as Dean noted in recalling an early wartime show in a factory, complete with the casual sexism of the era:

The canteen was packed: rows of faces, shining, work-tired faces on all sides, united in a simple expression of anticipation. Then in between the narrow dining-tables, dodging the canteen waitresses sniffing the food-scented air, came the artistes, five minutes late, the women in untidy slacks (women of a certain shape and age should take a backward glance at themselves in the mirror before adopting male dress) and the men in mufflers and caps. They made their way to the piano on the little platform with a self-conscious air of indifference to the hearty applause they were given.[24]

By 1941, ENSA had hundreds of companies and thousands of shows, both live and cinema (including mobile cinema) in war factories and military bases. Dean made them as professional as he could, and they were mostly pretty good. Bevin took with relish to compèring ENSA programmes for the BBC from his native Bristol, though 'not without raised eyebrows from ministerial colleagues'. He loved the reception, especially people calling out 'Hallo, Ernie'. Popular culture and self-promotion went hand in hand, with Bevin's ever-shrewd eye for self-aggrandising stunts and narratives.[25]

One of greatest popular memories of the war was ENSA performing, at Bevin's behest, in works canteens nationwide. ENSA was also instrumental in the creation of hugely popular programmes like *Workers' Playtime*, which was broadcast over the Tannoy in factories nationwide. As a historian of the Second World War and popular culture puts it:

Bevinism in industry was symbolised by the growing understanding of the value of music and entertainment in helping people to work faster. Besides peripatetic ENSA-tainments, there were the BBC's 'Workers' Playtime' and 'Music While You Work', which 'progressive' managements relayed over loudspeakers several times a day. These novelties appealed greatly to J.B. Priestley, who had coined the slogan 'Let The People Sing' which ENSA used as the title of its signature tune; new humanity, even new gaiety, emerged from the dourness and violence of war. Bevin himself liked to put in an appearance at a works' concert (and to sample personally the food in the canteen). 'Let The People Sing', it might be said, was the spiritual essence of Bevinism.[26]

Bevin understood that morale was crucial to mobilisation. He understood 'The White Cliffs of Dover' before Vera Lynn ever sang it. The wartime songs were popular hymns, written in spirit when Bevin was singing along in his Methodist and Baptist chapels before the First World War.

Bevin's intention from the outset of the war was to create a 'new deal' for the working class. 'I take no job that ends with the war,' he told the TUC General Council when asking their permission to enter the government in May 1940. 'I take a ministry whose value will be permanent to our people.' Direction by direction, regulation by regulation, he set up a new tripartite regime of bargaining between employers, unions and the state with strong ministerial reserve powers, all designed to continue after the war. As he put it in Bevinese: 'There is nothing I am doing without I am keeping an eye on its possible value when this war is over.'[27]

On voluntaryism, Bevin pointed out that Tory colonels, all in favour of corralling the working classes, were less keen on his policies for minimum wages, recognition of trade unions by government contractors, wages councils of employers and unions and compulsory industrial arbitration. A group of Tories fought a guerrilla war in the House of Commons against his 1943 Catering Wages Bill, which applied mandatory collective bargaining and arbitration to the huge catering and hospitality industry. Bevin won. He was particularly proud of his 1945 Wages Councils Act, the fruit of his wartime policy of enforced collective bargaining. By 1950, sixty councils were regulating conditions for 5 million workers.[28]

A group of Tories fought a guerrilla war in the House of Commons against
his 1943 Catering Wages Bill. Bevin won. © *Evening Standard*

Compulsory negotiation and arbitration were Bevin's main tools,
direction by the state his last resort. The radicalism of his policy was
precisely that it did not, for the most part, involve state direction, but
rather regulation. Bevin was well aware that state direction of wage
levels and employment conditions, beyond a minimum, would not
survive the war. By contrast, his framework of mandatory tripartite
negotiations on wages, conditions and production largely continued
after 1945, until the Thatcher government dismantled it in the 1980s.

Hardly a day passed without Bevin pushing this agenda. There
are hundreds of letters like the one he wrote to Lord McGowan,
chairman of Imperial Chemicals:

I am very anxious to secure your support and that of my colleagues
to a campaign for the establishment of what might be called a
'round table' in every factory. Present methods tend to emphasise
the 'two sides' of industry and therefore the apparently conflicting

interests, whereas if we could get the 'round table' idea accepted, we should get more emphasis on the community of interest between people engaged together in a common task.

He told a conference of industrial relation officers that he was seeking to build 'a new kind of industrial democracy', where the 'gap between management and operatives' was broken down and workers felt that joining management was not being 'disloyal'. In his TUC conference speech in 1946, his last before, appositely, taking up the chairmanship of the British Electricity Authority, Walter Citrine declared, 'We have passed from the era of propaganda to one of responsibility.'[29]

As Minister of Labour, Bevin was constantly attacking bad employers, both privately and publicly. In November 1940, Churchill sent him 'a very friendly hint' not to make speeches critical of private enterprise, which just produced a Bevin response by return that 'there is no hope of carrying the British people with us for a long war if they have to return to unemployment at the end'.[30]

Bevin's regulation of strikes was another pillar of his nascent corporately regulated state. His order 1305 of 19 July 1940 – maybe the most important he issued – outlawed strikes and lock-outs unless the dispute had been reported to him and twenty-one days had elapsed without his having referred the matter to independent arbitration. Breaches of the order were subject to up to six months in jail or a £200 fine for the individuals concerned. While apparently draconian, it was a great advance for the unions, forcing employers to arbitration. For the first time union activists in the workplace were given legally enforceable security from dismissal by employers. But for Bevin, neither side of industry might have accepted this package.

'Bevin left an indelible impact on the post-war settlement,' writes the historian and Labour MP David Marquand. 'Thanks to full employment the balance of economic power had shifted massively in labour's favour. But the shift might have been temporary: Bevin's achievement was to make sure that it would last.'[31] Jack Jones, a successor of Bevin's as T&G general secretary, went further in his 1981 Bevin Centenary Lecture, calling the wartime settlement a 'permanent alteration of the status of working people'. But nothing is permanent and, poignantly, the centenary of Bevin's birth in 1881 was when it started seriously to crumble.

Bevin said the same himself. Towards the end of the war he 'started repeating in many quarters a very significant wisecrack. "They say", he grinned, "that Gladstone was at the British Treasury from 1860 to about 1930. They'll say that Bevin was at the Ministry of Labour from 1940 to 1990."' This had a crucial political dimension too: insofar as it is true, as suggested by the historian Paul Addison, that political consensus about post-war domestic policy fell 'like a bunch of ripe plums' into Labour's lap in 1945, Bevin had planted and watered the plum trees.[32]

From the left, the chief wartime critic of Bevin's 'corporatism' was Aneurin Bevan, who claimed it undermined parliamentary democracy. This was the left-wing 'middle-class' parliamentarian arguing against the 'working-class' trade unionist, a damaging fault line in Labour politics since Bevin's and Bevan's social objectives were largely the same: a powerful democratic welfare state levelling up. Their achievements were also on a par: what Bevan did for health in the NHS, Bevin did for working conditions as Minister of Labour. By the late 1940s each had come grudgingly to admire the virtues of the other, thanks to Attlee's skill in uniting them.

'Every London newspaper blazoned: "BEVIN WANTS 100,000 WOMEN".
He roared delightedly at its ambiguity.' © *Punch Magazine*

The crux of Bevin's policy was an energised state, and the energy started with his strong personal leadership as its representative. The charismatic element was hugely important. 'Ernie' Bevin became a force of nature, ever present in wartime media and the popular consciousness as the man, alongside Churchill, driving the war effort. There are thousands of pictures of Bevin with different groups of workers, like the one on the front cover of this book. During the war he always broadcast on the BBC after the one o'clock news on Sundays, not after the nine o'clock news like other ministers, so he could speak to 'his' people, 'sitting down nice and comfortable to their Sunday dinner'.[33]

A journalist who went on a weekend tour with Bevin in the north-east recalls being summoned to the minister's hotel in Newcastle at nine o'clock on the Sunday morning. 'After sympathising with us for having to be astir so early, he calmly announced his call for volunteers from the women of Britain. Next day every London newspaper blazoned: "BEVIN WANTS 100,000 WOMEN." He roared delightedly at its ambiguity.'[34]

There were Bevinist wartime initiatives galore: training centres for engineers and technical specialists (thirty-eight open by 1941); 'humanising', in Bevin's word, the 800 labour exchanges nationwide; a big pay increase for miners, taking them to their pre-General Strike pay level; a dock registration scheme of the kind he had wanted for twenty years; statutory support for collective bargaining; all those canteens and popular entertainments described earlier – the list goes on and on of initiatives and schemes, many successful, some contradictory, others fitful, but all of them directed like a battering ram at mobilising the war effort. Bevin's Labour Ministry is reminiscent of Roosevelt's New Deal: constant energy, dynamism and initiative.

On voluntaryism, two powerful facts support Bevin's policy. Days lost to strikes in the Second World War were only a fraction of the level of the First World War. Between 1915 and 1918, an annual average of 4.2 million working days a year were lost through disputes; between 1940 and July 1945 it was 1.8 million. The same was true after the war, when strikes in the Attlee years were only a tiny fraction of the astronomic 39.8 million working days lost on average in 1919 and 1920, as bitter wartime industrial relations led to a complete breakdown under the post-war Lloyd George coalition.[35]

Then there is the case of the Bevin Boys. The need for them to go down the mines was to some extent Bevin's own fault, for allowing miners to join the forces in 1940–41, when coal production was sufficient and high pre-war unemployment persisted in the coal fields.

But by 1943 there was the threat of coal shortages, even coal rationing, because production could not keep up with war demand. Hence
the Bevin Boys – a group description for the 48,000 young men who
were allocated to the pits by ballot between 1943 and 1948, as well as
those who volunteered to serve in the mines or who simply took up
mining jobs as they probably would have done anyway because they
were brought up in mining communities.

Two things are striking about the Bevin Boys. The first is the
pride felt among many of those who volunteered for this dangerous
and often terrible work, particularly those from non-mining communities who had little idea what was in store. The fact they were
doing their bit for their country was voluntaryism personified. But
equally striking is the bitter discontent among many of the one-in-
ten young men who were conscripted to the mines at the end of the
war. It was like the reaction to the draft in Vietnam. Of the 16,000
youths selected by ballot to go down the mines by November 1944,
500 had been prosecuted for refusal to obey the National Service
Officer's order or for leaving their employment without consent. Of
these, 143 were sent to jail for desertion. This was a higher level of
disaffection than in any other sphere of war-time conscription, civil
or military, intensifying 'an atmosphere of bitterness which hung
over the mining industry like an acrid fog'.[36]

The psychology of crowds had been a Bevin study since his earliest
days as a lay preacher and a union organiser. He knew that collective
action by consent was ten times more effective than direction from
above, and he was a master of mobilising working men *en masse*. In
this, his entire life was a prelude to becoming wartime Minister of
Labour, as surely as Churchill's entire life was prelude to becoming
wartime Minister of Defence and Prime Minister.

In his first broadcast as minister, Bevin spoke of having to deal with 'the most difficult material to handle, the human being'. This was his art. As he put it when replying to critics of voluntaryism: 'Whatever may be my other weaknesses, I think I can claim that I understand the working classes of this country. I had to determine whether I would be leader or a dictator. I preferred and still prefer to be a leader.'[37] The date was November 1940, long before success was assured.

What of Bevin's art in handling his colleagues? Any view of him as a blunderbuss because he was a bruiser is wildly misplaced. He was a master of giving and receiving loyalty. He particularly cultivated the trust of Churchill and Attlee, the relationships that mattered by far the most to him during the war. He rarely criticised either of them in private and never in public, except for routine party politics in the case of Churchill at the end of the war. In both cases, loyalty begat loyalty.

Bevin accorded strong, measured praise to Churchill as war leader and never sought to second-guess the military conduct of the war. This was characteristic Bevin: once you have put someone in charge, let them get on with the job unless and until they fail. In May 1942, shortly after the fall of Singapore when anti-Churchill sentiment was in vogue, Bevin told a Barnsley audience:

> This is the best government you have ever had. I had been for many years in opposition to the Prime Minister. What I have found in Winston Churchill is that he is a great colleague, he is a great leader, he is tireless in his endeavour, and I have never worked with a man who is more determined to carry on this struggle, however long it lasts, until victory is achieved.[38]

Although a member of the War Cabinet, Bevin was not on the

Defence Committee and had little to do with military strategy. When Churchill, in dispute with the chiefs of staff, brought a matter to the War Cabinet, Bevin's response was the closest he came to a rebuke, couched in terms of loyalty. 'He knew nothing about the war himself,' Bevin declared,

> and doubted if the opinion of the other members of the Cabinet was worth having either. They had put the Prime Minister in to win the war. If they lost confidence in him, they would put him out. But as long as he had their confidence, he should get on with it and not come asking the Cabinet for its opinion on matters about which they knew nothing and which were too serious to be settled by amateur strategists.

At this, 'even Churchill was taken aback and pursued his manoeuvre no further'.[39]

Churchill stood just as resolutely by Bevin. When criticism rained down from the Tory benches about war production in mid-1941, he called a Commons debate in order to defend Bevin personally. 'It is the fashion nowadays to abuse the Minister of Labour,' he began, launching into a splendidly crafted tribute:

> He is a working man, a trade union leader. He is taunted with being an unskilled labourer representing an unskilled union. I daresay he gives offence in some quarters; he has his own methods of speech and action. He has a frightful load to carry. He makes mistakes, like I do, though not so many or so serious – he has not got the same opportunities. At any rate he is producing at this moment, though perhaps on expensive terms, a vast and

steady volume of faithful effort, the likes of which has not been seen before. And if you tell me that the results he produces do not compare with those of totalitarian systems of government and society, I reply by saying 'We shall know more about that when we get to the end of the story.'[40]

Which turned out to be fair comment, when we got to the end of the story.

So, Churchill and Attlee's trust in Bevin was well placed. In their darkest hours, his word to them was, as one Tory observer put it, 'as solid as the Bank of England'.

Bevin also respected and got on well with Anthony Eden as Foreign Secretary, his neighbour in the War Cabinet, and with Sir John Anderson, who was domestic affairs co-ordinator as well as Chancellor for the last two years of the war. These were crucial relationships, in the case of Eden also being important in maintaining bi-partisan support for his foreign policy after 1945. 'Hasn't Anthony Eden grown fat,' R. A. Butler used to joke on the Tory front bench when listening to Bevin's speeches as Foreign Secretary. After Bevin's death, Eden said, 'The harsher the times, and there were some hard times, the more stalwart was the resistance Ernest Bevin brought to our councils.'[41]

When crossed by lesser mortals Bevin was capable of bullying and bitter, even ridiculous rows, sometimes in public. But these were rarely knee-jerk, and were generally restricted to colleagues, not subordinates, as a deliberate means of control. Inside the government, anything with Morrison's name attached was sure to get a negative response from Bevin on principle. 'Don't you believe a word the little bastard says,' was his *sotto voce* refrain to his neighbours in Cabinet when Morrison ventured forth.

Particularly telling was a public spat Bevin entered into with Walter Citrine over manpower planning in the autumn of 1941, when he accused the TUC leader, one of his closest former partners, of a 'Quisling policy'. This was offensive and ludicrous in respect of a dispute over manpower planning. But that it was not – or not solely – an undisciplined emotional outburst is clear from the follow-up private correspondence, where Bevin went out his way to be truculent. It was really an argument about respect, and who owed it to whom now that Bevin was a national leader.

'Dear Bevin,' Citrine wrote in 'colleague to colleague' tone:

This is a difficult letter to write ... It is unfortunate that we do not see eye to eye on a number of matters connected with the war. My views, like your own, are sincere and deep, and I must stand by them until I have been shown where I am in error.

I have felt for some time past that you have been resentful of criticism ... I have never regarded you as a superman but definitely as the most outstanding personality in the Labour Movement.

What I have always felt is that you do not give sufficient credit to your colleagues and that you are inclined to regard those who do not agree with you, and stand up for their opinions, as enemies ... I for my part do not intend to indulge in any vendetta against you or anyone else.

The following day came this icy response:

Dear Sir Walter,

I am in receipt of your letter ... With regard to my reference to you, if the policy of the government is attacked, Ministers must answer...

I am glad you do not regard me as a superman, so no one will expect too much, but I am not concerned how people regard me personally. All I have lived for in this world has been for what I could leave behind for the benefit of the people I represent. My record in the Trade Union Movement is probably the best evidence.

Your statement about giving sufficient credit to colleagues and regarding as enemies those who do not agree with me I cannot treat seriously.[42]

Citrine never wrote another letter like that.

Bevin's worst relations, worse even than with Herbert Morrison if that is possible, were with the mercurial Canadian press baron Lord Beaverbrook. This was hardly exceptional: even Attlee's oil-on-troubled-water quality, invaluable to holding the wartime coalition together, stopped short of the gargantuan alter ego of Lloyd George in the First World War and Churchill in the second.

It wasn't possible for Bevin to avoid Beaverbrook because he came as an item with Churchill, who kept appointing him to key war government posts, and because 'The Beaver' had a public reputation for dynamism, assiduously cultivated by his own newspapers. That is where the bitter antagonism between them had started: Beaverbrook's *Express* and Bevin's *Daily Herald* were daggers-drawn rivals in the 1920s and 1930s when Bevin was constantly in the Labour-hating Beaverbrook's sights.

In the tempestuous early years of the war, Bevin and Beaverbrook had a relationship akin to two scorpions, Beaverbrook oscillating between flattery and attempted assassination, Bevin between contempt and hatred. As minister of aircraft production in the Battle of Britain, Beaverbrook let it be known that he was the only thing between the *Luftwaffe* and London. While Bevin sought agreement on a manpower strategy for all the key sectors of the economy, and worked through committees, Beaverbrook asserted that he should just be able to take anything and everything he needed for fighter aircraft building and repair. To try and compromise, Bevin took to holding meetings of the 'production executive' in Beaverbrook's own office. The aircraft supremo ostentatiously worked at his desk while the committee met 'but he could not avoid getting drawn into the discussion'.[43]

On the merits of the immediate Battle of Britain requirements Beaverbrook had a point – but Bevin never denied that: he was simply doing his job of seeking to reconcile competing labour demands, without which the whole war effort would be impaired. However, the argument wasn't really about aircraft production, but about ascendancy and competition for Churchill's ear. And in this battle, to the Beaver's fury, Bevin held his own. The fact that it was Beaverbrook, not Bevin, who kept resigning is testament to who was on top.

Beaverbrook was fascinated by and increasingly admiring of Bevin's sway, magnetised as he was by all wielders of great power. Bevin was 'the strongest man in the present Cabinet', he told Churchill in February 1942. He then did as he always did with men of power: tried to insinuate himself. As the fall, one after another, of Hong Kong, Singapore and Tobruk left Churchill increasingly vulnerable, he started making not especially Delphic overtures to Bevin about replacing Churchill. Bevin would not play. He cut him short and then told Churchill what had been said. Still, none of this damaged the Prime Minister's long-term relations with his double-dealing associate, who kept resurfacing in different roles until the end of the war and during the 1945 general election campaign. 'He's like a man who's married a whore,' Bevin said of Churchill's infatuation with Beaverbrook. 'He knows she's a whore but he loves her just the same.'[44]

Another inveterate plotter was Professor Harold Laski, a big figure of the day on Labour's National Executive Committee. At the same time as the Beaver was making his overtures, Laski joined in from the other side, suggesting to Bevin in March 1942 that he should replace Attlee. 'Unless you become the first man instead of the second, the confidence of the masses in this movement will rapidly die,' came the unctuous missive. Bevin didn't even reply. Laski was then writing what he thought was a great book, *Reflections on the Revolution of our Time*, while Bevin was drafting the Catering Wages Bill. 'There is much Labour history compressed into this contrast,' notes Bullock in a brilliant footnote.[45]

Bevin was loyal to his departmental officials: he was general secretary; they his union organisers and shop stewards. His pitch, repeated in speech after speech to staff in his headquarters and to 1,200 local employment offices as he toured the country, was this: 'If you make a mistake I will stand by you. One thing I will not forgive. That is inaction.' A journalist who went with him on tour reported thus of his meetings with local civil servants: 'Local men felt at ease with their minister. There was an air of informality about these conferences. Bevin handed his cigarettes around to those on the platform with him. Men from offices in little-known moorland towns or sleepy country market places got up to discuss their problems with their chief.'[46]

Bevin rarely needed – or took – advice from civil servants or advisers on broad strategy, either as Minister of Labour or later as

Foreign Secretary, because he knew his own mind, and it was rooted in so much practical personal experience. Godfrey Ince, the Ministry of Labour's director of manpower, said of him: 'Few ministers ever know as much about the business of their ministries as their permanent officials. Bevin did, and could surprise us by the information he would produce out of his head. He knew where he wanted to go, and how to get there.'[47]

The demobilisation plans for 1945 were crafted by Bevin and Ince, based on Bevin's scheme to balance age with length of service in order to meet the emotive concerns of skilled older men, mostly with families, who had joined up late in the war. 'One morning,' wrote a sympathetic journalist,

> Bevin sent for Sir Godfrey Ince and said excitedly, 'I've got it. It came to me in the middle of the night.' And there and then he outlined to Sir Godfrey the simple formula of age-and-length of service. Thus it transpired that Bevin not only fully mobilised the British, but organised their demobilisation too.[48]

Doubtless it didn't happen quite like that, but the fact that Ince said so, and that this was generally believed, speaks to Bevin's reputation in Whitehall at the end of the war. And it was justified in that demobilisation was much smoother in 1945–46 than in 1918–19. Churchill's Tory manifesto for the 1945 election pointedly sheltered behind Bevin: 'The broad and properly considered lines of the demobilisation proposals which Mr Bevin has elaborated will be adhered to.'

Schooled by Bevin, Churchill was fulsome in praise of the unions at the end of the war. 'We owe an immense debt to the trade unions and never can this country forget how they stood by and helped,' he declared.[49] From the organiser-in-chief who had been against Bevin and the trade unions in the General Strike less than twenty years before, it was akin to a recantation.

The wartime rapport between Churchill and Bevin went beyond war leadership to a common understanding that defeating Hitler was only stage one: dealing with a rampant and hostile Stalin and Stalinism thereafter was a perilous stage two. This bound them close even as party politics reasserted itself in the last months of the war, pointing the way to Bevin's foreign policy after 1945. The defining moment was the controversy over Greece at the end of 1944, where the threat of a communist takeover, of the kind that swept Central and southern Europe in the late 1940s, first became a decisive and then a divisive issue in Britain and America, after years of eulogising Uncle Joe.

Churchill's concern was to stop fascist dictatorships being replaced by communist dictatorships as Europe was prised from Hitler. It was hard, often impossible, to do this in the face of the Soviet advance from the East, with Stalin installing communist partisans in government, some from local and national resistance movements, some parachuted in directly from Moscow. Churchill sought to limit the damage by persuading Stalin to agree to free elections, but his leverage was virtually zero when British and American forces were weak or non-existent. Poland became the excruciating *cause célèbre*: the country whose freedom precipitated the war, yet which transitioned almost directly from Hitler to Stalin in 1945–46, while Western communists and the naive of the left excused or even justified the coup.

Before Poland came Greece. Trying to assert some leverage, in

October 1944 Churchill improvised his famous – or infamous – 'percentages agreement' with Stalin in Moscow, scribbled by him on a piece of paper with a big tick by Stalin. Churchill recognised the Soviet dictator's dominant interest in Rumania and Bulgaria, while Stalin indicated acceptance of a 50:50 power share in Hungary and Yugoslavia and a dominant British interest in Greece. This was hardly edifying; possibly it was even counterproductive in assuring Stalin of a free hand in Central Europe and the Balkans when he might otherwise have doubted Western intentions and acted more cautiously. Bevin, as Foreign Secretary, accorded 0 per cent trust to Stalin.

However, in Greece, a communist-inspired civil war broke out in late 1944, despite Stalin's big tick. Communist bands in recently liberated Athens were determined to take the country by force in the face of a weak and fractious alliance of liberals and monarchists. Churchill intervened decisively on 3 December, ordering the 5,000 British troops in the city to support – with firepower if necessary – Greek royalist police against the attempt by communist-led bands to seize key installations. In a ditty of the day:

> I want peace
> And part of Greece
> Said Stalin
> Snarling[50]

This immediately embroiled Churchill in controversy with the left at home, and less publicly but more delicately with Roosevelt in Washington. Cries of 'war-monger', 'neo-royalist', even 'neo-fascist', issued from Labour and the left, while FDR was almost as concerned about British imperialism as Stalinist imperialism. A reluctance to grasp the gravity of the Stalinist threat was general in American and liberal circles until 1947, and it continued on the hard left until the fall of the Soviet Union in 1989. However, in 1944–45, the 'hard centre' was as soft on Stalin as the hard left. *The Times* was highly critical of Churchill on Greece while *The Economist* accused him of reviving 'the Bolshevik bogy' and declared, in a spectacular misreading of the situation: 'Never once since its first appearance has the Red Scare led to a revolution of the Left. For twenty years the revolutions have come from the Right. How can British foreign policy be based on the Anglo-Soviet alliance and on the Red Scare at one and the same time?'[51]

The answer was that British foreign policy had to be based on those two premises because they were the ones that applied at the time. The solution was not to pretend there was no 'red scare', in Athens or elsewhere, when it was both very red and very scary. Churchill saw this clearly. In an act of considerable personal courage and leadership he flew to Athens on Christmas Day 1944, to the anguish of Clementine and their Christmas guests assembled at Chequers. His aim was to shore up the non-communist forces and reach an accommodation with the head of the Greek Orthodox Church, the tall, austere, dramatic Archbishop Damaskinos. This personal intervention stabilised the situation sufficiently for Greece to sustain a non-communist government, while still after the war dethroning its unpopular king, then in exile in London. It wasn't a great regime and civil war ensued, but it wasn't a communist dictatorship, or a dictatorship of any kind, until the coup of the 'Colonels' in 1967.

Bevin was not directly involved in these events, although he knew what was going on as a member of the War Cabinet. But he became critical to avoiding a coalition rupture over Greece in

December 1944. This rupture came close because, just as the controversy peaked, Labour was holding a pre-arranged party conference
in London, and a showdown could not therefore be avoided. Bevin
lined up the union block vote in support of a resolution avoiding
criticism of government policy. But a minister had to hold the line
for the government in the debate. It should have been Attlee, but he
didn't relish the prospect of taking on the left over 'liberation communism', so Bevin took on the task. It is possible that they agreed
between them that Bevin was best placed for a 'good cop, bad cop'
routine: the records are silent on precisely why Bevin, who had no
direct responsibility for foreign policy, was put up, but he was, and
he did not flinch.

In Bullock's account, following speech after speech savaging
Churchill,

> hunching his shoulders and sticking his hands in the pockets
> of his jacket, Bevin walked out on to the platform to face the
> concentrated hostility of the audience crowding Central Hall
> [Westminster] ... He kept his temper in the face of interruptions
> and argued his case with skill, but he was no less resolute, no more
> inclined to appease his critics than Churchill had been.[52]

In doing so, Bevin pointed the way to his own anti-Stalinist foreign
policy after 1945:

> If we win at the next election, as I hope we will, we shall find that
> we cannot govern the world with emotionalism. Hard thinking,
> great decision, tremendous will power will have to be applied, and
> the Labour Movement will have to learn to ride the storm as these

great issues arise … These steps which have been taken in Greece are not the decision of Winston Churchill. They are decisions of the Cabinet … and I say to the public – boldly, I hope, because I am not going to hide behind anybody – that I am a party to the decisions that have been taken, and looking back over all the efforts that have been made, I cannot bring it to my conscience that any one of the decisions were wrong.

Bevin was immediately and bitterly attacked by Bevan, who got the applause in the hall. But with the trade union block vote, the leadership won by 2,455,000 to 137,000. And Bevin had demonstrated 'that if Labour was looking for a leader capable of standing in comparison with Churchill, it would come nearest to finding him in Ernie Bevin'.[53]

By the end of the war, Churchill and Anthony Eden, his heir apparent, were in such admiration of Bevin and his political sway that they mistakenly thought he might 'do a MacDonald' and support Churchill in a new 'national' government. They noted Bevin's earlier support for continuing the war coalition. Bevin had told Eden on a visit to the D-Day ports in June 1944 that this was what he wanted.

He would not care which office either of us held … there was however one thing that he must have. 'What?' I asked. 'The nationalisation of the coalmines: The trade unions would have to have that.' When Eden repeated these remarks to the South African general and Churchill confidant Jan Smuts, his reaction was: 'Cheap at the price.'[54]

Yet Bevin never even flirted with leaving the Labour Party in 1945, and it was a fundamental misreading of his character and politics to believe he was ever going to do so. What he wanted was for Labour, as a united party, to continue the coalition. This was principally because he thought Churchill would win the election, as did almost everyone. He was also, towards the end of the war, semi-estranged from the Parliamentary Labour Party; he even stopped attending its meetings. This was for a classically Bevinist reason: the rebellion of ninety-seven Labour MPs on the Beveridge Report in May 1943, which offended against the sanctity of party loyalty. Worse, the rebellion was led by Bevan, who by now was almost as great a *bête noire* to Bevin as Morrison.

The Beveridge Report of November 1942, an immediate best seller, was to be at the heart of Labour's vision for post-war Britain. But when Labour MPs started agitating for wartime commitments, Attlee and Bevin asserted the War Cabinet's decision to postpone controversial domestic issues until victory was secured. It wasn't going to be possible to get the War Cabinet to commit to Beveridge during the war, not least because, as R. A. Butler put it, there was a feeling among Tories 'that Beveridge is a sinister old man who wants to give away a great deal of other people's money'.[55] Bevin was perfectly prepared to argue against this position when it suited him, as he did to secure the passage of Butler's own 1944 Education Act, which would not have been brought forward without his strong support within the War Cabinet – particularly its provision to raise the school leaving age to sixteen, unfortunately discarded by Attlee's post-war government. The 1944 Employment White Paper also owed much to him, with its commitment to the 'maintenance of a high and stable level of employment', which Keynes described as 'a revolution in official opinion'. But Bevin wouldn't tolerate back-benchers trying to do the same. He rationalised this as the difference between leadership and followership, and the need for collective discipline. He had a point, but so did his critics.

There was also an underlying grievance, utterly characteristic of Bevin. Beveridge had been a senior official in the Ministry of Labour, but Bevin found him condescending, a cardinal sin, and had him moved out. It was as a result of this that Beveridge ended up doing his famous report, which was billed around Whitehall as just a tidying-up exercise for the co-ordination of social services. Bevin wasn't taking any nonsense from *him*, even if it wasn't nonsense.

At a special meeting of Labour MPs after the Beveridge rebellion, Bevin warned of the political dangers if the coalition broke up, and when he was heckled 'began to shout, protest and threaten', according to Dalton. Maybe because he had planned to do so, or maybe in a fit of temper, he declared that, according to the rules of the Parliamentary Labour Party, he had broken the rules by voting for the government against the party's whip. Since this was the case 'he demanded to be expelled from the party or, if not expelled then publicly acquitted'. Then 'after having his say, Bevin left abruptly, not attempting to conceal his anger'. It was to be a year before he attended another meeting of the PLP.[56] This did not impede the work of the War Cabinet and Attlee astutely carried on throughout as if nothing was amiss. But everyone noted this public display of Labour disunity and the Minister of Labour's semi-detached position in his own party.

I suspect there was also a personal factor in Bevin's readiness to continue the war coalition: a sense that he did not have long to live and that his career was virtually over. In early 1945 he was sixty-four and in poor and declining health, with a serious heart condition and fainting fits. His health had been getting steadily worse since his first heart complaints seven years previously.

But for all this, Bevin had no intention of repeating 1931 by splitting the Labour Party. Nor did he mistake post-war solidarity against Stalin, where he was at one with Churchill, with agreement on domestic policy. He was not going to be another Lloyd George, let alone MacDonald. The solidarity and advancement of the Labour Movement – he always used capitals – was the core of his being. When Attlee thanked him for his wartime service in May 1945, Bevin's reply focused on this point: 'One thing it should have done is to remove the inferiority complex amongst our people.'[57]

Bevin made all this clear on 7 April 1945 in a speech to the Yorkshire Regional Council of the Labour Party. 'There have been lots of suggestions about my future. I do not know why,' he began, a bit disingenuously. 'I do not wear Loyalty as a band on my hand, but nevertheless I have been loyal to this party for forty years ... A lot of the Tory propaganda seems to have forgotten that I am a member of the Labour Party.' He then spelt out his position: 'I have profound admiration for the Prime Minister as a war leader – unfettered. I gave him my loyalty in that position: I never gave it to him as leader of the Conservative Party.' As for future policy, nationalisation, housing and fair shares were the imperatives, and they would never come from the Tories.

The *Manchester Guardian* noted the significance of Bevin's words. 'The Tories have done quite a lot to encourage the notion that Labour was leaving the coalition against Mr Bevin's will and that it was quite on the cards he would throw over his party and remain at Mr Churchill's side,' wrote the paper's political correspondent two days later.

Had he stayed, the consequences might have been disastrous for

Labour unity. Some other Labour ministers might have been tempted to do likewise and 1931 would have been repeated. That would have sealed the hopes of Labour for another decade at least. Now Labour goes into the fight as a completely united party.[58]

On VE Day a month later, Bevin came out onto a Whitehall balcony overlooking the Cenotaph, standing next to Churchill, and led the roaring London crowds in 'Three Cheers for the Prime Minister' and 'For He's a Jolly Good Fellow'. But it was to celebrate the comradeship of the past, not the future.

Churchill still wanted to delay the election until after the defeat of Japan, which was thought to be six or so months away. So did Bevin and Attlee, to protect British strength abroad at this critical juncture, although now only on the basis that, when the election came, Labour would fight it independently. But the rest of the Labour leadership and the National Executive Committee were for an immediate election, and with Labour's conference about to meet, this tide was unstoppable. So on 23 May 1945, almost exactly five years after it had been formed, Churchill's coalition government resigned and an election was called for 5 July.

It was the termination of the most successful British government in history. 'The light of history will shine on all your helmets,' Churchill said at a reunion of coalition ministers in No. 10 on 28 May.[59] After Churchill and the generals, Bevin was the leader who had done most to win the war. Now he had to win the peace.

CHAPTER 8

VICTORY

WHAT'S THE HURRY?

The electoral mountain for Labour seemed impossible. © *Evening Standard*

It is hard to know which was more surprising: that Labour won the 1945 election or that Bevin became Foreign Secretary.

Even the day before the votes were counted, both seemed improbable. Returning from the Potsdam conference on 25 July for the declaration of the results, three weeks after polling day to allow service personnel abroad to vote, Churchill told King George VI that he thought he had won an overall majority of between thirty and eighty.[1] Attlee and Bevin shared this view. So did the media and virtually every commentator.

The electoral mountain for Labour seemed impossible. It was only fourteen years since the party had crashed to just fifty-two seats. In the 1935 election, the last before 1945, its tally recovered to only 154 – forty-nine seats fewer than Jeremy Corbyn secured in 2019. Had Labour doubled this number in 1945, historians would have written of a remarkable Labour revival, despite the comfortable Tory majority. To nearly treble Labour's strength to 393 seats in one election, with the Tories reduced to just 197, was seen by contemporaries as a virtual miracle. For this victory was won against Winston Churchill, the saviour of his country, whose election meetings and rallies in 1945 were the greatest political hero worship in Britain since Gladstone's Midlothian campaign of 1880. And no one was comparing Attlee to Churchill or Gladstone.

'Everyone was stunned with surprise,' wrote George Orwell.[2] The electoral turbulence at constituency level was phenomenal. Bevin's south London seat of Central Wandsworth had gone solidly Tory in the two previous general elections, by majorities of 11,647 in 1931 and 4,323 in 1935. A narrow Labour victory by 485 votes in a 1937 by-election made it available for Bevin in 1940 when he was returned unopposed, but it was thought to be marginal in 1945. In the event, his majority was 5,174 and his share of the vote 61 per cent, more than double Labour's 28 per cent in the seat in 1931, the year Ernie was humiliated in Gateshead and reduced to yelling insults at Ramsay MacDonald's voters in nearby Seaham.

Bevin played a central part in Labour's 1945 campaign, and its success owed more to him than to anyone else apart from Attlee. In the short campaign in May/June, Attlee was the rapier, Bevin the bludgeon. Responding to Churchill's 'Labour Gestapo' attack in his election broadcast of 4 June, Attlee parried brilliantly: 'The voice we heard last night was the voice of Mr Churchill, but the mind was that of Lord Beaverbrook.' He then focused on the domestic record Churchill would prefer to forget. 'He has forgotten many things, including, when he talks of the danger of Labour mismanaging finance, his own disastrous record over the gold standard.' Bevin was less subtle. 'Your vote,' he broadcast, 'will determine whether or not this country will go back to unemployment, means tests, and all the things from which we suffered between the two wars, and whether abroad, we shall drift back to international chaos and war.'

Bevin kept up a running duel with Beaverbrook. 'Mr Bevin has been hitting hard without any respect for persons and is building up a big reputation for knowing what he wants and how to get it,' wrote *The Economist*, 'while Lord Beaverbrook has been giving his audience the impression that if it were not for Mr Bevin's labour controls, there would be unlimited housing, food and clothing by tomorrow morning'.[3]

This was the fundamental domestic issue of the 1945 election: whether post-war Britain would have a planned economy and welfare state or whether it would return to a *laissez-faire* system, however benign the packaging. It was a debate that Labour comprehensively won and it was Bevin's victory pre-eminently. It was a victory won not in the short election campaign but in the five previous years of government, where no one had done more than Bevin to make the state and collectivism the answer and not the problem, where no one had done more to make Labour the party of competence and sound administration, and where no one had done more to make Labour and the trade unions patriotic, responsible, democratic, anti-communist and radical – all at once. The title of Trevor Evans's biography of him, published in the first year of the 1945 government, says it all: *Bevin of Britain.*

'Ernie Bevin' was Labour's brand in 1945, summed up by the *Observer* quotation that headed the four-page newspaper delivered across his Wandsworth constituency: 'The first British statesman to have been born a working man and remained one.'[4] This was a half-truth, as we have seen, since 'Ernie' had long since ceased to remain 'a working man', but the fact that he was universally thought to be so, and that this was seen as a fundamental strength, was another Bevin–Labour triumph.

No one recognised all this better than Churchill's own daughter Sarah. 'Socialism as practised in the War did no one any harm and quite a lot of people good,' she wrote to her father as the election campaign intensified.

> The children of this country have never been so well-fed or healthy. The rich did not die because their meat ration was no larger than the poor and there is no doubt that this common sharing and feeling of sacrifice was one of the strongest bonds that unified us. So why, they say, cannot this common feeling of sacrifice be made to work as effectively in the peace?[5]

It was during the course of Thursday 26 July that the startling election results were announced constituency by constituency. Thereupon, an electric 24-hour saga of intrigue, chance events and split-second decisions took place, which set the whole course of post-war Britain, the world – and the last six years of Bevin's life.

It was a play in two acts.

Act One, in the afternoon of 26 July, opens with Attlee, Bevin, Morrison, Laski, Deakin and the Labour Party general secretary Morgan Phillips, in Bevin's room in Transport House, the wireless on in the background reporting Labour gain after Labour gain in the later election results. The three politicians were London MPs; they had already been to their constituency declarations in the morning.

A brief but intense power struggle erupted as Morrison sought to supplant Attlee as party leader and Prime Minister-elect. It failed because Bevin quashed the coup decisively and immediately.

The attempt to oust Attlee had begun just before the election campaign when 'Professor Laski', as Bevin called the chair of Labour's National Executive Committee in a term of non-endearment, issued one of his portentous letters to Attlee calling on him to resign. 'Just as Mr Churchill changed Auchinleck for Montgomery before El-Alamein, so, I suggest, you owe it to the Party to give it the chance to make a comparable change on the eve of this greatest of our battles.'[6] This produced Attlee's famous put-down. 'Dear Laski, Thank you for your letter, contents of which have been noted.' Laski's analogy was off-beam: Attlee was actually a pretty good character imitation of the taciturn but relentless Montgomery, and Monty's reply to Laski would have been equally laconic.

Morrison, for whom Laski was plotting, renewed the charge after the election. On 24 July, as Attlee was about to return from Potsdam with Churchill, Morrison wrote to say that he intended to 'accept nomination for the leadership of the Party' at the first meeting of Labour MPs in the new Parliament.[7] Attlee did not reply, so Morrison told him in this meeting in Transport House on the afternoon of 26 July that he should not agree to form a government until Labour MPs had met to elect their leader. The issue came to an immediate head because a message was brought in to Attlee that Churchill would be resigning at 7 p.m. and would recommend that the King send for him immediately afterwards. This was earlier than expected. It had been thought that Churchill would wait until the following day, which would have given Morrison more time.

The next few minutes decided the leadership of the country for the next six years. Morrison repeated his pitch, adding that he could not commit to serve under Attlee until the leadership had been decided. Attlee and Bevin said it was out of the question that the leader of the party that had just won a landslide majority should decline to accept the King's commission to form a government. At one point Arthur Deakin, prompted by Laski, suggested that Bevin might himself stand for the leadership. If this was a well-meaning attempt by Deakin to promote his boss, Bevin cut him dead. 'How dare you come and talk to me like that,' he said to Deakin. As the discussion continued Morrison left the room to take a call from Cripps, on the same subject of the leadership. While he was out, Bevin asked Morgan Phillips: 'If I stood against Clem, should I win?' Phillips replied: 'On a split vote I think you would.' Whereupon Bevin turned to Attlee and said: 'Clem, you go to the Palace straightaway.'[8]

Attlee went to the Palace soon afterwards, at 7.30 p.m., without further conversation with Morrison, driven by his wife Vi in their family car, and was appointed Prime Minister. From the Palace he went straight to the Labour victory rally in Central Hall Westminster, opposite Parliament, to be acclaimed by an ecstatic crowd singing 'England Arise'. Few present had any idea of the shenanigans behind the scenes. With Attlee now in No. 10, the Morrison/Laski plot rapidly fizzled out, although it wasn't until a meeting of Attlee and the senior officers of the PLP at 3 p.m. on the following day, when Morrison raised the issue of a leadership election but was given short shrift by the others present, that it died.[9]

The impregnable Attlee–Bevin partnership was thus literally the foundation of the 1945 Attlee government.

Why did Bevin not want the top job himself? He certainly didn't lack the requisite self-belief or capacity until he became seriously ill in 1949. Partly it was because, from his inter-war experience of Baldwin and MacDonald, he regarded the Treasury and the Foreign Office as the key peacetime departments of state, and controlling them directly was the way to manage policy and its implementation. Just as his trade union power always lay in his leadership of the T&G, not the General Council, so he saw No. 10 and the Prime Minister as co-ordinating as much as leading. Since this was largely the role Attlee played in the 1945 government – although not, crucially, in respect of India, as we shall see – he had a point.

Bevin had also given his word to Attlee, and unusually in politics, his word was his bond, like all agreements he negotiated at the T&G. Since Attlee's commitment to Bevin was equally unflinching and remained so until early 1951, when he felt he had no choice but to replace him as Foreign Secretary because of incapacity, it was a reciprocal pledge. In Bullock's words:

> Disloyalty was the blackest crime in his calendar, and all his old suspicions and dislike of Morrison were aroused. He saw Attlee as the Campbell-Bannerman of the Labour Party, the man best fitted by temperament to hold a team of ministers together as C.B. had done after the Liberal victory of 1906. To Bevin who, as he told Dalton, wanted no more personal leadership like Churchill's – or MacDonald's – this was a strong recommendation.[10]

This accords with Bevin's oft-repeated respect for Campbell-Bannerman, the gruff but amiable Scots Liberal laird with a streak of steel, who held together a team including Lloyd George, Asquith, Churchill and, not least, John Burns, a leader of the 1889 Dock Strike alongside Ben Tillett who became the first 'working man' Cabinet member in 1905. 'Sir 'Enry, you never did a more popular thing in your life,' Burns reputedly said to C. B. when the offer was made, as Bevin would have known from dockers' union folklore.

It was shrewd to see Attlee as 'Labour's C. B.' and it speaks to Bevin's deep knowledge and grasp of the political culture in which he worked. It is hard to see who else besides Attlee could have held together Morrison, Cripps, Bevan, Dalton and Bevin himself for six years, while boldly creating a welfare state and equally boldly standing up to Stalin. Bevin probably also intuited that, with his shortcomings as a parliamentarian, he would struggle in the top job. Bevin was full of himself but he rarely over-reached. For all his egocentricity, he was more self-aware than most top politicians, maybe because he was a semi-outsider in the claustrophobic world of Westminster. Maybe also because he thought, from the late 1930s, that he was living on borrowed time health-wise.

The Attlee–Bevin relationship was 'quite exceptionally trouble free', wrote a close observer after 1945. 'Ernie was scrupulous about consulting the Prime Minister on all important decisions, and he knew he could almost invariably get full backing from him for whatever he wanted to do.' Attlee consulted Bevin just as much. He generally stayed behind after Cabinet meetings and between them they sorted out 'the line' on the big issues of the moment. When in the depths of the financial crisis of September 1947 there was another coup attempt against Attlee, this time started by Cripps, Bevin stamped it out immediately. 'Why should I do him out of a job?' was his response. 'What's Clem ever done to me?' Again, he resisted the temptation to try to seize the crown. 'What a man,' he said of Attlee to one of his aides. 'He plucked victory from defeat. I love the little man. He is our Campbell-Bannerman.'[11] For Bevin, all politics was personal.

However, having installed Attlee as Prime Minister on 26 July, Bevin neither expected nor wanted to be Foreign Secretary on 27 July. Here starts Act Two of the two-day drama.

Bevin wanted to be Chancellor. As Labour's foremost Keynesian in the 1930s, he had big plans in mind for post-war reconstruction and the welfare state. He said all this to Attlee at Transport House on the afternoon of the 26th, before the Labour leader went to the Palace. Attlee appeared to assent and told the King that his intention was to make Bevin Chancellor and Dalton Foreign Secretary. He said the same to Dalton himself on the morning of the 27th, who records Attlee telling him that he would 'almost certainly' go to the Foreign Office.[12] They even discussed what clothes Dalton should pack for Potsdam the following day.

During or after lunch, though, Attlee changed his mind and told Dalton and Bevin so at about 4 p.m. Bevin promptly went home to Flo, who had planned a week's holiday for them in Devon. 'It's not Devon for me tomorrow but Potsdam,' he called up the stairs. 'Potsdam, what on earth is that?' she replied.[13]

So it was that Bevin, not Dalton, went with Attlee to meet Stalin and Truman on 28 July. This probably changed history. Dalton, in the mainstream Labour tradition of the 1930s and 1940s of being strongly anti-fascist but not nearly so anti-communist, would almost certainly not have taken Bevin's tough, unyielding line against Stalin, particularly on the future of West Germany. A Dalton foreign secretaryship might not have accomplished any of West Germany, NATO or the Marshall Plan.

Why did Attlee change his mind?

When Attlee told the King of his choice of Dalton as Foreign Secretary, George VI, according to his private secretary Sir Tommy Lascelles, 'begged him to think carefully about this, and suggested that Mr Bevin would be a better choice'.[14]

This was an unusually strong royal intervention in politics, maybe the most decisive by any monarch in the past century besides his father George V's intervention to persuade MacDonald to form the 'national' government in 1931. It flowed from George VI and his wife's unusually strong antipathy to Dalton, which had little to do with foreign policy. They knew Dalton well as the chippy Etonian-class renegade son of John Dalton, who had been tutor to George V and chaplain to Queen Victoria, and who had served into old age as a canon of Windsor with a house by St George's Chapel at Windsor Castle. In contrast, the King and Queen got on well with the working-class, bluff, respectful Bevin. They would have to see far more of the Foreign Secretary than the Chancellor of the Exchequer, so this mattered to them.

Hugh Dalton's biographer, Ben Pimlott, says that George VI's easily aroused temper was 'inflamed' shortly before the end of the war, by Dalton selling royal gifts that had been given to his parents. The King asked for these gifts to be returned.[15]

In retirement, Attlee said it wasn't the King's intervention that caused him to change his mind, rather that Bevin would be better at standing up to Stalin. 'I thought affairs were going to be pretty difficult and a heavy tank was what was going to be required rather than a sniper,' he told Alan Bullock. However, this was after Bevin's success in containing Stalin had become a near-universally applauded legacy of Attlee's government, and it was in the context of refuting claims, now public, that the King had made up his mind for him. It was an *ex post* justification, contradicted by other post-retirement statements by Attlee. On another occasion, he said he decided it was best to keep Bevin and Morrison apart on the home front to avoid 'trouble' between them, while on another he wrote: 'I naturally took into account the King's view which was very sound.'[16]

Morrison also claimed in his memoirs to have influenced the decision. He was one of a group of senior Labour MPs who met Attlee at lunchtime on Friday 27 July, at the meeting mentioned earlier which finally killed his leadership bid. He said that he warned the new Prime Minister – this was probably in the margins of the meeting itself – about Dalton's 'uncontrollable temper' and the diplomatic problems this would cause. The Labour Chief Whip agreed, he wrote, 'And so the appointments were made.'[17]

There are also contemporary accounts of top civil servants and diplomats lobbying Sir Tommy Lascelles and the Cabinet Secretary Sir Edward Bridges for Bevin to go to the Foreign Office. Eden, the outgoing Foreign Secretary, was strongly pro-Bevin and said so to all comers. So did the permanent under-secretary at the Foreign Office, Sir Alec Cadogan. The mandarinate was anti-Dalton partly because of personal dislike, on class grounds similar to the King's, particularly among those who had worked for him when he was Henderson's deputy at the Foreign Office in the 1929–31 government. But concern to have a strong minister to stand up to Stalin was another factor that weighed with Cadogan, who was at the time still in Potsdam awaiting the new government's representatives. It is also possible that Churchill personally urged Bevin's appointment on the King in his resignation audience immediately before Attlee's audience on 26 July. If so, Churchill's support for Bevin would have been in part because of his former Labour colleague's robustness in the face of communism, not least in the Greek crisis. He also rated Bevin far higher than Dalton, as did Attlee, who would probably have proposed Bevin as Foreign Secretary initially were it not for Bevin's specific request to become Chancellor.

There is also the factor of 'the dog that didn't bark'. Although Bevin expressed a preference to Attlee to be Chancellor in their discussion at Transport House on the afternoon of 26 July, he didn't follow it up either in person or in writing, and when Attlee told him the following afternoon that he wished him to go to the Foreign Office, he did not demur or argue. Bevin was strong enough to have insisted on becoming Chancellor, but he did not do so. Maybe his own mind was changing; maybe some of the people above had spoken to him.

Historical reconstruction is art, not science. Piecing together all these statements, meetings and views, I cannot say categorically why Bevin became Foreign Secretary on 27 July 1945. Ben Pimlott, who suggests that George VI's intervention may have been critical, remarks elegantly: 'It is a curious reflection that such an act, with its world-wide repercussions, may have occurred because of an emotion that derived in part from the turmoils of the Dalton nursery and the Saxe-Coburg-Gotha schoolroom, and from the strange interlocking of the two dynasties, more than half a century before.'[18]

Even in the Saxe-Coburg-Gotha schoolroom, however, Bevin was not passive. He cultivated the nervous and impressionable King

George VI every bit as much as Dalton alienated him. A Foreign Office private secretary gives this glimpse:

> Ernie got on particularly well with George VI for whom he had a warm regard. He was most punctilious about keeping the King informed about what was going on in the field of foreign affairs. On various occasions when I saw them together Ernie would put a large hand on the King's back and lead him to a corner where he would tell him some story which usually evoked roars of laughter.[19]

Once these key appointments were made, the changing of the guard could not have been more emphatic. On the morning of Saturday 28 July 1945, all 393 Labour MPs gathered in Central London. Attlee and Bevin joined them directly from Buckingham Palace, where they had been sworn as First Lord of the Treasury and Secretary of State for Foreign Affairs. As soon as they were seated, William Whiteley, the Chief Whip, rose. 'The Foreign Secretary,' he announced to a standing ovation. Whereupon Bevin moved a vote of confidence in the new Prime Minister that was 'finely phrased and magnificently delivered', according to Chuter Ede, the new Home Secretary. Attlee's ovation lasted several minutes.

Attlee spoke briefly, saying he must return to Potsdam. Then, he handed the meeting over to Morrison while he and Bevin set off for Berlin to meet Stalin and Truman. The most transformational phase of Bevin's life was about to begin.

JOINT OCCUPATION

["We are in Berlin as of right. It is our intention to stay there."—*Mr. Bevin, speaking in the House of Commons on Foreign Affairs.*]

Bevin stood up to Stalin sooner and more effectively than any other post-war Western leader. Better than Churchill and far better than Roosevelt and Truman. He was decisive in keeping Stalin out of Western Europe. © *Punch Magazine*

CHAPTER 9

STALIN

Bevin stood up to Stalin sooner and more effectively than any other post-war Western leader. Better even than Churchill and far better than Roosevelt and Truman. He was decisive, maybe indispensable, in keeping Stalin out of Western Europe, and in the process he led the creation of the Federal Republic of Germany, NATO and the transatlantic Western alliance that continues to this day.

The policy of 'containment' – seeking to contain Soviet Russia, rather than appease it – was Bevin's unwavering policy from his first day as Foreign Secretary, 27 July 1945, until his last day, 9 March 1951 – the six years which made modern Europe. He was successful because of his adroit exertion of Britain's continuing world power and the decision of the United States to adopt the same policy from 1947 rather than continuing to seek an accommodation with Stalin. This US policy change was nurtured and then exploited to the full by Bevin.

Containment is usually credited to George Kennan, American deputy ambassador to Moscow, in his 'long telegram' of 22 February 1946. But containment was Bevin's strategy from July 1945, and it was another crucial year after the February 1946 long telegram before containment was fully embraced by the Truman administration. Until then, particularly on the future of Germany, the United States triangulated between Britain and Soviet Russia. But for Bevin, Stalin might have been long past containment by the time the United States became converted to it. And but for him, the consequence might have been a Soviet-dominated Germany, that is West Germany as well as East, destroying political freedom and the whole balance of power across Western Europe.

Bevin had the measure of communism and Stalinism long before he became Foreign Secretary. As we have seen, from his earliest days leading the T&G in 1922, he grasped communism as an existential threat to the labour movement and democratic politics. He sought to root communism out of the British labour movement at every turn. After 1933, he saw communism and fascism as equal threats to democracy, peace and international order. He never made the mistake of thinking that Hitlerite fascism was worse than Stalinist communism. As totalitarian ideologies with criminal, murderous thugs as leaders, they were the same.

He set out his uncompromising views on international communism as far back as the 1927 TUC conference in Edinburgh, when he opposed the creation of joint international trade union institutions with the Soviet Union. This process was already underway until he and Walter Citrine, the new TUC general secretary, put a stop to it.

'Bevin looked pale and grim, as he always did in major debates, when he got up to speak,' recalled an observer. 'You have to appreciate that running through these things there are two distinct moral standards,' Bevin told the conference, getting straight to the heart of the matter.

One is the moral standard accepted by the British movement: to differ but to hammer out their differences, and when a decision is arrived at, to loyally and honourably abide by it. That is the British standard. The Russian standard, as I see it, is that the end justifies the means. That has been our experience on the General Council. Now these two moral standards cannot be reconciled in the promotion of a unified movement.[1]

The next passage of his 1927 speech is prophetic and compelling on how Stalin and his henchmen Molotov, Beria and Vyshinsky behaved before and after 1945, and why Bevin got the measure of them from his first day at the Potsdam conference:

If you turn down this resolution [rejecting collaboration with Soviet trade unions] it means that the General Council would be expected to meet the Russians on the joint committee. How would we meet them? If you had been called a traitor, a twister, a liar, and everything else that can be thought of, and you had to meet the man that called you that, would you meet him as a friend or as an antagonist? That does not promote international unity; that is the wrong way to assemble for a conference.[2]

Bevin's resolution was carried by four to one. Britain's trade unions kept clear of their Soviet counterparts thereafter and the central plank of Bevin's foreign policy after 1945 was in place.

So far as I am aware, Bevin never once expressed admiration for Stalin while Foreign Secretary, as opposed to his bromides about seeking a working relationship. He issued the bromides in the cause of unity in a Labour Party with strong pro-communist elements and, like much of the international community, an overwhelming belief in the early post-war years that unity was possible and necessary between East and West. But he didn't actually believe this himself and he didn't let it affect policy, in sharp contrast to Roosevelt, Truman and Byrnes, Truman's disastrous Secretary of State for Bevin's first two years at the Foreign Office.

Roosevelt regarded Stalin in 1945 not just as an ally but as a comrade. 'Of one thing I am certain,' he told the exiled Polish Prime Minister of the Yalta agreement, 'Stalin is not an imperialist.' And to the former American ambassador to France:

> I have a hunch that Stalin doesn't want anything other than security for his country, and I think that if I give him everything I possibly can and ask for nothing in return, noblesse oblige, he won't try to annex anything and will work for a world of democracy and peace.[3]

Churchill was not immune to the Soviet monster's charms and Bevin was privately critical of him on this score, even while the war was ongoing. 'Stalin I'm sure means well to the world and Poland,' Churchill told the War Cabinet after the Yalta conference in February 1945. The Cabinet note-takers record him continuing: 'Premier Stalin had been sincere. He [Churchill] had a very great feeling that the Russians were anxious to work harmoniously with the two English-speaking democracies,' particularly after Stalin 'had given the Polish people a free and more broadly based government to bring about an election'. This alarmed Bevin, who knew all about communist 'elections'. He told the Tory cabinet minister Leo Amery that he was 'fed up with Winston over a good many things', including his softness towards Stalin. Five months later, Foreign Secretary Eden thought Churchill's opening performance at the Potsdam conference was appalling: 'He is again under Stalin's spell. He kept repeating "I like that man" and I am full of admiration of Stalin's handling of him.'[4]

However, both Bevin and Churchill grasped Stalin's essential barbarism. The same was not true of Potsdam's novice in international communism, Harry Truman. The new American President, on arriving in Potsdam on 16 July, was polite to Churchill but wary of him. 'He gave me a lot of hooey about how great my country is and how he loved Roosevelt and how he intended to love me etc., etc.' Truman wrote in his diary of their first meeting. 'I am sure we can get along if he doesn't try to give me too much soft soap.' Whereas the following day, meeting Stalin for the first time, he was starstruck and took all the beguiling Soviet dictator's soft soap. 'I can deal with Stalin. He is honest – but smart as hell.'[5] Truman proceeded over the next fortnight to triangulate between Churchill and Stalin on the fate of Poland and much else, as had Roosevelt at the Yalta meeting of the Big Three five months previously. He also stuck to Roosevelt's policy that the United States would withdraw entirely from Europe within two years.

'After ten days in Potsdam, Truman was much taken by the Russian dictator,' writes the editor of his papers. 'A dozen years later, the President in retirement recalled in a letter to Dean Acheson [Secretary of State after 1949] how he had been an innocent at Potsdam, believing that the Soviets desired peace; as for Stalin, he had "liked the little son-of-a-bitch".'

The one thing Bevin wasn't, at Potsdam or later, was an innocent, and he never liked the little son-of-a-bitch. Almost every other democratic leader who met Stalin was worsted by him, as by the equally magnetic Hitler. Bevin had no personal dealings with Stalin in the last years of the war, which was probably a blessing as Russia was then, of course, Britain's ally, which was obviously a factor with Churchill and Roosevelt. But Bevin was always unimpressed by the charisma of others, and he was not remotely attracted to Stalin, or impressed by him, in his personal dealings after 1945. From Potsdam onwards, he was blunt and direct with the Soviet dictator, and still more so in his constant dealings with his coffin-faced foreign minister Molotov.

By the time Bevin and Attlee arrived at Potsdam in the afternoon of 28 July, it was too late to affect the big decisions. The conference had already been going for ten days. There had been nine plenary sessions, and Stalin and Truman were anxious to get away. Soon after the start of the conference, Truman had learned of the successful test of the US atomic bomb and its potential to bring a rapid end to the Japanese War: the atomic bomb was dropped on Hiroshima on 6 August, four days after the Potsdam conference ended.

But this didn't stop Bevin putting down markers. 'I'm not going to have Britain barged about,' he said to General Pug Ismay on landing in Berlin.[6] In particular he wasn't going to be barged about by Stalin. 'He said he was quite familiar with the tactics of the Communists because he had had to deal with them in his own labor unions in England,' he told James Forrestal, Truman's Secretary of the Navy, soon after arriving, and he made this immediately plain in the first plenary session with Stalin and Truman.

As soon as the plenary started at 10.30 p.m., Bevin 'repeatedly questioned Stalin's remarks in an aggressive manner'. When the dictator made a vaguely worded proposal to recognise Soviet-controlled governments in Eastern Europe, Bevin replied that in order to be 'perfectly straight with the House of Commons' he would not 'quote things in words of doubtful meaning'. Attlee nodded throughout but left the talking to his Foreign Secretary, demonstrating his adage: 'If you had a good dog like Ernest Bevin, there was no point barking yourself.'[7]

The following morning, 29 July, Stalin developed a 'cold' that resulted in a two-day suspension of plenary sessions. It was an anti-Bevin chill: 'His cold may have been a device to avoid having to deal with the truculent Bevin while working out compromises with the more accommodating Americans,' writes a historian of the Cold War.[8]

When Stalin's 'cold' abated sufficiently for him to return to the conference table, Bevin did not let up. © *Evening Standard*

When Stalin's 'cold' had abated sufficiently for him to return to the conference table on 31 July, the penultimate plenary, Bevin did not let up. To get a sense of the drama, here are the heated Stalin–Bevin exchanges on the Soviet dictator's claim for massive reparations from Germany, at the heart of his strategy to plunder and control the Ruhr in British-occupied north-west Germany. There had already been a provisional agreement on reparations earlier in the summit between Stalin, Churchill and Truman, but Bevin was setting out his stall. Even in the dry official transcript it comes alive:

Mr Stalin said he hoped the British and Americans would meet the Soviet wishes. Mr Bevin should have in mind that the Russians have lost much equipment. They should receive a small part of it back then.

Mr Bevin said that the British had had in mind equipment after determination of the amount needed for the maintenance of the [German] economy.

Mr Stalin said this was in his proposal. If he thought it over, Mr Bevin would accept it.

Mr Bevin replied that he could not. He had used the words 'equipment not needed for peacetime economy'. This was not in the Soviet document.

Mr Stalin reread the Soviet proposal on this point.

Mr Bevin said he did not give the basis on which the determination would be made.

Mr Stalin insisted it was the same thing.

Mr Bevin asked if he would then accept the British wording and said he did not want a misunderstanding.

Mr Stalin said the Russians had in view 15 per cent of the equipment to be removed which was not necessary for the peacetime economy but was not clear about it.

Mr Bevin again cited the British language which he said reflected the views agreed upon by the British and American delegations...

Mr Stalin observed that the U.S. was willing to meet the Soviet wishes – why was Britain unwilling?

Mr Bevin said that because they were responsible for the zone from which the Soviet claims were to be satisfied [i.e. the Ruhr]. They were also responsible for satisfying the claims of France and other countries.

Mr Stalin pointed out that France had signed an armistice with Hitler and had suffered no real occupation. France should be satisfied with a small amount. He said that 150 divisions had been sent to Russia from France or had been supplied from France.

Mr Bevin repeated that they had to satisfy France, Belgium, Czechoslovakia and Holland. The British wanted nothing except raw materials ... He said that the percentage the Soviets asked plus reparations from their own zone gave more than 50 per cent.

Mr Stalin insisted that it would be less than 50 per cent and pointed out in addition that they were supplying goods to the equivalent of 15 per cent. The Soviet proposal was a minimum. The Soviets received only 10 per cent – the others got 90 per cent. He agreed to 15 per cent and 10 per cent and thought it fair. The Americans agreed. He hoped Bevin would support them.

Mr Bevin said 'All right then.'

Mr Stalin expressed his thanks.[9]

The final exchange is especially significant. Bevin's problem in resisting Stalin in the crucial first year after the war was that Truman and his Secretary of State Jimmy Byrnes had already conceded the points at issue, which made it hard for Britain to revisit them. American appeasement of Stalin was one of Bevin's biggest problems at Potsdam and after.

Byrnes reciprocated the distrust. Bevin's manner at Potsdam was 'so aggressive', he wrote, 'that both the President and I wondered how we would get along with this new Foreign Secretary'. The answer is that they didn't try too hard. Truman and Byrnes saw Britain as 'a bankrupt imperialistic power', in Giles Radice's brutal description, and they acted to hasten insolvency. Within a month of Labour taking office, on 21 August, they ended Lend–Lease financial support to Britain, which had provided an open-ended credit card for vital British imports from the US. This caused the 'financial Dunkirk', which forced Britain to seek a large emergency US loan, secured by Keynes over the next year with immense difficulty and on onerous terms. Truman also declined to share atomic research with Britain when Attlee flew to Washington in November 1945, which was a decisive factor in his and Bevin's decision to initiate a British nuclear weapons programme.[10]

Bevin's elemental skill, knowledge and grasp of the international scene is captured in James Forrestal's full account of their conversation at Potsdam.

Found Bevin in very good form. He said in answer to my question that the only industries they proposed to nationalise were power, railroads, mines, and textiles up to the spinning mills. He indicated he had no use for Laski. He spoke highly and appreciatively of Anthony Eden. He said he was quite familiar with tactics of the Communists because he had had to deal with them in his own labor unions in England.

I asked him a question about the Emperor in Japan, whether he thought we ought to insist on destruction of the Emperor concept along with the surrender. He hesitated and said this question would require a bit of thinking, but he was inclined to feel there was no sense in destroying the instrument through which one might have to deal in order to effectively control Japan. He then made a rather surprising statement—for a liberal and a labor leader: 'It might have been far better for all of us not to have destroyed the institution of the Kaiser after the last war—we might not have had this one if we hadn't done so. It might have been far better to have guided the Germans to a constitutional monarchy rather than leaving them without a symbol and therefore opening the psychological doors to a man like Hitler.'

He said he was determined to get going what he called the three historic axes of European trade—the Baltic axis, that is to say, the old Hanseatic League; the Antwerp axis, and the Genoa axis. He said these three were the classic foci of European trade for hundreds of years back, that if they could be restored to activity, it would do much to bring about revival of commerce in Europe.[11]

Bevin knew how to cultivate the tough Forrestal, who was soon to become US Secretary of Defence and a crucial ally. At home Labour would be bold, but not extreme. Abroad, he wasn't any taking nonsense from Stalin, and he knew the Soviet game. The priority was to get Europe working again, reviving its principal trade routes. The comments about the Kaiser and the Emperor of Japan are arresting: a bit left field, like much of Bevin's conversation, but making striking points on what had gone wrong after the First World War and the lessons. He was possibly right about constitutional monarchy in Germany. As on reparations, he sought to avoid repeating the mistakes made after the First World War and he had thought through what they were. He pointed the way towards the decision to keep the Emperor of Japan: seventy-five years later, that looks a good decision.

Germany was the main battleground on which Bevin fought Stalin for the whole six years of his foreign secretaryship.

Hitler had committed suicide in his Berlin bunker only eleven weeks before Potsdam and the Reich was now divided and governed by Britain, Russia and America. North-west Germany was to be Britain's last major colony and maybe the only one where British rule was an unmitigated success, ending in 1949 with the creation of a strong, democratic West German state. The Federal Republic of Germany was essentially Bevin's creation. From this distance it all seems inevitable, yet it was anything but. It resulted from an intense six-year struggle for power which Bevin won and Stalin lost, and at every stage it was incredibly close-run.

It is impossible to overstate the physical and moral wreckage of Germany in May 1945. The cities were piles of rubble, the devastation and desperation akin to Hieronymus Bosch's vision of hell. Column after column of civilians, soldiers and concentration camp inmates marched and shuffled with little but their clothes towards home, or towards somewhere, anywhere, because they had to go somewhere, anywhere. Starvation, desperation and death were everywhere. Never before in Germany had so many people been killed in so short a time, not even in the Thirty Years' War. 'Everywhere there is great demand for poison, for a pistol and other means of ending one's life,' reported the SS at the end of March. 'Suicides due to depression about the real catastrophe which is expected with certainty are an everyday occurrence.'[12]

For Germans conquered by Stalin, it was like the fall of Constantinople to the Ottomans in 1453: panic, rape, murder, pillage, frenzy, violence, destruction, arbitrary horror at any place and at any moment. Millions in eastern Germany fled from the Russians in fear for their lives. Millions of Germans in territories further east marched and shuffled westwards, brutally expelled from their *Heimat*.

In 1944, Churchill, Stalin and Roosevelt decreed that after unconditional surrender Germany would be dismembered, with each of them governing a third of the country. The plan, drawn up by FDR's adviser Henry Morgenthau Jr, was for swathes of Germany to be given to France in the west and Poland in the east. The industrial Ruhr, its plants and factories, would be dismantled and then turned into an international zone, with its inhabitants encouraged to migrate. What was left was to be divided into two rump, rural states of northern and southern Germany.

The Morgenthau Plan was adopted by Churchill and Roosevelt at the British–American Quebec conference of September 1944. Churchill did one of his masterly rewrites of history in the light of future events, but the record is clear that he and FDR agreed to a dismembered, de-industrialised Germany. They committed to 'eliminating the war-making industries in the Ruhr and the Saar, looking forward to converting Germany into a country primarily agricultural and pastoral in its character'.[13]

Roosevelt, for all his wide and generous sympathies, was a Germanophobe at the end of the war, drawing on his unhappy schooldays as a nine-year-old in Germany. In one of his last conversations, in April 1945, he told General Lucius Clay, about to depart for France as Eisenhower's deputy, of his 'early distaste for German arrogance and provincialism'. FDR wrote to Queen Wilhelmina of the Netherlands in August 1944:

There are two schools of thought, those who would be altruistic in regard to the Germans, hoping by loving kindness to make them

Christians again – and those who would adopt a much 'tougher' attitude. Most decidedly I belong to the latter school, for though I am not bloodthirsty, I want the Germans to know that this time at least they have definitely lost the war.[14]

He and Stalin had little difficulty agreeing on this point.

If Roosevelt and Truman had been the lead players in Germany in 1945, events might thus have panned out very differently than with Bevin in the lead. But a key decision at Yalta in February 1945 was the allocation of the economic heart of Germany – the Ruhr, the Rhine, Hamburg and Bremen – to Britain as its zone of occupation. The British zone was also in population terms by far the largest of the four, and by far the most strategic in its proximity to France and the Netherlands. It became still more so after the flight of Germans westwards. The Yalta zone allocation decision reversed the previous plan for Britain to take the more rural south of Bavaria, Baden and Württemberg, while the US occupied the industrial north-west. Churchill negotiated hard for this exchange, which gave Britain the dominant role in post-war Germany and Europe. By mid-1945, 29,000 British officials were in Germany, taking control of the huge British zone under the leadership of Field Marshal Montgomery, who was appointed by Churchill as its governor on 8 May.

By Potsdam, Britain's military and Foreign Office analysts had few illusions about Stalin's intentions. Alan Brooke, Churchill's chief of the Imperial General Staff, wrote in his diary as early as 27 July 1944:

Should Germany be dismembered or gradually converted to an ally to meet the Russian threat of twenty years hence? I suggest the latter ... Russia is the main threat. Therefore, gradually build her up and bring her into a Federation of Western Europe under the cloak of a holy alliance of Russia, England and America. Not an easy policy.[15]

The Potsdam Declaration, agreed by Stalin, Truman and Attlee on 2 August, was Morgenthau-lite, based on 'four Ds': de-militarisation, de-nazification, de-industrialisation, and democratisation. It was the first three that mattered immediately; democratisation was last and least. The immediate step was the abolition of all existing German government and the dismemberment of the Reich. The Polish/German border was shifted 120 miles west and Alsace-Lorraine returned to France, reducing German territory by a quarter compared to 1937. Germans east of the Oder-Neisse line were summarily expelled, as were all Germans in Poland, Czechoslovakia and Hungary. Berlin, like the rest of Germany, was divided into four zones under the colonial rule of the Big Three and France.

Bevin's approach to containing Stalin after Potsdam was his classic formula of hard, egotistical but pragmatic trade union bargaining with all comers – the Soviets, the Americans, the French and the Germans, but also the Treasury, fellow ministers and parliamentarians at home – on the basis of not giving an inch to Moscow except where *force majeure* left no choice.

This required a robust attitude not only to the US but also to France, which in the immediate post-war years sought to stop the creation of a viable West Germany. De Gaulle had been Churchill's *bête noire* almost from his first day in London in 1940. Now, together with Georges Bidault and Robert Schuman, his successors as leader of France after he retreated to Colombey-les-Deux-Églises in

January 1946, de Gaulle sought to enlarge France, beyond the Yalta and Potsdam agreements, at the expense of western Germany. This caused constant tension with Bevin.

For Bevin, the problem with the United States in 1945 was fundamental. Truman inherited FDR's commitment to leave Europe within two years, and the general view of his policy makers, especially Secretary of State Jimmy Byrnes, was that this required a peace treaty with Stalin. This would include concessions on Central and Eastern Europe, agreement on emasculating the British Empire and a joint administration for the whole of Germany.

Bevin was never anti-American when it came to resisting Stalin. '49th STATE? NO THANK YOU, MR CHURCHILL' was *Tribune*'s headline after Churchill's Iron Curtain speech of March 1946, which applied equally to its view of Bevin.[16] Bevin's view of the United States oscillated. Britain was the 'last bastion of social democracy in Europe', he argued in a Cabinet paper of 1946, and the British Empire was all that stood between 'the red tooth and claw of American capitalism and the communist dictatorship of Soviet Russia'.[17] But when it came to resisting Stalin he never doubted that it had to be 'two against one', and he regarded much criticism of America as profoundly ignorant. With his knowledge of the American trade union movement dating back to his first fraternal visit to the American Federation of Labor convention in 1916, he saw America, for all its libertarian zealots, as a republic teeming with workers fighting the same fight as the workers of Britain, France, Germany and the world over. In an exchange about Marshall Aid in the House of Commons with a communist MP, one of the few elected in 1945, Bevin let rip:

When you strip all these things down which produce political ideologies and get down to the masses, what do they want? They want to live! They want to be free, to have social justice, to have individual security, to be able to go home, turn the key in the lock and not be troubled by a secret police. Why not let them live? Why set them at each others throats? That is the basis of my approach to the problems of a war-scarred Europe and world.[18]

But in 1945 Marshall Aid was still two long years away. After Potsdam, Bevin had to contain Stalin, entice America and stabilise Germany. These were huge parallel challenges: stabilising Germany and encouraging the US were critical to curbing Stalin and *vice versa*. And they had to be done in the teeth of opposition from much of the British left, which wanted to appease Stalin or positively supported him. And the right was not immune. Lord Halifax, having spent the late 1930s appeasing Hitler, wanted to do the same with Stalin after 1945 as ambassador to Washington. He pronounced himself 'intensely irritated' with Churchill's Fulton speech in March 1946, which was 'a waste of Churchill's commanding position' and 'simply cut off any progress towards an accommodation with Russia'.[19] Bevin was with Churchill.

As the new colonial power in the Ruhr and the industrial north-west of Germany in 1945, Britain's immediate objective was, in the words of General Brian Robertson, Montgomery's deputy governor of the British zone, 'not to batter Germany down – she was sprawling in the dirt already – but to rebuild her up and do so wisely. We had to save Germany physically from starvation, squalor and penury, and spiritually from despair and communism.'[20]

To replace anarchy with stability, the factories, the mines and the farms of West Germany had to start working again. In the summer of 1945, Germany was importing 70 per cent of its food: famine was the looming catastrophe. Bevin's policy was to empower Montgomery and his administration in Germany to act with ruthless pragmatism to restore normality to the British zone, while resisting Stalin's relentless campaign for punitive reparations. Bevin's economic adviser, Alec Cairncross, told him: 'At the end of the last war Lord Keynes familiarised us with the truth, which experience is now reiterating, that Germany was the heart of the entire European economy and that upon her prosperity the prosperity of Europe in large measure depends.'[21] Bevin made this the core of his policy. It meant stopping Russia and France from seizing coal and steel from the Ruhr. It also meant lifting production quotas, which had been capped tightly at Potsdam and immediately afterwards, against Bevin's better judgement.

Having confronted Stalin personally, Bevin wasn't fazed by Molotov, his foreign minister. He deliberately mispronounced the apparatchik's name ('Mr Mowlotov'), and told him straight-out in one bruising early encounter that his attitude and policies were 'reminiscent of Hitler'.[22] Bevin and Molotov crossed swords throughout the first four years of his foreign secretaryship in the institution of the Council of Foreign Ministers, the rolling summit of the four victorious allied powers charged at Potsdam with negotiating the post-war peace treaties and managing great-power diplomacy. The council held nine summits between 1945 and 1949, each lasting between ten days and six weeks. Bevin, the only minister of the four powers to be a member of the council throughout the four years, was its dominant personality.

London hosted the first meeting of the council in September 1945. From the outset Bevin's strategy was to keep Stalin completely out of West Germany and West Berlin, despite the Potsdam Declaration which stated the opposite. He also sought to contain Stalin across the rest of Europe and the Middle East. Obviously all this put him in conflict with Molotov. More problematically, it also put him on a collision course with Jimmy Byrnes, Truman's Secretary of State.

Now historically overshadowed, Byrnes was a key figure of the Roosevelt and Truman administrations. Variously congressman, senator and governor of South Carolina in the heart of the old confederacy, he had expected to be FDR's vice-presidential nominee for the 1944 election before losing out at the last minute to Senator Harry Truman of Missouri, who was unencumbered by southern political baggage. Dubbed 'my assistant president' by FDR, Byrnes was an assertive director of war mobilisation at the end of the war, becoming Truman's Secretary of State just before Potsdam.

Byrnes had been at Yalta with Roosevelt and inherited FDR's belief that compromise deals could be done by personal diplomacy with Stalin, although he was lacking the maestro's subtlety and intuition. He was 'prima-donnish' – the reason FDR gave for not appointing him to succeed Cordell Hull as Secretary of State at the end of 1944 and why he and Truman ultimately fell out (he called the President 'Harry' even in front of subordinates). However, for the crucial nineteen months between July 1945 and January 1947, Byrnes was the principal diplomat of the United States and the main shaper of its foreign policy. This wasn't just because 'Byrnes had decided that he was going to run foreign policy and he would casually tell the president about it', as Truman's press secretary recalled. It was also Truman's express will. On appointing Byrnes, the President said in his diary that he would go with Byrnes, the 'hard hitting trader on the home front', and not with 'the smart boys in the State Department' including Edward Stettinius Jr, the Secretary of State sacked to make way for 'Jimmy', and ambassadors and diplomats like George Kennan and Averell Harriman.[23]

'I know how to deal with the Russians, it's just like the US Senate,' Byrnes breezily told his delegation on board the *Queen Elizabeth* travelling to the London Council of Foreign Ministers in September 1945. 'You build a post office in their state, and they'll build a post office in our state.'[24] Bevin was as 'prima-donnish' as Byrnes, but he had no illusions about happily building post offices with Stalin across Europe.

At the London conference, Bevin could not get Byrnes to support a joint Anglo-US statement refusing to recognise Stalinist regimes in Romania and Bulgaria. Even on Austria and Yugoslavia, where they did briefly co-ordinate, Byrnes attributed Russian obstructionism to Molotov rather than to Stalin, telling an aide that there was 'no hope of stopping Molotov except by appealing to Stalin', naivety akin to his description of the Soviet monster as 'a very likeable person'. One Cold War historian notes drily, 'Byrnes came to London with one illusion and left with another.'[25]

Illusion soon became dangerous delusion, for in November 1945 Byrnes instigated an unscheduled pre-Christmas meeting of the Council of Foreign Ministers in Moscow, after liaising with Molotov but without even consulting Bevin. He thought he would be able to rapidly broker comprehensive peace treaties, and that he could do this through personal chemistry with Stalin. He told an associate he would achieve 'further progress with Stalin in Moscow by means of the compromising American diplomacy of mutual accommodation already practiced by the Hopkins mission [sent by Truman to Stalin

in June 1945] and at the Potsdam conference'. According to his biographer, 'Byrnes presumed that he could "get through" to almost
any individual if only they could meet personally. Hence ... on his
own initiative shortly after Thanksgiving Day he called on Molotov
to agree to a second meeting of the Allied foreign ministers before
the end of December 1945.' And he suggested that they meet in
Moscow, 'where the US Secretary could, if necessary, meet personally with Stalin'.[26]

This explicit triangulation, in Moscow itself, astonished and
alarmed Bevin, particularly when Byrnes told Stalin, in a conversation relayed to British diplomats, that he had intentionally blindsid-
ed Britain. France was excluded even from attending the Moscow
conference, at Molotov's instigation. Bevin told Byrnes bluntly that
Stalin's aim was to dominate Europe from the Baltic to the Adriatic.
He said the same to Stalin himself. When the dictator remarked
that Britain and the US had 'spheres of influence but the USSR had
nothing', Bevin countered that 'the Soviet sphere extended from
Lübeck [on the German Baltic coast] to Port Arthur [on China's
east coast]'.[27]

The Moscow conference signified the high-water mark of Byrnes's
accommodation of Stalin. By Christmas Eve, after eleven days of
sessions and two tête-à-têtes with the Russian dictator, Byrnes had
only two tangible achievements: agreement on a United Nations
Atomic Development Authority, which rapidly fell apart at the UN
on issues of scope and control; and, in return for US recognition
of Stalinist regimes in Romania and Bulgaria, the token concession
– which Byrnes saw as far more significant – that there should be
two opposition ministers included in their communist-dominated

governments. Bevin deliberately blocked any accommodation on Germany. For him, the most contentious issue in Moscow was Soviet destabilisation and threats to Iran. Bevin pressed Stalin to withdraw from northern Iran and proposed a mutual early with-drawal of troops. Stalin refused, saying he needed to protect the oil wells at Baku, 'whereupon Bevin asked sardonically whether he feared an Iranian attack'.[28]

In 1952, by which point Truman had moved decisively against Stalin and sought to deny that he had ever sought accommodation with Moscow, a bitter dispute erupted between Byrnes and Truman about precisely what had happened in 1945 and 1946. Truman claimed he hadn't known what Byrnes was up to in Moscow and, when he learned, 'read him the riot act', particularly about turning Romania and Bulgaria into 'police states'. He claims to have read aloud a letter to his Secretary of State, which included the following: 'I am not going to agree to the recognition of those governments unless they are radically changed.' Byrnes responded that Truman was lying and rewriting history.

There is indeed no contemporary written or third-party record of Truman saying any of this to Byrnes at the time. On the contra-ry, the circumstantial evidence suggests that Truman supported his chief diplomat at the time. Byrnes did an NBC radio broadcast on 30 December 1945 defending the Moscow conference. 'It must be recognised that the Soviet government has a very real interest in the character of the government of these states,' he said of Romania and Bulgaria. This broadcast came after he had seen Truman, and the President praised it in front of guests the following evening when Byrnes was present again. Byrnes said that, had Truman criticised him, 'I would have resigned immediately ... with my deep conviction that there must be complete accord between the President and his Secretary of State,' just as he had in fact walked out of previous posts under FDR, Beaverbrook-style, and just as he was to resign thirteen months later.[29] Byrnes's account is the more convincing.

Tellingly also, Truman praised the Moscow conference in his State of the Union address to Congress on 21 January 1946 and made no criticism of Russia. 'The agreement reached at Moscow preserves this [human rights] in the making of peace with Italy, Romania, Bulgaria, Hungary and Finland. The United States intends to preserve it when the treaties with Germany and Japan are drawn.' All of which was of little comfort to western Germany. The US proceeded to recognise the Stalinist government of Romania on 5 February, nine months before an 'election' there inaugurated a 43-year communist dictatorship.

Churchill's seminal 'Iron Curtain' speech of 5 March 1946, hosted by Truman in his hometown of Fulton, Missouri, made some impression on the President but it set out only a partial strategy for dealing with the Stalinist menace it identified. Its stirring call for a 'fraternal association of the English speaking peoples' was not a policy to resolve the immediate future of Germany, where Stalin already had a firm and growing foothold thanks to Russian domination of the east and the provisions of Yalta and Potsdam.

All this is vital to appreciating the significance of Bevin's stalling tactics in negotiation after negotiation with Byrnes and Molotov throughout 1945 and 1946. In the case of Romania and Bulgaria, occupied by Russian troops, Bevin did not ultimately seek to block the US/Russia deal, but he sought to avoid any US/Russia deal on Germany which might have increased Stalin's leverage and led to the United States withdrawing troops and economic support, as it did after Versailles in 1919.

Molotov trying to crush Bevin. 'The danger of Russia has become certainly as great as, or possibly even greater than, that of a revived Germany.' © *Daily Mail*

Bevin was negotiating on a second front too: with Attlee at home. Although Attlee stuck strongly behind Bevin in public and in Cabinet, he was nervous about an overt split with Russia and periodically in 1946 pushed back on Bevin's determination to block any agreement with Stalin. But he shared Bevin's basic assessment of the Soviet dictator and stepped back when Bevin responded robustly. A decisive moment was Bevin's Cabinet paper of 3 May 1946 on the government's negotiating position for the forthcoming reconvened Paris meeting of the Council of Foreign Ministers.

Bevin spelt out the extent of the Soviet threat and made an explicit case for the containment of Stalin and building up western Germany as a counter to Soviet Russia. 'Until recent months,' he told the Cabinet in the 3 May 1946 paper, we have thought of the German problem solely in terms of Germany itself, our purpose having been to devise the best means of preventing the revival of a strong aggressive Germany. But it can no longer be regarded as our sole purpose, or indeed perhaps as our primary one. For the danger of Russia has become certainly as great as, or possibly even greater than, that of a revived Germany.[30]

In west Berlin, British support for the social democrats was crucial in saving them from 'fusion' with the communists, as happened in east Berlin and the whole of Soviet-occupied eastern Germany with the creation of the 'Socialist Unity Party' in February 1946. When John Hynd, the Minister for Germany, warned Bevin privately that Germany's social democrats and Christian democrats were 'rapidly losing their grip on Western Germany and the Communists are going ahead', Bevin agreed. 'I never understood why we could not proceed with our own policy in our own zone in the same way as the Russians were proceeding with their policy in their zone,' he responded. When Hynd went on to say: 'the question must be faced whether we should now proceed to establish a [West] German government,' Bevin was cautious about timing: 'This means a policy of a Western bloc and that means war.' But the groundwork for turning the British zone into a self-governing entity had begun by April 1946 and soon became Bevin's next step in containing Stalin in Germany. The alternative was 'Communism on the Rhine', said Orme Sargent, a tough anti-Stalinist recently appointed by Bevin to succeed Alec Cadogan as the Foreign Office's permanent under-secretary.[31]

Communist subversion was now relentless across Central and Eastern Europe. Poland, Hungary, Czechoslovakia, Romania and Bulgaria were under intense Stalinist assault and fell one by one to communist police states operating by murder, expropriation and mass persecution. At the United Nations in London in January 1946, a bitter dispute took place between Bevin and Vyshinsky over Iran and Greece. Byrnes stayed silent. John Foster Dulles and Senator Arthur Vandenberg, the leading Republicans present, noted this and were 'impressed with Ernest Bevin's impassioned stand against Vyshinsky'. In a Senate speech on the question 'What is Russia up to now?' back in Washington on 27 February, Vandenburg pointedly praised Bevin as 'sturdy' while not mentioning Byrnes.[32] Days later, a Stalinist coup, with Russian tanks and troops, was narrowly averted in Tehran, with Bevin and Byrnes working closely in tandem for the first time because of the imminent threat to the Persian Gulf and Iranian oil supplies.

In public, Bevin continued to pay lip service to the quest for a new global order in partnership with Russia. But in private and semi-private he gave no ground whatever to left-wing appeasers of communism. By now, mainstream Labour MPs could see the pattern of events across Europe and responded positively when rallied by Bevin. But a hostile minority was increasingly vocal and there were many fence-sitters. At a meeting of Labour MPs on foreign policy on 22 March 1946, 'after lashing the British Communists as fellow travellers and rounding abusing his critics', he carried the room.[33] Stalin helped with a rare speech in Moscow, on 9 February, asserting that a peaceful co-existence of capitalism and communism was impossible.

The Council of Foreign Ministers reconvened in Paris on 25 April, the first of three meetings in 1946, two in Paris and one in New York, which occupied fourteen weeks between them. Byrnes was still hoping that Paris would yield his peace treaty with the

Soviet Union. Since the Iranian crisis, Byrnes had been more alive
to the real Stalin behind the façade, but the Soviet–Iranian agreement of 4 April, which ended the immediate threat in Tehran, gave
him renewed confidence in his deal-making powers. He still sought
a treaty on Germany with the Soviet dictator, which most American
diplomats and administrators in Germany also thought necessary as
they couldn't commit to keeping US troops and administrators there
long term. Byrnes's 6 September speech in Stuttgart, announcing
that troops would stay for the time being, was notably equivocal: 'As
long as there is an occupation army in Germany, American forces
will be part of that occupation army.' This begged the question:
how long was 'as long'? When, in Paris in July 1946, Byrnes asked
Bidault what he thought Stalin was trying to achieve in Europe, the
Frenchman replied bluntly: 'Cossacks on the Place de la Concorde.'[34]
Byrnes did not respond.

The first Paris conference accordingly saw Byrnes side with Bevin
against the punitive reparations demanded by Molotov from western
Germany's steel and coal production. But to Bevin's consternation,
the US sided with Molotov in support of setting up pan-German
institutions, including possible four-power control of the Ruhr.
Bevin rejected this outright. Worse still, Byrnes published proposals
to reduce US, British and Russian military forces in Germany, which
he proposed would pave the way for a demilitarised Germany to be
policed by inspectors. Bevin didn't need Stalin to ask the question,
'How many divisions have the inspectors got?'

Bevin kept stalling, making a blunt move to break up any US/
Russian bromance on Germany by threatening Molotov with
re-opening the question of the Polish–German border. 'It has only
been agreed that Poland should occupy certain areas pending final

settlement,' he warned Molotov, 'and the United Kingdom ... would have something to say in view of their experience when the time came to fix them.'[35] By these and other feints he managed to get the council adjourned on 16 May without progress on Germany.

Time was Bevin's ally as the situation in Germany went from bad to worse during 1946. The food crisis, with more severe rationing, was leading to a breakdown in relations with German leaders and people in both the British and the American zones, while the subsidies needed to maintain the zones were unsustainable. British and American administrators on the ground were ever more convinced of the need to empower the West Germans themselves. When Montgomery left Germany in May, handing the governorship of the British zone to General Brian Robertson, he reported to Bevin and Attlee:

> The whole country is in such a mess that the only way to put it right is to get the Germans 'in on it' themselves. We must tell the German people what is going to happen to them and their country. If we do not do these things, we shall drift towards possible failure, and that 'drift' will take the form of an increasingly hostile population which will eventually begin to look east.[36]

Byrnes's attempts at triangulation continued when the Council of Foreign Ministers reconvened in Paris on 15 June. Bevin accordingly kept up the belligerence. In five long and acrimonious sessions on the future of Germany, he used every argument and ploy he could to forestall US/Russian agreement, which again led to a deadlock, as he had hoped. Bevin also had France against him: Bidault wanted to annexe the Saar and put the Rhineland under four-power control separate from the rest of Germany. So tense and exhausting were these weeks that Byrnes had a near breakdown and Bevin had a heart attack on returning to London. All this was on top of his other preoccupations, including the bombing of the King David Hotel in Jerusalem on 22 July. 'All the world is in trouble and I have to deal with all the troubles at once,' was his characteristically egocentric worldview.[37]

What started out in Paris as a precarious holding operation ended up with a tentative advance. On the penultimate day of the summit, 11 July, in reply to Bevin's robust statement the previous day that Britain would 'organise' its zone of Germany in the absence of a four-power agreement, to which he had no intention of agreeing, Byrnes made an offer to join the American zone with any other zone 'for the treatment of our respective zones as an economic unit'. In practice, this could only mean unity with the British zone. It was a crab-like move towards Bevin's policy of a 'bizone' – that is, a united British/American zone with joint political and economic institutions, possibly paving the way for a *de facto* western German democratic state.

However, Byrnes was still riding two horses, for he followed up this bizone suggestion with another proposal for four-power central administrative institutions in Berlin, which Bevin continued to block. More than a year after the war there was still no fundamental agreement between Byrnes and Bevin on how to handle Germany, and the United States was still not committed to staying in Europe to contain Stalin.

This intense Anglo-American mistrust is vital to the momentous October 1946 decision, taken in secret by Attlee, Bevin and a small number of Cabinet colleagues, to equip Britain with nuclear weapons. Bevin's famous remark that 'we've got to have this thing over here whatever it costs, we've got to have the bloody Union Jack flying on top of it', is routinely quoted. However, equally important was Bevin's previous sentence: 'We've got to have this. I don't mind for myself, but I don't want any other Foreign Secretary of this country to be talked at or by a Secretary of State in the United States as I have just had in my discussions with Mr Byrnes.'[38] It wasn't only opposition to Stalin and the Soviets which precipitated the decision to adopt the British nuclear deterrent, but also acute concern about the United States.

The 26 October 1946 decision to adopt nuclear weapons has become a *cause célèbre* to students of British government, because it wasn't taken by or even notified to the Cabinet, let alone Parliament. But this misses the main point. Decisions of this kind in British government have always been taken by small groups of ministers in secret, whether or not notified to Parliament soon afterwards. In this case, it was not long before the decision was known. The point of substance is what the decision actually *was*. And the point of significance is that, but for Bevin, the decision might have been different. We know this because, by the account of an official present, Bevin arrived late for the meeting, saying he had fallen asleep after a good lunch. Dalton and Cripps argued against a nuclear programme on grounds of cost, and were carrying the point when Bevin reversed the decision in his most brutal method, described here by Roy Jenkins: 'He simply stopped the engine in its tracks, lifted it up, and put it back facing in the other direction.'[39] He barged in, saying, 'That won't do at all, we've got to have this,' as he proceeded to make the remarks quoted above, ending in the decision to go ahead.

So had Bevin not been Foreign Secretary in 1946, Britain might not have proceeded with the nuclear deterrent. Perhaps Attlee would have driven the decision anyway, over-ruling Dalton and Cripps, and maybe if Dalton had been Foreign Secretary he would have acted differently. All we know is that, at the time, Bevin was crucial to this decision being taken, and his reasons were directly related to the containment of Stalin.

If the nuclear decision was taken in secret from the British Parliament and media, it was not secret from the White House or the higher echelons of the Truman administration, where it was seen as a statement of British resolve, personified by Bevin, to stand up to Stalin. This can only have encouraged the US to do the same. In the autumn of 1946 Byrnes engaged more positively on the bizone concept, although money remained one of several sticking points. The Americans wanted the bizone financed 57 per cent by Britain, as per the larger population in its zone, while Dalton, as Chancellor, proposed that the US pay four-fifths.

Bevin leapfrogged these disputes with another bold move. On 22 October 1946, in the same week as the nuclear decision and just before leaving on the *Aquitania* for the next Council of Foreign Ministers in New York, he told the House of Commons of his resolve to turn the British zone into a self-governing state, while also lifting the cap on industrial production in the Ruhr. Damning Stalin with faint praise ('we are extremely glad of Marshal Stalin's categorical denial of the idea that Russia might be intending to use Germany against the west'), he went well beyond his previous language of 'organising' the British zone to set out a detailed plan to turn it into a *de facto* state in defiance of East Germany and the Soviet Union. This 'Bevin Plan' set out virtually the entire constitutional structure of what became the Federal Republic of Germany three years later.

'We are striving to stimulate habits of orderly self-government among the Germans,' he told MPs, continuing,

> There have recently been elections in the British zone for local councils. There have also been elections in Berlin. Next spring there will be elections for the provincial councils ... we are decentralising German administration as far as possible. We have set up a new province of North Rhineland-Westphalia, and we intend reorganising the remainder of our zone into two other provinces, Schleswig-Holstein and Lower Saxony. The Hanseatic towns of Hamburg and Bremen will remain separate. Looking further ahead, we contemplate a German constitution which would avoid the two extremes of a loose confederation of autonomous States and a unitary centralised state ... The central Government might consist of two chambers, one of which would be popularly elected, and the other consisting of representatives of the regional units. There might be a Supreme Court like the United States Supreme Court, with justification to give rulings on the powers of all central and provincial legislatures.[40]

Bevin was building, as he always built. Here, only seventeen months after the end of the war, are all the key constitutional principles of the Federal Republic of Germany as it functions successfully today: the regional states (*Länder*); power-sharing between the *Länder* and a federal government; a two-chamber German Parliament comprising an elected lower chamber (the *Bundestag*), which appoints the Chancellor; and an upper chamber (the *Bundesrat*) representing the *Länder* to cement the federation. Together with a 'mixed member' form of proportional representation, which kept individual constituencies while providing a proportional top-up, it was a constitution that learned from the best of Germany's past and from the best of the Westminster model. It launched West Germany with a constitution now long regarded as a model in its democratic credentials and its spread of political and economic power over a large and diverse country.

R. A. Butler, the post-war Tory moderniser, immediately welcomed the Bevin Plan. 'Today we have achieved in the Foreign Secretary's speech the moral purposes which will always be the basis of British foreign policy at its best,' he said, recognising also the great significance 'that the Rhineland and the Ruhr are to be included in the general bounds of what will amount to a federalised Germany'.

This was only a fraction of the work now underway in the British zone to turn it into a successful society and economy – 'Trying to beat the Swastika into the parish pump,' as one British official put it.[41] Under Bevin's *imprimatur*, German trade unions, media, banks, arts, schools, universities and industry were all revived and modernised to guard against the experience of the Nazis while also applying some British practice. From the creation of *Der Spiegel* and Germany's free media, to industrial partnership between unions and employers (*mitbestimmen*), British engagement was deep and constructive, in many respects deeper and more constructive than in the modernisation of post-war Britain itself.

Armed with parliamentary support for turning the British zone into a *de facto* state, Bevin renewed discussions on the bizone a fortnight later, with Byrnes in the margins of the next protracted Council of Foreign Ministers in New York from 4 November to 12 December 1946. Crucially, they resolved the money issue. Bevin initially tried a weak bluff at Dalton's behest, that Britain might withdraw from its zone if the US did not finance the majority of the bizone. Byrnes called his bluff by offering to swap zones, adding waspishly – and revealingly of his stand-offish attitude to Britain even at this late stage – that 'with American organisation and the potentiality of the British zone they would make it a success in a very short time'.[42] The deal was done on 1 December for 50:50 cost sharing. Attlee worried that this was still unsustainable, so weak was Britain's financial position as the American loan ran out. But since the deal paved the way to America's continuing engagement in Germany, Bevin seized it. The 50:50 burden sharing also helped justify an equal partnership between the UK and the US in the crucial decisions ahead. In the event, it was to be supplemented by Marshall Aid, and also by the setting up of NATO with a massive, indefinite US military commitment to Germany, so the US ended up picking up the lion's share of the costs.

On the key issue of Germany, Bevin succeeded in keeping the Council of Foreign Ministers stalled for the whole six weeks of the New York meeting. He was still not in agreement with Byrnes, and the absence of France from New York made him all the more anxious to play for time. The reason for the French absence went to the heart of the issues at stake. In the second post-war French election, held on 10 November, a week into the conference, the pro-Stalin French communists became the largest party in the French National Assembly with 28 per cent of the vote. Bidault never made it to New York because of the horse-trading required to put together a precarious anti-communist government. But while the French election made the dynamics of New York more difficult for Bevin, it also demonstrated to the US the gravity and imminence of the Soviet threat deep across Western Europe, not just in Central and Eastern

Europe. The threat of communist, even Stalinist, governments across the entire continent, including in France and Italy, was very real.

Another game changer was the mid-term US Congressional elections, held the day after the council opened (5 November). Truman lost control of both Houses of Congress. The rising tide of anti-communism among the victorious Republicans, and their determination to weaponise it against the Democrats, decisively shifted US policy. Joseph McCarthy became senator for Wisconsin in this election and Richard Nixon won his first congressional seat after a ruthless red-baiting campaign in California, in which the future president alleged that his Democrat opponent – the incumbent – was backed by Radio Moscow. Days after the end of the New York summit, on 19 December, Byrnes told Truman he was resigning, although it was a month before he was replaced by George Marshall.

'Any man who would want to be secretary of state would go to hell for pleasure,' was Byrnes's parting shot. It was a commentary as much on divisions within Truman's Washington as on the job itself. Unlike Bevin, who never resigned from any major post and never willingly gave up on any major endeavour, Byrnes had no stomach for the struggle ahead: 'He realised that the German negotiations would involve even longer and more arduous meetings, not to mention political hazards,' writes his biographer.[43]

Political hazards were pretty strong in London too. The left of the Labour Party was now in open revolt at Bevin's anti-Stalinism, tabling a hostile motion in the House of Commons while he was in New York, to his fury. Attlee replied to this debate personally, loyal as ever to Bevin, but 120 Labour MPs abstained in the vote and the mood was sour. This made no difference to Bevin's policy, nor did the *Keep Left* attack, a pamphlet published in early 1947 by Michael

Foot and Richard Crossman. Unlike Byrnes, and Beaverbrook before him, Bevin had both power and staying power in resisting his adversaries. In this, as Attlee's spokesman Francis Williams noted, he had more than a passing resemblance to the strong man he was confronting in the Kremlin.

Bevin's negotiating brief for Moscow, set out to the Cabinet in a paper of 27 February 1947, was deliberately couched in terms he knew Stalin would not accept. It reiterated the Bevin Plan for the British zone in Germany, raising for the first time the necessity for a new currency for the Western zones as part of the bizone plan, which, he said explicitly, 'would be tantamount to splitting Germany into two'. He ruled out any early resumption of reparations to Russia until the West German economy was on its feet and gained Cabinet agreement for substantial and immediate increases in West German industrial production. The brief was explicit that the Bevin Plan was compatible with a single state covering the whole of Germany if Stalin accepted all his conditions. But, 'If, as is very possible [certain, in Bevin's view] we fail to agree, we could proceed without difficulty to implement the conclusions recommended in this memorandum in respect of the British, American and the French zones only.'[44] In other words, the Cabinet was giving the green light to create a fully-fledged West German state.

Bevin's strategy for dealing with Stalin in East Germany was also spelt out in the same Cabinet paper. His priority now was 'to keep the Iron Curtain down unless we get satisfaction on all our conditions and build up West Germany behind it'. Then, he argued, 'there is more chance of drawing Eastern Germany towards the West than vice versa' – a prophecy of what actually happened before and after the collapse of the Berlin Wall in 1989.

Characteristically, Bevin told Attlee and Cabinet colleagues that 'the principles at stake are too important for compromise'. What he was setting out was in reality a plan of action, not a negotiating brief. He was determined, he said, 'to bring matters to a head'.[45]

Attlee, as ever, supported Bevin in the face of continued sniping from Dalton, Bevan and Morrison. 'We shall have to let them [the Russians] do most of what they like in Eastern Europe and Germany,' was Dalton's comment on Bevin's paper, which shows how different the fate of Germany and Europe might have been with him as Foreign Secretary.[46] At the same time, Bevin took complete charge of running the British zone, merging the Control Office, which since 1945 had overseen the administration of the British zone, into the Foreign Office. Hynd was sacked as Minister for Germany and Robertson, as governor, became directly responsible to Bevin, a change of form rather than reality.

Bevin's weakness from 1947 onwards was not in his policy, nor in commanding the requisite Cabinet and parliamentary support. He dealt with the Foot/Crossman *Keep Left* attack with a robust rebuttal pamphlet, *Cards on the Table*, written by Denis Healey, by then head of Labour's international secretariat and on his way to becoming a pugilist of Bevinist proportions. The title was a deliberate echo of Bevin's successful speech on foreign affairs to the May 1945 Labour Party conference, when he had said bluntly to Russia and the US: 'Do not present us with *faits accomplis* when we arrive [at the peace conference] ... If I may use a Cockney phrase, there should be "cards on the table, face upwards".'

Bevin's problem, rather, was that he was in terrible physical shape in the run-up to the Moscow conference. His now perennial heart condition was exacerbated by the worst winter in living memory in

1946–47 and a fractious Cabinet beset by fears of imminent British bankruptcy. He was so ill, finding it difficult even to get up and down stairs, that he wasn't allowed to fly to Moscow. It took him five days to get to the Russian capital by train, with his personal doctor Alec McCall in attendance. Dalton thought he might not return. Six weeks in Stalin's lair did not look auspicious.

However, once in Moscow, Bevin's spirits and health revived. The British ambassador Sir Maurice Peterson and his wife took great care of Bevin, and isolation from the hurly-burly of London, without the social whirl of Paris or New York, had a positive effect. The advent of spring raised Bevin's spirits further. 'It cheers one up to see the great thaw and the trees breaking into bud,' he wrote to his T&G secretary Ivy Saunders, almost poetically, on 30 March. 'Looking out of the windows we look across to the Kremlin with its great golden domes, hideous yet beautiful. Round it is the great wall which is symbolic of its secrecy. Few people enter and who does no one knows what happens within it.'[47] There was a run-in with Dr McCall over Bevin partaking of too much champagne at a reception at the Greek embassy: Bevin had to stop the doctor packing his bags. But when they left Moscow he was in better shape than when he arrived, to the relief of Attlee, who badly wanted him to continue at the Foreign Office.

As in Paris and New York, the formal sessions of the Moscow conference were protracted, tense and deadlocked. Molotov gave little ground. Nor did Bevin, who bigged up his verbal confrontations with 'Mr Mowlotov' for media consumption. It was a six-week trial of strength (10 March–24 April) which, again, Bevin won. He prevented, for the last time as a realistic possibility with American support, a punitive Soviet reparations regime on West Germany and the creation of a single demilitarised and neutral German state. Molotov helped, with his continued insistence on huge reparations, his opposition to lifting the cap on industrial production in the Ruhr and his insistence on a strong central government based in Berlin – in the middle of the Soviet zone – as part of a new German state, repudiating the power-sharing federalism of the Bevin Plan.

Bevin's big success in Moscow, of all places, was in striking up a good relationship with the new American Secretary of State. George Marshall initially found his British counterpart's aggression off-putting, but over the next six weeks, as he came to understand Bevin better and what he was up against in Stalin and Molotov, he became increasingly sympathetic and friendly.

Dubbed by Churchill 'the organiser of victory' as FDR and Truman's military chief of staff, Marshall was a military genius in the way that Bevin was a trade union genius. They forged a strong two-year partnership from 1947 to 1949, which became transformational with the launch of the Marshall Plan only a few weeks after the Moscow conference. It was all the more remarkable given that each had a precarious domestic base: Marshall was the fourth Secretary of State in just twenty-six months, serving an inexperienced US President apparently heading fast towards the electoral rocks. Meanwhile the situation in Attlee's government was barely stronger in 1947–48 as bankruptcy vied with exhaustion. Rarely have two foreign ministers risen further above the fray to do great constructive work.

Tellingly, after their first meeting, Bevin told Ivy Saunders that Marshall was 'quiet and firm and very direct with a voice and manner like Ashfield was ten years ago'.[48] This was the highest praise. Lord Ashfield was the British–American founder of what became today's Transport for London, with whom Bevin did deal after deal in the

1930s. Bevin and Marshall similarly did deal after deal in the late 1940s.

The three Western foreign ministers each had audiences with Stalin in Moscow outside the plenary sessions. Bevin spoke fairly bluntly to Stalin when he saw him in the Kremlin on the night of 24 March. 'I had a good talk, and understandings on many points,' he wrote the day after to Ivy Saunders.[49] He appreciated the sensation of dealing directly with Stalin. But never one to mistake words for deeds, he saw no thawing of Stalin's totalitarian ambitions in Europe and Bevin's policy changed not one iota after his last personal encounter with the Soviet dictator.

Crucially, Stalin made a wholly negative impression on Marshall, who delayed his night-time audience in the Kremlin until towards the end of the conference, 15 April, when he could see the cards on the table. The dictator was smoothly emollient ('These are only the first skirmishes and brushes of reconnaissance fire,' he told the American) but, after five weeks of Molotov, Marshall was unimpressed, particularly as the sessions of the conference the following week were the worst of all. Molotov proposed a big cut in American forces in Germany while leaving Russia's intact. Since the main issue Marshall had discussed with Stalin was the impasse on the demilitarisation of Germany, this convinced him that the Soviet dictator did not want a compromise but instead thought he could force the Americans out of Europe and take over Germany. He told Stalin bluntly that he 'had reached the conclusion that the Soviet Union did not want such a treaty [based on full demilitarisation in Germany] and would report accordingly to the President'.[50]

The breakthrough moment was a Bevin–Marshall meeting on 18 April 1947, after five weeks together and a week before the end of the summit. They had already met privately several times outside in the interminable plenary sessions, but crucially Marshall had by now met Stalin. He had also by now sized up the warring factions in his own delegation. Travelling with a bipartisan delegation in the wake of the Republican takeover of Congress, there were sharp divisions between John Foster Dulles, later Eisenhower's Secretary of State, who saw a fundamental battle with Stalinist communism that had to be won in Europe, and General Lucius Clay. Clay was the imperious governor of the American zone in Germany, who had been close to Byrnes and thought Germany – including West Germany – was ungovernable without agreement on joint institutions with the Russians. This co-existed with a jaundiced view of the British, particularly the Labour government's plans for public ownership in the Ruhr, which, Clay told Marshall, 'would not be acceptable to the American businessmen and bankers'.[51] He didn't spell out how having Stalin in control of the Ruhr would be an improvement on a few nationalised industries, a point Marshall quickly grasped, and Clay left Moscow early.

'The Soviet government were just fooling,' Marshall told Bevin in their 18 April meeting. 'The US was not going to humiliate herself by remaining in that position [of continuing to seek a German treaty with Stalin]. He was going to tell the President that he did not believe the Russians wanted Four Power Agreement.'[52] This was music to Bevin, and what he had been waiting to hear from a US Secretary of State for two years. He and Marshall resolved to press ahead with the bizone on the basis of practically the entire Bevin Plan, including two crucial advances: firstly, there would be only one political and administrative centre for the bizone, and secondly, the chairman of the bizone's executive committee would hold executive authority. This pointed the way to the creation of a fully-fledged West German government.

In parallel with these crucial discussions in Moscow, Bevin's diplomats in Washington paved the way for the Truman Doctrine, announced by the President to Congress on 12 March 1947. This was a breakthrough for what it said about 'the policy of the United States to support free peoples who are resisting attempted subjugation by armed minorities or by outside pressures'. But it was also significant because it went hand in hand with the US implementing this doctrine immediately on taking over from Britain in Greece and Turkey, in order to sustain their precarious governments under constant threat of communist coups.

In Greece, British action to prevent a communist coup in 1944 had been a key play by Churchill supported by Bevin, as we saw earlier. The significance of the US taking over from Britain in Greece and Turkey is brought out in Francis Williams's account of Bevin's diplomatic manoeuvres:

Bevin shrewdly assessing in his mind the current of American opinion and the cumulative effect upon it of Russian policy decided the time had come to force the American Administration to a major policy decision. On 24 February he instructed the British Ambassador in Washington to deliver to Mr. Marshall, the Secretary of State, a memorandum informing him that Britain's economic position would no longer allow her to continue as the reservoir of financial and military support for Greece and Turkey. The memorandum created a profound shock in the State Department. It faced the United States with a decision that it had so far been unwilling to meet. The first response was a strong telegram of protest from Marshall demanding to know whether this indicated a fundamental change in British policy. Bevin replied that it did not. He made it clear that the British view remained that freedom of Greece and Turkey, as also of Iran and Italy, from Russian domination was absolutely essential to Anglo-American and Western European security and to the stability of the Middle East. But Britain could no longer carry the burden alone. America must now be prepared to play her part.[53]

This overdoes the 'Bevin masterstroke' narrative but testifies to the growing American–British partnership in Europe.

From the end of April, back in Washington and London respectively, Marshall and Bevin set off a chain reaction that was to transform Western Europe and seal the containment of Stalin. The initiating move was Marshall's commencement address at Harvard University on 5 June, proposing American economic assistance to stabilise Europe. 'I need not tell you, gentlemen, that the world situation is very serious,' he told the Harvard students. He then set out pretty much the entire argument that Bevin had been making about Germany and Europe for the previous two years:

Recovery in Europe has been seriously retarded by the fact that two years after the close of hostilities a peace settlement with Germany and Austria has not been agreed upon ... The truth is that Europe's requirements for the next three or four years of foreign food and other essential products – principally from America – are so much greater than her present ability to pay that she must have substantial additional help or face economic, social, and political deterioration of a very grave character. The remedy lies in breaking the vicious circle ... the initiative, I think, must come from Europe.

It is what happened next that precipitated the chain reaction. Marshall had not informed Bevin of what he was going to say, and the Foreign Secretary only heard about the speech from the BBC news on his bedside wireless set. But he immediately grasped its potential to rally and rebuild Western Europe. At the Foreign Office the next morning he gathered his officials and, seizing on the words 'the initiative must come from Europe', he 'threw all his energy into conjuring up a European response of sufficient weight and urgency to give substance to Marshall's invited offer of American support'.[54]

Bevin had to seize on these words because that's all there was in early June. The 'Marshall Plan' was, as a State Department official put it as late as 28 July, 'a flying saucer – nobody knows what it looks like, how big it is, in what direction it is moving, or whether it really exists'.[55]

Bevin determined to convert the flying saucer into a concrete long-term US commitment to Britain and Western Europe. He immediately proposed a joint response to the French, the Italians, the Belgians and the Dutch and flew to Paris to lead it while sending strong personal messages of encouragement and support to Washington. 'Britain for eighteen years after Waterloo practically gave away her exports but this resulted in stability and a hundred years of peace,' he told the US deputy ambassador in London.[56] It was dubious history but excellent politics.

'The speech which Mr Marshall delivered at Harvard may well rank as one of the greatest in the world's history,' Bevin told London's Foreign Press Association on 13 June. 'When the United States

throws down a bridge to link east and west it is disastrous for ideological and for other reasons to frustrate the United States in that
great endeavour.' He addressed directly the concern that Britain
would not work in partnership with the rest of Western Europe.
'We are in fact, whether we like it or not, a European nation and
must act as such, as a link and bridge between Europe and the rest
of the world,' he told the assembled international journalists. It was
classic Bevin: realism and idealism jostling, never more so than in
this garbled yet crystal clear piece of Bevinese:

> We have been the first in the ring and the last out [in the First
> and Second World Wars]. Therefore it has been impossible to
> maintain our economic and financial position. But if anybody
> in the world has got it into his head that Britain is down and
> out, please get it out. We have our genius and science; we have
> our productivity, and although we have paid the price, I venture
> to prophesy that in a few years' time we shall have recovered our
> former prosperity.[57]

'The guiding principles that I shall follow in any talks on this will be
speed,' Bevin told the House of Commons on 19 June. 'I spent six
weeks in Moscow trying to get a settlement. I shall not be a party
to holding up the economic recovery of Europe by the finesse of
procedure. There is too much involved.'[58]

Soviet involvement in any American aid plan was an immediate
issue. Publicly, Bevin encouraged a positive response from Moscow,
but privately he was relieved when Stalin refused, following an
exceptionally truculent performance by Molotov, ending in a walk-
out, at the foreign ministers' meeting in Paris in late June to discuss

the response to Marshall. After Molotov's boycott, Bevin countered French moves to maintain dialogue with Moscow on the evolving plan. As he argued, Stalin's decision to impoverish Eastern Europe rather than accept American aid demonstrated why it was so essential in the first place. After the Paris meeting, Bevin moved swiftly to set up a bespoke West European organisation to plan and administer Marshall Aid with no Soviet involvement: what became the Organisation for European Economic Co-operation (today's OECD). He was anxious to avoid a role for the existing United Nations Economic Commission for Europe because of Soviet membership. Having closed the front door to Stalin, he wasn't going to admit him through the back door.

By leading Europe, forcing the pace and painting the big picture, Bevin rose to the level of Marshall's vision. As with his own plan of 22 October 1946 for a *de facto* West German state, Bevin leap-frogged the all too many issues dividing Europe, and Britain, from the US, to make the bold transformational response that produced Marshall Aid.

Until Marshall Aid, Bevin's fear was that France and Italy, in particular, were on the precipice of communism and that only what he called the 'outer crust' of Europe might be saved. Given the trend of elections and politics in Europe from the mid-to-late 1940s, this was no fantasy. As late as April 1948, a strong 'popular front' of communists and socialists was fighting the Italian elections, led by the socialist Pietro Nenni, with fellow-traveller support from the Labour left in England in the 'Nenni telegram', which was signed by thirty-seven Labour MPs. Bevin, fiercely opposed to popular fronts with the communists since the 1930s, supported the expulsion of the organiser – John Platts-Mills, a long-time campaigner for friendship with Stalin – from the Labour Party. It was only two months since the Stalinist coup in Czechoslovakia, which Bevin had earlier thought might be saved from Stalin. The Czech foreign minister colleague of Bevin's, Jan Masaryk, a liberal who survived the Stalinist coup of 25 February 1948 but not the subsequent purge, was found dead in the courtyard of the foreign ministry in Prague dressed only in pyjamas, having 'jumped out of a window'. It was said that 'Jan Masaryk was a very tidy man, such a tidy man that when he jumped he shut the window after himself.' Bevin had no hesitation spelling out what had happened and who was to blame. His first Foreign Office private secretary, Bob Dixon, had gone to Prague as ambassador in January 1948 and reported to him after the coup: 'The whole character of the state had been changed in less than a hundred hours.'[59]

The communists were kept out of government in Italy in 1948, helped by a socialist split over the formation of the Nenni Front with the communists, and by covert British and American support for De Gasperi's Christian Democrats. But the Nenni Front got 31 per cent and as late as 1951 the communists polled 26 per cent in French parliamentary elections. After Marshall Aid, though, the communists generally looked less attractive to working-class elec- torates in Western Europe; and after the creation of NATO, West Germany and the European Coal and Steel Community over the next three years, the prospect of Stalinist coups receded. And Stalin ended Stalinism by dying suddenly on 5 March 1953. But no one could have securely predicted any of this in the late 1940s.

Bevin shored up his domestic position after the 'failure' of the Moscow conference with his melodramatic 'stab in the back' speech to the Labour Party conference at Margate in May 1947, which

Dalton said 'swept away all opposition'. Left-wing MPs and intellectuals had 'stabbed me in the back', he declared, by undermining his foreign policy while he was negotiating in New York and Moscow. 'If you are to expect loyalty from Ministers, then Ministers however much they make mistakes have a right to expect loyalty in return. I grew up in the trade union movement, you see, and I have never been used to this sort of thing.'⁶⁰ The latter point was quite untrue, of course, but the trade unionists in the hall loved it.

The US Embassy in London reported to Washington on 11 June 1947, as Marshall and his deputy Dean Acheson weighed up how far to back Bevin's response to Marshall's speech: 'We believe that as matters now stand [with Bevin in post], Britain will be on our side in any serious issue.'⁶¹ This assessment was crucial to Truman and Marshall's decision to press ahead, despite the Byzantine difficulties of winning the support of the Republican Congress in the autumn of 1947. Bevin made an initial play for Britain to be regarded as a Marshall Aid recipient in its own right, not just as part of Europe, in order to secure a larger share without necessarily creating new European co-operation machinery. His argument was that Britain was Europe's only strong and reliably anti-Stalin democracy. This was true, but it was a pretty humiliating admission of Britain's economic plight, particularly as Truman demurred. Instead, Britain essentially became the lead European co-ordinator when the five-year $12 billion aid programme started in April 1948.

The details of Marshall Aid, and the sums involved, were always secondary in Bevin's mind to the fact that it turned into hard political and economic currency the concept of a 'Western Europe' of liberal democracy and rising prosperity, equipped to resist the allure of communism. The Marshall Plan for European aid and the Bevin

Plan for a West German state were two sides of the same coin, and both depended on seamless British and American action. As Bevin whispered to his private secretary during the opening of the Paris foreign ministers meeting to discuss Marshall Aid in late June, 'We are witnessing the birth of the western bloc.'[62]

A string of British–American agreements followed in the summer and autumn of 1947. The 'convertibility crisis' of July/August was resolved on 20 August, when Washington agreed to the suspension of the convertibility of pounds into dollars, which for a month had been draining Britain's foreign reserves at an alarming rate. A week later, Bevin agreed with Marshall to substantially increase the level of coal and steel production in the Ruhr, overriding strong objections from Bidault of France, who wanted less German steel and more German coal but only if the coal was for French consumption. There was also agreement that the Western zones of Germany would receive Marshall Aid because, as the Committee of European Economic Co-operation reported with strong British encouragement after the Paris summit, 'Other Western European countries cannot be prosperous as long as the economy of the Western Zone [of Germany] is paralysed, and a substantial increase of output there will be required if Europe is to become independent of outside support.'[63]

A critical issue, where Bevin and Bidault both compromised with the US in the summer of 1947, was on plans for coal and steel nationalisation in the Ruhr. This was a personal cause of Bevin's and symbolically important to Labour. But on 12 September he agreed with the US that in place of indefinite public ownership there would be a five year 'trusteeship' of the coal mines in the Ruhr, with ownership vested in the *Land* of North Rhine-Westphalia. After this, the elected *Land* government could, but not necessarily would, be allowed to decide how the mining industry was to be managed in the future. Bevin agreed this convoluted formula with reluctance. The French did not like it either, fearing it would give too much power to the Germans. It ignited Jean Monnet's seminal thinking on a West European political union, which became official French policy and led to the European Coal and Steel Community as the first step on the road towards today's European Union. But the short-term imperative to secure American goodwill persuaded Bevin to drop mandatory nationalisation. The biggest American concern about the West German bizone was now resolved.

Bevin was now making little pretence of a shared project with Stalin, or of any desire for substantive four-power negotiations for the united Germany presaged at Potsdam. But he did not want a complete diplomatic breakdown with Molotov, which would only heighten tensions further and antagonise the left in Britain and across Western Europe. He handled the second Council of Foreign Ministers meeting of 1947, held in London in November and December, accordingly. As he explained to Bidault beforehand: 'At Moscow [in March/April] he had not been entirely certain of public opinion at home. Since then the [Labour] party meeting at Margate and the TUC conference had shown that the country were squarely behind him. People in this country realised what the Russian game was.' Marshall told Bevin on 4 December that American public opinion 'was now baying for blood' and he could 'break off and tell the Russians to go to the devil'.[64] This for the first time put him on the hawkish side of Bevin, who lapped it up while agreeing with Marshall not to bring the London conference to an actual breakdown.

Before the conference opened, Bevin and Molotov had a no-holds-barred confrontation in the Foreign Secretary's residence in

Carlton Gardens. It was vintage Bevin, at least in his retelling of it to the diplomat and diarist Harold Nicolson at a Buckingham Palace reception soon afterwards:

'Mr Molotov, what is it that you want? What are you after? Do you want to get Austria behind your iron curtain? You can't do that. Do you want Turkey and the Straits? You can't have them. Do you want Korea? You can't have that. You are putting your neck out too far and one day you will have it chopped off. You are playing a very dangerous game. If war comes between you and America in the west, then we shall be on America's side. Make no mistake about that. That would be the end of Russia and of your revolution. What do you want?'

'I want a united Germany,' said Molotov.

'Why do you want that? Do you really believe that a unified Germany would go communist? They would say all the right things and repeat all the correct formulas. But in their hearts they would be longing for the day when they would revenge their defeat at Stalingrad. You know that as well as I do.'

'Yes,' said Molotov. 'I know that but I want a united Germany.'[65]

But a united Germany under Soviet tutelage is precisely what Molotov did not get. He and Stalin were never going to get it from Bevin without a war. And not, by now, from the Americans either.

The bizone was now functioning and work was underway on a new West German currency, which was to be another crucial underpinning of the new West German state. The launch of the Deutschmark on 20 June 1948 has gone down in history as the work of Ludwig Erhard, West Germany's founding economic minister, but it was largely the work of British technical experts over the previous two years. Equally vital was the promotion of capable, untainted political leaders for the new West German parliament and government. By late 1947, two leaders were establishing themselves as authentic West German leaders, both of them from the British zone. Konrad Adenauer, the pre-1933 Mayor of Cologne, became leader of a Catholic centre-right alliance, the Christian Democratic Union, while Kurt Schumacher, a pre-1933 Social Democratic Party (SPD) leader based in Hanover after 1945, became leader of an SPD that embraced all the Western zones and West Berlin, refusing to 'fuse' with the communists as in East Germany and East Berlin.

Neither Adenauer nor Schumacher had easy relations with the British authorities. They were tough, seasoned politicians who had survived Hitler without compromising themselves, which maybe explains why they were to be so successful in guiding the new West German state after 1949. Adenauer was even briefly banned as Mayor of Cologne in December 1945 after falling out with a British general, which he wore as a badge of honour. Governor Robertson and his team made the relationship work thereafter, and in 1948 Adenauer was elected chairman of the new bizonal executive committee, making him *de facto* leader of the emerging West German state. He went on to be elected founding Chancellor of the Federal Republic at its inauguration on 15 September 1949. Bevin did not seek to influence the election to make a social democrat the first Chancellor. The Attlee and Truman administration supported the new West German government thereafter, not exercising most of the reserve powers they continued to hold. It was a supreme act of democratic statecraft.

'Our task was to save western civilisation.' Bevin, 1948. © *Daily Mail*

To bring it about Bevin had to work hard to secure French consent, first to put the French zone into the new amalgamated Western zones, and then to agree the Federal Republic, which was ultimately approved by the French National Assembly by a majority of only six votes. 'Our task was to save western civilisation,' Bevin told Bidault in early 1948. 'He [Bevin] himself felt that we should have to come to some sort of federation in Western Europe whether of a formal or informal character. As an Englishman, he hoped it would not be necessary to have formal constitutions. Everything should be flexible, but we should act quickly.'[66] This appeal to 'saving western civilisation' while 'acting quickly' is the essence of Bevin at his most masterly. He understood that unless the West became a cause it was nothing, and its rallying cries were freedom, democracy and prosperity. Hence his support for the Council of Europe, established in

1949 with Churchill in the vanguard, despite his opposition to fed-eral arrangements for Europe.

All this took place as relations with Stalin plunged from acute tension to deep crisis. In September 1947, Cominform, the 'Infor-mation Bureau of the Communist and Workers Parties', was formed from Moscow to unite Stalin's Eastern bloc, amid vitriolic attacks on Western socialist leaders, including Bevin and Attlee who were 'attempting to cover up the rapacious essence of imperialist policy under a mask of democracy'. Bevin replied in kind. 'The free nations of western Europe must now draw together,' he told the House of Commons in January 1948. 'We shall not be diverted by tyrants, propaganda or fifth-column methods from our aim of uniting by trade, social, cultural and all other contacts of these nations of Europe and the world who are ready to cooperate.'[67]

'We shall not be diverted by tyrants, propaganda or fifth-column methods…'
Bevin, 1948, here with Robert Schuman and George Marshall. © *Daily Mail*

On 20 March 1948 Berlin's three-power control council collapsed. Stalin withdrew on the pretext that the introduction of the Deutschmark was undermining the unity of Berlin. On 24 June he blockaded the Western zones of Berlin, which were deep inside the Soviet zone of East Germany and entirely surrounded by it. He also cut off the supply of electricity from East Berlin. This was a bold play by Stalin to expel both Britain and America from Berlin, to take over the entire city and maybe stop the creation of a West German state. His gamble was that Britain and the US would sooner abandon Berlin than undertake the almighty struggle and expense required to maintain their zones, risking another European war. He sensed rightly that unless he evicted the Americans from Western Europe quickly, before they took up permanent residence, he and his communist puppets would be permanently shut out. A thriving democratic West Berlin in the heart of East Germany and Soviet-controlled Eastern Europe was an existential threat to his whole project, so he judged the blockade a risk worth taking.

But Bevin and Marshall never flinched from the moment Russia closed West Berlin's surrounding land borders. They were adamant that Berlin had to be kept – and kept open to the West. In a renewed D-Day spirit, British and American forces worked as one, sustaining a dramatic eleven-month airlift of food, fuel and people. It was heroism, risk and mission to match the greatest moments in history. Up to 7,000 tons of goods were flown into West Berlin every day for 323 days to supply the 2 million inhabitants. Bevin and Attlee's key decision, to allow the US to station in Britain B-29 bombers that were capable of carrying atomic weapons, convinced Stalin of the British–American determination to stay in Berlin. After weeks when the world held its breath, Stalin did not interfere with the airlift and did not escalate to war.

The siege of Berlin was lifted on 12 May 1949, the highpoint and vindication of Bevin's resistance to Stalin.

The Berlin blockade accelerated progress towards a permanent transatlantic military alliance. The North Atlantic Treaty setting up NATO, signed by Bevin in Washington on 4 April 1949, was a phenomenal negotiating achievement. It began as a serious project when Bevin appealed to Marshall on 11 March 1948, a fortnight after the Stalinist coup in Prague, for the British and US governments 'to consult without delay' on establishing a transatlantic security pact. Marshall immediately replied, after consulting Truman: 'Please inform Mr Bevin that in accordance with your aide memoire of 11 March we are prepared to proceed at once in the joint discussions on the establishment of an Atlantic security system.'[68]

American willingness to commit to the defence of Europe in time of peace 'marked a revolutionary step in US policy', said Oliver Franks, sent to Washington as British ambassador after successfully executing the negotiations for the Marshall Plan. Franks also negotiated the 1951 agreement by which US military bases became permanent in the UK. Bevin's objective throughout was to create not just reciprocal transatlantic defence and security commitments, but also an institution that would promote lasting solidarity and a real community of interest between leaders and peoples on both sides of the Atlantic. Hence NATO, with the emphasis on the last word: 'Organisation'. This included a parliamentary assembly drawn from all the member states. 'If only I'd had time to make the Atlantic Pac … into something large, into a wider organism, with a budget and other things for the whole area,' he told Nico Henderson in his last conversation as Foreign Secretary, six weeks before his death. But he did pretty well. Seventy years later the 'organism' is alive and well.

It now has thirty members: North Macedonia is the latest country to join, in 2020, in one of the most disputed and unstable regions of Europe in 1945, which had caused Churchill and Bevin so much grief after 1944.[69]

The road to NATO included both the Berlin blockade and the Brussels Pact between Britain, France and the Benelux states, signed just a month before the NATO treaty, in March 1949. The Brussels Pact was itself an enlargement of Bevin's Anglo-French Dunkirk Treaty of March 1947, a binding mutual defence commitment, so it was the piecing together of a jigsaw. Vital too was Attlee and Bevin's decision to commit to the Korean War in June 1950, which for all the trauma it caused in sending British troops, demonstrated to the US, in the fraught end-game of Stalinism, that Britain would stand by the United States as well as *vice versa*. In this crucial and intense period of British–American collaboration, as the only two global democratic powers, it was a genuine 'special relationship', however misused the term later became. The new partnership extended to agreement on the devaluation of sterling and further economic support for Britain in September 1949, negotiated by Bevin and Cripps together in Washington in an atmosphere far warmer than for Keynes's loan negotiations of 1945.

This Anglo-American co-operation was enhanced by Bevin's exceptionally close rapport with Dean Acheson, who took over from George Marshall as Secretary of State on 21 January 1949. Acheson had been Marshall's deputy and served in previous foreign policy roles for Roosevelt and Truman dating back to 1941. In 1949, a large part of which they spent in each other's company at long summits in Washington, New York, London and Paris, he and Bevin were almost telepathic, building on four years of shared endeavour and discussion of the Soviet menace dating back to the days of Jimmy Byrnes, whom Acheson had distrusted from the start. It was an uncle–nephew relationship, but with the nephew holding the cheque book. Bevin took to calling Acheson 'me boy'. After one particularly obscure Bevin intervention in the crucial North Atlantic summit of September 1949, where Bevin couldn't quite bring himself to endorse German rearmament, Acheson suavely remarked: 'If Mr Bevin means what I think he means but not what he said, we are in agreement.'[70]

Of all Bevin's achievements, the greatest was the one about which he was most reticent: the creation of the Federal Republic of Germany. Here with Schuman and Acheson. © *Daily Mail*

Of all Bevin's achievements in his life, the greatest was the one about which he was most reticent: the creation of the Federal Republic of Germany. His goal throughout was to stop Stalin dominating

Europe and undermining Western democracy; for Germany itself he had no love. 'I tries 'ard, Brian,' he told General Robertson, Governor of the British zone, 'but I 'ates them.'[71]

Throughout these six turbulent years, which focused so much on the future of Germany at the heart of post-war Europe, Bevin only went there once, apart from the Potsdam conference, and that was to Berlin to show solidarity with British troops in the struggle against Stalin during the 1949 blockade. He only met Adenauer once. The new German Chancellor took great offence when, in 1950, Bevin blurted out in the House of Commons that 'the Hitler revolution did not change the German character very much. It expressed it.' When Churchill protested, it led to some telling Bevinese: 'I had to deal with them as well as the right honourable Gentleman, as employers, and in shipping, and in many other things where I got into close contact with these gentleman.'[72] Everything came back to the Transport and General Workers' Union.

But Adenauer respected Bevin. When, again in 1950, Bevin intimated that he wanted to speak to the Ruhr miners, the Chancellor responded with an invitation to address the *Bundestag*, the first foreign visitor to be accorded this honour. Bevin was by now too ill to accept.

As for Stalin, he outlived Bevin by just two years. And he kept out of Western Europe.

Bevin won; Stalin lost.

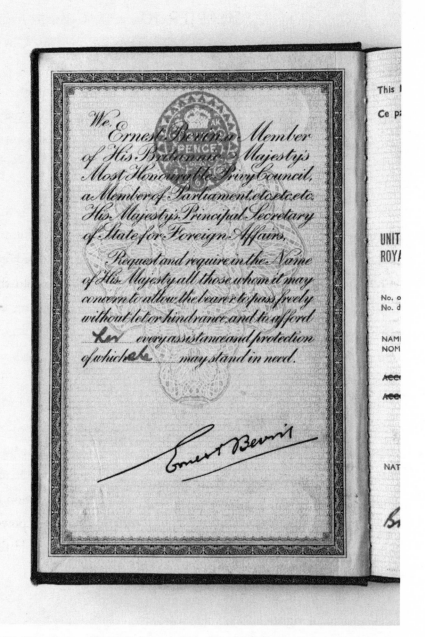

'We, Ernest Bevin ... His Majesty's Principal Secretary of State for Foreign Affairs, Request and require...' Symbolically for the imperialist in him, which believed Britain could still 'request and require' globally, Bevin was the last Foreign Secretary to issue passports in his own name.

CHAPTER 10

FAILURES

'We will have to form a government at the centre of a great Empire and Commonwealth of Nations,' Bevin told the 1945 Labour Party conference.'[1] And he didn't intend to give it up. By the end of the war he was an unreconstructed imperialist, which led to his greatest failures as Foreign Secretary, particularly on Israel/Palestine and the failure to engage with the initiation of the European Union.

Maybe Bevin's failures were the obverse of his successes and inseparable from them. The view that 'I'm not going to have Britain barged about' gave him the indomitable will to resist Stalin and build a welfare state. But it went hand in hand with an assertion of the Empire as the continuing fulcrum of Britain's post-war power and prosperity. Maybe it was akin to Churchill, who fought Hitler with as much passion and certainty as he resisted Indian and Iraqi independence and the General Strike; or LBJ, who fought so ruthlessly for civil rights and so desperately too in Vietnam; or Tony Blair, whose missionary liberalism secured democracy in Northern Ireland and Kosovo and sought to do so too with George Bush in Iraq. Political leaders, like all human beings, come as a job lot.

Whatever his motivation and psychology, Bevin's rejection of European unity and his equation of British security, prosperity and values with a resolute post-war defence of imperial power, or as much of it as could be maintained without excessive opprobrium, established a post-war mindset that dominated British politics for the next decade until the Suez crisis. Its influence persists today. Dean Acheson's jibe of 1962, that 'Great Britain has lost an empire and has not yet found a role', dates back, fundamentally, to Attlee and Bevin.

On decolonisation, the Attlee government made one bold move: Indian independence in 1947. However difficult and bloody to implement, Attlee did quickly what otherwise would inevitably have been done slowly and with greater trauma. Indian independence substantially delegitimised the rest of the Empire. But, largely because of Bevin, it did not lead to equally bold decolonisation elsewhere.

During the war Churchill put a veto on Indian independence and Bevin supported him. The Minister of Labour thought 'politically minded' Indians could be 'sidetracked by just paying no heed to them', while, with rising living standards, 'the Indian peoples as a whole would not trouble their heads about political development'. In the post-war government, Indian independence was the one notable case of Bevin criticising Attlee directly. 'We are throwing away the Empire because of one man's pessimism,' he said in Cabinet when Attlee proposed, on 31 December 1946, to set an early departure date. Dismissing the capacity of India for self-government, he opposed 'scuttle without dignity or plan' and even talked of sending a new British army to India, made up of the recently demobilised. 'We knuckle under a first blow,' he wrote to Attlee, accusing him of defeatism. This irked Attlee, who replied robustly: 'I am not defeatist but realist. If you disagree with what is proposed, you must offer a practical alternative. I fail to find one in your letter.' After meeting Bevin, Lord Wavell, the Viceroy of India, concluded that he and other Labour ministers 'were in reality imperialists and dislike any idea of leaving India'.[2]

Far from proposing to scale back the British Empire after 1945, one of Bevin's first acts as Foreign Secretary was to seek to take over Libya and Italy's other former colonies in North Africa, on the argument that 'they flank our main line of Imperial communication by sea and air to India, Australia and New Zealand through the Mediterranean and the Red Sea and provide bases from which Egypt, the Sudan and Kenya would be attacked'. As imperial historian William Roger Louis puts it: 'These were words that could have been written just as well by Lord Curzon in 1919,' and Bevin's imperial policy thereafter 'more often than not' pitted Britain against nationalist forces in league with 'the forces of reaction'.[3]

Bevin's imperialism went back to 1929 when he became a member of a new Colonial Development Advisory Committee. This soon had him championing imperial development as the 'socialist' alternative to decolonisation. Two years later, after the 1931 crisis and the introduction of trade tariffs in conjunction with 'imperial preference', he came to regard this set-up as better and more viable than the French foreign minister Aristide Briand's plan of 1929 for a European customs union developing into a broader political and economic union. This is despite the fact that he himself had championed such a plan at the 1927 TUC conference and it was pretty much the plan taken forward by France, Germany, Italy and Benelux in launching the European Coal and Steel Community (ECSC), precursor to today's European Union, in the last year of Bevin's foreign secretaryship.

In 1927 Bevin called for 'a policy having for its object the creation of a European public opinion in favour of Europe becoming an economic entity'. He declared,

> I have recently been to the continent of America. I found there were 130,000,000 people within one economic entity, with no tariffs, with a mobility among the people to move about without the boundary handicaps that apply in Europe. I found a frontier three thousand miles long without a gun, with commerce passing to and fro pretty freely, and I came to the conclusion that if we are to deal with the problems of Europe we have got to try and teach the people of Europe that their economic interests, their economic development have to transcend merely national boundaries. I am a little bit of a dreamer: I think it is necessary.
>
> The labour movement should carry on a great educational work in the way of promoting the development of all forms of national culture, and yet trying at the same time to inculcate the spirit of a United States of Europe – at least on an economic basis, even if we cannot on a totally political basis.[4]

This stands comparison with Churchill's Zurich speech of 1946 calling for 'a kind of United States of Europe'.

Of course, there could be no customs or economic union including Germany and Italy in the 1930s. But Bevin's view did not change after 1945. He saw Europe's continuing travails as ruling out a postwar European customs union, just as he saw the continuation of Empire as inevitable and essential even after Indian independence. It was partly a matter of conviction, partly realpolitik. This imperial realpolitik was soon less tenable than the European alternative it claimed was unrealistic, but in the late 1940s you could read the future of Europe and of the non-Indian Empire two ways, and Bevin stuck to the book of the past. He did so, too, in his support for the reimposition of French colonial power in Vietnam and of Dutch colonial power in Indonesia, both of which involved Britain in ugly military engagements.

'Ernest Bevin, the Somerset labourer's boy risen to be foreign secretary, turned out to be almost as much of an imperialist as Churchill,' writes historian Simon Schama:

It was almost uncanny how exactly the map of Middle Eastern oil reserves resembled the old Disraeli-ite map of strategic links between the Mediterranean and India; and how ardent Bevin was to keep that map red or at least pinkish. Bases were built or consolidated along the Persian Gulf and round the southwestern tip of the Arabian peninsula from Iraq to Aden...

The far-flung stations of Bevin's empire, to be sure, were called things like the Overseas Food Corporation and the Colonial Development Corporation but it was designed to finance the British economy in ways that did not look all that different from its nineteenth-century predecessors. The flow of crucial raw materials, now including oil of all sorts – palm from West Africa, ground nuts from East Africa, petroleum from the Gulf and Iran – would be guaranteed in return for the blessings of receiving Morris Minors; Sanderson's wallpaper; Liberty soft furnishings; sterling payment accounts; an aircraft fleet, humming with Rolls-Royce engines, on which countries could paint their 'flagship' colours; for the sheikh a Bentley, also humming with a Rolls-Royce engine; a visit from Yehudi Menuhin, courtesy of the British Council; and good seats at the coronation in 1953.[5]

Far from making him less imperialist, Indian independence simply led Bevin to regroup. He now asserted that India was the exception which proved the imperial rule because of its unusually politicised culture, and that the Middle East and Africa could, with a will, be conditioned to become the heart of a refashioned British Empire. Middle Eastern oil was one element, African minerals another. So was the maintenance of troops and bases in most of the forty countries where they had been present when Labour came to power in 1945, sustained by the controversial and unpopular decision in 1947 to continue indefinitely with military conscription ('national service') for the first time in British peacetime history, in order to sustain the largest army in British peacetime history.

The continuation of conscription led to the biggest backbench revolt of the Attlee government: 148 Labour MPs voted against or abstained. Bevin and the chiefs of staff, led by Montgomery, had been adamant on eighteen months' conscription as necessary to maintain British forces in the Mediterranean and the Middle East. Attlee was sceptical about such extensive military commitments, particularly in Egypt and the Middle East, and he used the revolt, and Bevin's absence at the Council of Foreign Ministers in Moscow, to reduce the term from eighteen months to twelve. As a historian of the incident puts it, 'The alacrity with which Attlee responded to parliamentary criticism suggests that he saw an opportunity to weaken the opposition of the chiefs of staff ... and to bring down the cost of conscription.'[6] However, Attlee supported Bevin on the need for conscription to maintain Britain's broad imperial reach.

Among the generation coming of age in post-war Britain, the Attlee government was remembered more for national service than for the National Health Service. At its end in 1951, the Labour government was spending more than twice as much on defence as on the NHS. This wasn't only because of the Korean War and the defence of Germany; it was also the cost of refusing to scale back the British Empire in Egypt, the Middle East, the Mediterranean and the Far East, which, with skill, could have been done without weakening the defence of Europe or the transatlantic security alliance.

Why did Indian independence not jolt Attlee and Bevin? Particularly followed as it was in the space of one year by the chaotic abdication of responsibility for Palestine, the Malayan uprising, Smuts losing the South African election to D. F. Malan, the progenitor of apartheid, and the treaty leading to Ireland becoming a Republic and leaving the Commonwealth in 1949? The Irish treaty was signed by Attlee himself while on holiday in Dublin in August 1948. 'I signed a treaty while the family shopped,' was his typically laconic remark on this fundamental reconstitution of the United Kingdom and its Empire.[7]

My best explanation is that the defensive imperialism of the late 1940s, for all its immediate crises and long-term failure, was at the time just about sustainable except in India, and that Bevin and Attlee, Victorians both, couldn't conceive a viable alternative. They also didn't want to be seen as unpatriotic, and empire and patriotism were then very much the same thing. Bevin was notably more gung-ho than Attlee, but the difference was of degree not kind. History rarely proceeds in straight lines, and the imperial calculus strengthened in one key respect after Indian independence in 1947: the rise of anti-communism. This gave a new rationale for resisting independence movements and brought the Truman administration not only to support but to urge British resistance to supposedly 'communist' nationalist movements everywhere from Malaya and Indonesia to Iran, Egypt and Cyprus.

'Development' to boost the lot of the colonial poor was a Bevin shibboleth, and how he reconciled imperialism and socialism. He appears to have believed in it, not just said it, unlike Dalton who, when offered the Colonial Office by Attlee after the 1950 election, recoiled with horror: 'I had a horrid vision of pullulating, poverty-stricken, diseased n***** communities, for whom we can do nothing in the short run, and who the more one tries to help them, are querulous and ungrateful,' he wrote in his diary. Instead, he took the Ministry of Town and Country Planning. Bevin had higher ideals, but his primary goal was transparently empire not equity. If Africa's mineral wealth was developed, Bevin told the Cabinet in March 1948, 'We could have the US dependent on us and eating out of our hand in four or five years.'[8]

The imperial grandeur of the Foreign Office, and the vibes of global power emanating from the Foreign Secretary's vast ornate office overlooking St James's Park, certainly impressed themselves on Bevin. He joked that he only kept the huge portrait of King George III over the fireplace as a mark of gratitude to that unwise monarch for freeing the American colonies to fight with Britain after 1941, but he undoubtedly felt spiritual continuity with the 'great' imperial Foreign Secretaries who had gone before. By 1950 he was referring to 'Old Palmerston' and 'Old Salisbury', and quoting their dispatches, as if they were friends and fellow pioneers.[9]

Attlee and Bevin set store by the newly formed British Commonwealth. They thought this new club of colonies, plus the white 'dominions' of Canada, Australia, New Zealand and South Africa and the newly independent republics led by India, would be a significant political and economic bloc. In the context of a continuing sterling area, and Commonwealth trade still accounting in the late 1940s for nearly half of British trade, this was plausible. The magic of royalty was sprinkled liberally by King George VI, who was given the title Head of the Commonwealth in 1949 and engaged himself and his daughter Princess Elizabeth in extensive imperial tours. She was on one such tour when the King died in February 1952, ten months after Bevin. Alan Bullock writes that India's membership of the Commonwealth after independence 'made a great impression on Bevin as well as Attlee' and 'strengthened their belief in a continuing world role for Britain as the leader of a multi-racial Commonwealth of self-governing nations, with major consequences for British foreign policy vis-à-vis Europe and the USA'.[10]

However, the major consequences turned out to be delusion and complacency. The worst effects came after Bevin's death with the Suez catastrophe of 1956, which exposed and accelerated the disintegration of the Commonwealth as a serious bloc. Attlee was all along more sceptical than Bevin about sustaining the Empire in the Mediterranean and the Middle East; he thought it was a losing game, particularly in Egypt, where, as in India, nationalism was strong and the cost of maintaining imperial forces in such a large country debilitating. But as late as 1960, by which time West Germany was fast overtaking Britain economically, he delivered an Oxford lecture series on 'Empire into Commonwealth' which lauded its continuing vitality. 'There have been many great Empires in the history of the world that have fallen,' Attlee began, but 'there is only one Empire where the majority of the people liberated have continued in political association with their former rulers'. The quality of his argument about the 'very real family feeling' and economic power of the Commonwealth is summed up by his paean in praise of cricket:

The game of cricket is confined to the Commonwealth, and with the exception of Canada, where climate stands in the way, it is played with enormous enthusiasm in India, Pakistan, the West Indies, South Africa, Australia and New Zealand. Everywhere this very distinctive British game evokes enthusiasm. Perhaps this last point may serve to emphasise the very peculiar character of the British Commonwealth of Nations; perhaps also it illustrates the difficulty to the foreigner of understanding its nature.[11]

Alas, by 1960 cricket could not sustain the British economy or Britain's place in the world.

TWO COOKS ARE BETTER THAN ONE.
"Remember my future as a chef is involved."

On Palestine he was both stubborn and provocative. © *Punch Magazine*

In 1945 the position was nowhere near so clear and Bevin could and did plead realpolitik. Even at the time, however, realpolitik was never less realistic than in his policy on Palestine, which led to the precise opposite of its declared intention of stability and the peaceful co-existence of the Jewish and Palestinian communities within one state at peace with its neighbours. Instead, Bevin's legacy was a Jewish state of Israel, much larger than even most of its advocates previously favoured, in periodic war and perpetual tension with both its native Palestinians and its Arab neighbours. The démarche came in May 1948, after three years of failing to negotiate a settlement between Jewish and Palestinian Arab leaders on no clear principle besides maintaining British imperial power in the Middle East, in the face of popular uprisings and stark unreconciled differences with the United States.

Imperialism was at the heart of Bevin's policy on Palestine from the outset. As late as February 1947, when the partition of Palestine to create a Jewish state looked unavoidable, he was still warning the Cabinet that this course would 'contribute to the elimination of British influence from the whole of the vast Moslem area lying between Greece and India. This would not only have strategic consequences it would also jeopardise the security of our interests in the increasingly important oil production of the Middle East.'[12] Roy Jenkins, generally an admirer of Bevin, was damning:

> On Palestine he was both stubborn and provocative. He believed that British influence in the Arab world was of great importance both to the security of the Commonwealth and to our standard of living. But by the time he was responsible the Balfour Declaration was a thirty-year-old fact. He always claimed to be a

great man for dealing with 'facts'. This fact he tried to ignore. And he showed a lack of imagination in his failure to appreciate the force of the Jewish determination to establish a state in Palestine. Furthermore, to put it at its lowest, he allowed his handling of the Palestine question, a difficult but peripheral issue, gravely to endanger his central policy objective of good relations with the United States. This at the very least showed a lack of proportion.[13]

Why did Bevin get Israel/Palestine so wrong? In the first place, because, during the three key years 1945–48, he did not agree that his central policy objective was 'good relations with the United States'. His central objective, rather, was to sustain British power. Only with the Berlin blockade, starting in June 1948 – a month after Britain left Jerusalem – did he come to regard British power as absolutely inseparable from American foreign policy, partly because of the military emergency in Berlin and partly because US policy on Stalin and Europe had by then shifted substantially in his direction. Before 1948, as we have seen, resistance to Stalin, a core Bevin–British interest from the start, set him frequently and seriously at odds with Truman.

On Israel/Palestine, Bevin's view on taking office in July 1945, shared initially by a large part of the political and imperial establishment, was that Britain could and should retain suzerainty and continuing control by forging an agreement on local self-government acceptable to Palestine's existing Jewish and Arab communities. Even in 1945, the Attlee government's opposition to large-scale Jewish immigration looked simply wrong to many observers and put Britain publicly at odds with the US. But with 100,000 British troops and the full apparatus of imperial rule still present in Palestine, the policy was just about sustainable for around a year until the 'facts' of pressure for large-scale Jewish immigration and a Jewish state became almost irresistible.

Both in retrospect, and to many observers at the time, the right and viable course by mid-1946 was for Britain to broker or simply announce a partition and the creation of two states in Palestine, with as much United Nations and American support as possible to enforce it. And to permit unlimited Jewish immigration to the new Jewish state.

Before Hitler came to power, Jewish immigration to Palestine was running at below 10,000 a year. It rose dramatically after 1933, not only from Germany but from across mainland Europe, including Poland. Britain permitted this under pressure, and in 1936 a Palestinian Arab uprising, fiercely anti-Jewish as well as anti-British, was quelled with difficulty and serious bloodshed. A subsequent commission of inquiry under Lord Peel recommended partition. After the war, pressure for substantial Jewish immigration became overwhelming, both due to the legacy of the Holocaust and because of Truman, who backed large-scale Jewish immigration into Palestine. Before the 1945 election Labour had been supportive too: a party policy declaration of 1944 declared that there should henceforth be no such thing as a 'Jewish illegal immigrant'.[14]

Palestinian Arab demands for self-government were also escalating, in line with Arab demands in the other Western 'mandate' colonies of Syria, Lebanon, Iraq and Jordan, the last two also ruled by Britain. The MacDonald/Baldwin government gave quasi-independence to Iraq in 1932, extended to Jordan by Attlee and Bevin in 1946, where the newly installed King Abdullah I, brother of King Faisal of Iraq, traded subservience for independence. There are lots of pictures of Bevin and King Abdullah conferring over tea and smiles in expensive London hotels.

'If I don't get a settlement I'll eat my hat,' Bevin told Dalton in late 1945.[15] But he didn't get a settlement, and at the same time as the government was yielding decisively to the 'facts' in India, Bevin would accept neither the April 1946 recommendations of the Anglo-American commission in favour of 100,000 Jewish immigrants being allowed into Palestine, nor the UN vote for the partition of Palestine in November 1947. Yet he had no viable alternative to either policy. All the while there was an escalating catalogue of violence, grief and diplomatic humiliation, including the lynching of British soldiers from lamp posts and the bombing, on 22 July 1946, of the King David Hotel in Jerusalem, headquarters of the British administration in Palestine, which killed ninety-one people.

After the United Nations vote for partition, the government simply announced on 11 December 1947 that, rather than acquiesce in a Jewish state, Britain would hand back the Palestine mandate to the UN. This happened on 14 May 1948. David Ben-Gurion, the Jewish militia leader who was to become Israel's first Prime Minister and Minister of Defence, announced the formation of the state of Israel on the same day and made it a fact over the following months by winning a succession of conflicts with Israel's Arab neighbours. It was the greatest failure of Bevin's career.

Bevin's key decisions on Palestine were endorsed by Attlee, who at no point, including the rejection of Jewish immigration and partition, suggested a different course. The only difference between them was that Attlee's trenchantly anti-Jewish remarks were kept in private. So the question must be asked whether, in acting thus, they were motivated partly by antisemitism.

'One of the great tragedies of the world has been the persecution of the Jews,' Bevin told the 1937 TUC conference.[16] He had Jewish friends, he lived in Golders Green for a decade before the war and he did not manifest a personal dislike of individual Jews beyond his ability to take strongly against critics of any race and party and play the man as well as the ball.

However, neither Bevin nor Attlee showed much sympathy for the Jewish plight after 1945. 'The Jews are a religion, not a race or a nation,' they both said repeatedly, and they sought to drastically curb post-war Jewish immigration to Palestine. 'Illegal' immigrants were interned in Cyprus. In the shocking SS *Exodus* incident of July 1947, they insisted on returning a Jewish refugee ship to France, where the passengers refused to disembark. They ended up in Hamburg, from where they were taken to a prisoner-of-war camp. The images of the refugees behind barbed wire were reminiscent of the concentration camps and shocked international opinion.[17]

Bevin and Attlee were also into tropes about Jews and money. 'It is a game of Shylock versus the people, with Shylock getting the pound of flesh every time,' Bevin told the 1931 TUC conference about the financial crisis. When Bevin, returning from the Council of Foreign Ministers in New York in December 1946, complained about the intense criticism he had faced from Zionists, Attlee reported Bevin's anger in a letter to his brother. 'It appears that Zionism has become a profitable racket over there.' A Zionist, Bevin had told him, 'is defined as a Jew who collects money from another Jew to send to another Jew in Palestine', with the collector taking a good percentage.[18]

More importantly for policy on Palestine, Bevin believed Jews did not do enough to integrate and had themselves partly to blame for antisemitism. He wrote thus to the German-Jewish writer Emil Ludwig in 1938:

I have continually observed how easily, even in a country like this, anti-Semitic feeling is stirred up.

What does worry me, and a good many of my friends who have fought against the anti-Semitic feelings, is the difficulty that we have often been placed in due to what appears a lack of appreciation on the part of the Jew to appreciate the freedom in the country where he enjoys it. I am not referring to the 'working Jew' but chiefly to the 'nouveau Riche' or moneyed person, and even many of the cultural classes.[19]

This passage was omitted by Bullock from his discussion of Bevin's attitude to Jews in his official biography, although he quoted another part of the letter which set out a novel argument that 'the great colonial empires of Europe should pool their colonial territories', which might, among other things, improve the 'German national character'. However, it is crucial for it is not an isolated expression of Bevin's view that Jews court victim status and should do more to integrate into their host societies, implying there would then be no need for a Jewish state. He repeated this in a press conference in 1946: 'I am very anxious that Jews shall not in Europe over-emphasise their racial position. If the Jews, with all their sufferings, want to get too much to the head of the queue, you have the danger of another antisemitic reaction through it all.' And in his June 1946 Labour Party conference speech he said of American enthusiasm for Jewish immigration into Palestine: 'I hope it will not be misunderstood in America if I say that this was proposed with the purest of motives: they do not want too many Jews in New York.' Comments like these shocked Bevin's contemporaries, even those uttering casually antisemitic remarks that then abounded. In protest New York's dockers to refuse to handle his luggage when he arrived there later in the year.[20]

Only by ignoring such statements, and by claiming that many other public figures thought similarly, could Bullock reach this convoluted conclusion about Bevin not being antisemitic on Israel/ Palestine:

> The answer, I suggest, is not that Bevin or Attlee any more than George Hall and Arthur Creech-Jones (the two Colonial Secretaries) or Morrison (as Chairman of the Cabinet's Palestine Committee) were moved by hatred of the Jews or anti-Semitism, but that the British alone among the Western nations, because they were responsible for the government of Palestine as the Mandatory power, could not ignore the political consequences of the Zionists' demand to create a Jewish state there and the bitter opposition to it, already expressed in the Arab revolt before the war, of the majority of the population.[21]

Simply stated, Bullock is arguing that many responsible Brits at the time believed that a Jewish state in Palestine was wrong or impossible. But this is untrue. The Peel Commission of 1936–37, chaired by a former Tory Secretary of State for India after the Arab revolt Bullock mentions, recommended 'two sovereign independent states' in Palestine precisely to resolve this question as to how Britain, as the responsible power, could reconcile 'the political consequences of the Zionists' demand to create a Jewish state and the bitter opposition to it'. The Attlee government repeatedly considered this option but chose to reject it. It is, of course, what happened.

RECOGNITION
A Possible Scene in the Bulrushes

When Bevin delayed recognising Israel in 1949, Churchill claimed it was due to 'a very strong and direct streak of bias and prejudice'. © *Punch Magazine*

It seems clear to me that there was a significant strand of antisemitism in Bevin and Attlee's anti-Zionism. This is not discounted by some of Bevin's associates, who mostly shared his views, insisting the contrary. Anyway, others close to Bevin thought he was antisemitic and attributed his policy on Palestine to this cause. 'I must make a note about Ernest's anti-Semitism,' wrote his junior Foreign Office minister Christopher Mayhew in his diary in May 1948.

There is no doubt in my mind that Ernest detests Jews ... He says they taught Hitler the techniques of terror and were even now paralleling the Nazis in Palestine. They were preachers of violence and war. He says, 'What could you expect when people are brought up from the cradle on the Old Testament.'[22]

This was no sour grapes: young Mayhew was a protégé of Bevin's who, after losing his seat in the 1950 election, inherited Bevin's constituency of Woolwich East on his death and cherished his memory.

There is a Churchillian coda. Israel/Palestine was one of Bevin's few foreign policy departures that Churchill attacked hard. When Bevin delayed recognising Israel in 1949, Churchill claimed in Parliament that it was due to 'a very strong and direct streak of bias and prejudice'. As protests started on the Labour side, he added: 'I do not feel any great confidence that he has not got a prejudice against the Jews in Palestine,' pointing out that in May 1948 Bevin had rejected a Jewish state and predicted that the Arab League 'would win if fighting broke out'. But, Churchill went on, Bevin was wrong: 'Wrong in his facts, wrong in the mood, wrong in the method and wrong in the result, and we are very sorry about it for his sake and still more sorry about it for our own.'[23]

'When I say I am not prepared to sacrifice the British Empire, what do I mean?' Bevin asked the House of Commons rhetorically in 1946. His answer: 'I know that if the British Empire fell, the greatest collection of free nations would go into the limbo of the past and it would be a disaster.'[24]

Since the idea of 'free nations going into the limbo of the past' was meaningless in the context of British imperialism – they weren't free and they weren't going into limbo – what Bevin really meant, and what suffused his thinking as Foreign Secretary, was a refusal to 'sacrifice' Britain's existing imperial power. This was for two reasons: firstly, he did not believe that British living standards could be maintained without an imperial hinterland, and secondly, he could see no other means of maintaining British security, apart from the alliance with the United States, which he successfully put in place, but which he thought would be vulnerable to American caprice unless Britain could call on the power of its empire.

However, there was another post-war answer to Bevin's underlying question of how to sustain British prosperity and security in alliance with the United States. It was to seek to do so in partnership with the rest of Western Europe, and to build up and unify its economies and democracies accordingly. This did not require clairvoyance: the immense industrial potential of West Germany, France, the Netherlands and Belgium were hardly secret, and Bevin's own policy on the Ruhr and the Rhine restored German economic power with all deliberate speed. But he would not entertain a European economic and political strategy even when, at the end of his foreign secretaryship, it was presented by the Schuman Declaration of 9 May 1950. Why not?

Bevin's attitude to Europe was contradictory even as he forged West Germany and NATO. General Pug Ismay, Churchill's chief military adviser and first Secretary-General of NATO, said the alliance's purpose was 'to keep the Americans in, the Russians out, and the Germans down'. Bevin went partly along with this, even after creating the Federal Republic. He distrusted and disliked 'the Germans'. He never bonded with Adenauer or its other leaders, and among his final actions was a half-opposition to German rearmament. Yet, since it was also his fundamental policy to build an economically and politically strong West Germany, which on past form would inevitably soon become a powerhouse, there had to be a comprehensive policy of engagement with the new West Germany once he had created it. His policy after 1949 of treating the new West Germany as essentially still a colony was obviously unviable and self-defeating.

Leider alle Hände voll . . .

'Unfortunately all our hands are full.' Attlee and Bevin's response to Adenauer and Schuman's plan for a 'United Europe'. © *Hamburger Abendblatt*

Bevin rejected the Schuman Declaration of 9 May 1950 without giving it any serious consideration. © *Daily Herald*

Bevin rejected the Schuman Declaration of 9 May 1950 without giving it any serious consideration whatever, 'a far cry', writes the normally sympathetic Giles Radice, 'from the Bevin who responded so imaginatively and promptly to George Marshall's Harvard speech, or who worked so resourcefully and creatively to help create NATO.'[25] By 1950, as his deputy Kenneth Younger put it, Bevin was spending as much time in hospital as in the Foreign Office and was 'only half alive'. But had he been 'wholly alive' he would probably have taken the same fateful decisions in relation to European integration in 1950–51.

Bevin, Attlee and the entire Labour high command of 1950–51 chose to see the ECSC as a threat to coal and steel nationalisation in Britain, which is what Herbert Morrison meant in his celebrated response – 'the Durham miners won't wear it' – when he was tracked down to the Ivy restaurant to give the government's immediate response (Bevin was in hospital). Bevin also opposed the federal elements in the Schuman Plan, as Eurosceptics, and latterly Brexiters, were to oppose every constitutional manifestation of the European Union over the next seven decades. 'I am not a very strong believer in Constitutions,' he remarked about the proposed European institutions. 'I like the thing that grows, the thing that evolves.'[26]

Bevin's opposition was also geo-political. He knew that the Schuman Plan came in 1950, and not before, because it was the French Plan B. Plan A had been a far weaker West Germany with the industrial Ruhr and Saar, adjoining France, either under French or separate international control. Bidault and Schuman had even been willing to trade Soviet influence in West Germany to achieve Plan A, until Bevin stopped this.

But none of this was conclusive. After all, the 22 October 1946 'Bevin Plan' for the British zone of Germany was a blueprint for a federal constitution of West Germany far more novel and elaborate than anything proposed for the ECSC. So too was the constitution of the Transport and General Workers' Union devised by Bevin in 1922, with its deliberate echoes of the constitution of the United States. The fundamental point was that Bevin did not regard Schuman as serious, or if he was, he did not think that his plan would come to anything. He thought it was a ploy, not a plan. The fact that Schuman did not inform Bevin of it before it was launched, still less seek to discuss it, and that he told the Americans before the Englishman, reinforced in Bevin's congenitally suspicious mind the idea that it was just a French diplomatic feint, and he was pretty contemptuous of French politicians anyway. Meanwhile the Empire, and Commonwealth, was the here and now. As Labour's National Executive Committee declared in 1950, on the day of the rejection of the Schuman Plan, in a statement written for Bevin by international secretary Denis Healey:

> Britain is the nerve centre of a worldwide Commonwealth which extends into every Continent. In every respect except distance, we in Britain are far closer to our kinsmen in Australia and New Zealand on the far side of the world than we are to Europe. We are closer in language and in origins, in social habits and institutions, in political outlook and in economic interest.[27]

Bevin was not out on a limb in taking this view in 1950–51: it was the general view in British policy circles. Attlee backed him, and later, after the 1957 Treaty of Rome turned the ECSC into the Common Market, he opposed that, too, until his death in 1967. At its foundation, the *Financial Times* thought the ECSC 'a cross between a frustrated cartel and a pipe dream'. Even Churchill, after his Zurich speech of September 1946 calling for 'a kind of United States of Europe', blew hot and cold over the Schuman Plan in 1950–51 and ultimately did not join the ECSC when he took office in October 1951. As he put it in one of his first Cabinet papers: 'We help, we dedicate, we play a part, but we are not merged and do not forget our insular or Commonwealth-wide character.'[28]

However, even historically, there is no safety in numbers when you are wrong. The Schuman Plan soon turned out to be far more than a ploy. Bevin's alternative imperial strategy soon proved unviable. And on the economic arguments, his aversion to the ECSC jarred with his lamentations on the state of Britain's coal and steel industries, which had a lot to gain from a European strategy. 'Give me a million tons of coal and I'll give you a foreign policy,' had been his refrain since 1945.[29]

The key question is how far he should have foreseen this at the time. Churchill had himself already made a panic offer of independence to India in the wartime crisis of 1942. In his compelling account of British imperial decline, David Reynolds pinpoints the fall of Singapore to Japan in February 1942, with the surrender of 80,000 British and Empire soldiers, as the moment when British imperial overstretch was exposed to all:

Newsreel film and press photos of British officers in their baggy shorts signing the articles of surrender in Singapore and then marching off into Japanese prisoner-of-war camps were beamed around the world, shattering the image of racial superiority that was so essential to British power. No longer could imperial loyalty be assumed. And the panic offer of independence to India in the crisis of 1942, though not enacted then, had to be honoured after the war, beginning the domino-like process of decolonisation.[30]

Those dominoes again! Reynolds says that after India they were all bound to fall and this was, at the time, obvious for those with eyes to see. And the strongest supporting evidence came from Bevin himself, who said precisely this in his plea to Attlee against setting a date for leaving India on New Year's Day 1947:

> You cannot read the telegrams from Egypt and the Middle East nowadays without realising that not only is India going, but Malay, Ceylon and the Middle East is going with it, with a tremendous repercussion on the African territories. I do beg of you to take a stronger line and not give way to this awful pessimism.[31]

Maybe, had Bevin adopted his own logic, and made it a cause of optimism not pessimism, the post-war decade under Bevin and then Churchill might have seen Britain leading its continent into 'a kind of United States of Europe', instead of seeking to sustain a defunct empire. But it was not to be.

The irony is, it was Bevin who made today's European Union possible, doing more to lay its foundations in West Germany, NATO and a free Western Europe than either Monnet or Schuman. Nico Henderson, Bevin's greatest diplomatic protégé, who we have encountered so often in these pages, made precisely this point to Jim Callaghan, then Foreign Secretary, when trying to encourage him to enlarge his European vision in the economic crisis of 1974. 'I produced the emotive card of Ernest Bevin's name,' he recalled, 'recounting how Bevin had supported and even inspired the concepts of the Marshall Plan and NATO without knowing in detail how they would work or what exactly they would achieve.'[32]

The last long international summit of Bevin's foreign secretaryship, in January 1950, was richly symbolic. It had nothing to do with Europe or the transatlantic alliance. It was a Commonwealth conference held at his instigation in Colombo, the capital of Ceylon/Sri Lanka, which had recently become independent alongside neighbouring India. Most of the Prime Ministers and foreign ministers of the eight independent member states of the Commonwealth were there, apart from Attlee. Bevin was the chairman.

By now an institution as much as a person, Bevin was treated with the deference of a monarch. Literally so when he was conveyed up the stairs into the conference room in Colombo on a palanquin, being too infirm to walk. But it was form not substance. A prickly Pandit Nehru, India's first post-independence Prime Minister, told Bevin's private secretary, Roddy Barclay, stories of his time at Harrow School, where Barclay, like his father and his son, also went. But little meaningful power politics was done. The 'Colombo Plan', agreed with difficulty because of resentment at British imposition, was a modest initiative for economic development, in line with Bevin's attempt to position the Commonwealth as an agency for improving what was soon to be called the 'third world'. But it was no strategic plan for the future of Britain itself, let alone for its remaining empire.

On the return trip, Bevin and his entourage stopped off in Cairo for a lavish lunch with King Farouk. Prince Philip, then a young naval lieutenant stationed in Malta, joined the party. It was very grand but very unproductive, because 'nothing less than the complete and unconditional evacuation of Egyptian territory by British forces would have been acceptable to the Egyptian politicians, and we were not then prepared to concede this', recalled Barclay.[33] Instead, evacuation plus humiliation took place two years later when Farouk, a playboy around London with Edward, Prince of Wales, before they both inherited their thrones in 1936, was overthrown by Colonel Nasser, Eden's nemesis in the ensuing Suez crisis. Farouk fled his palace in such haste he didn't even have time to destroy his huge collection of pornography.

There is a Churchillian coda here, too, painful to British Cypriots like me. Jock Colville, Churchill's wartime private secretary, returned to the Foreign Office in 1945. 'One day,' he recalled,

> I wrote a memorandum suggesting that as in the long run we should probably have to abandon Cyprus, it would save a lot of trouble if we did so right away, on condition that the British were allowed to retain their military bases in full sovereignty and local autonomy was provided for the small Turkish minority.

This advice went up to Bevin:

> The telephone rang. Mr Bevin wished to see me ... 'Look 'ere, Colville, what's all this nonsense you've written about Cyprus? Churchill said Cyprus was British and on things like that Churchill is always right. While I'm Secretary of State, Cyprus stays British. And I say, you're looking rather peaky. You ought to 'ave a 'oliday. 'ose the 'ead of your department?'
>
> 'William Hayter, Sir.'
>
> 'Well, go and tell 'ayter from me that you're to 'ave a 'oliday. Take my advice. Go to 'ove. The air at 'ove is wonderful. Mrs Bevin and I went there last year and it did us all the good in the world. Now, be a good boy, go off to 'ove and when you come back you won't look 'alf so peaky and you'll stop writing all that bloody nonsense about Cyprus.'[34]

Britain stayed in Cyprus for another fifteen years, and fought a bloody war to resist independence, yet was still forced out in 1960. Like Ireland and Malta, Cyprus now belongs to the European Union.

'I have not become the King's first minister to preside over the liquidation of the British Empire,' Churchill declared in 1942. Bevin took the same view of the Empire. In this too he was Labour's Churchill and it was equally misplaced. The only thing to be done with British imperialism in the 1940s was to end it as soon as possible, and the only thing to be done with Western Europe was to engage with it as fully as possible. That had been Bevin's view too, before the trauma of the 1930s. Perhaps fittingly, his wider achievements as Foreign Secretary made it the policy that people like him almost universally supported within another generation.

CHAPTER 11

BEVIN TODAY

B evin died on the afternoon of 14 April 1951 of a massive heart attack while in bed reading official papers. It was a Saturday and he had been due to go to the football at Wembley with Flo, but his chest pains were so severe he could not leave the Foreign Secretary's official residence where he still lived.

He was found with the key to his ministerial red box clasped vice-like in his hand. Death imitated life, raging against the dying of the light. It was four months into his thirtieth year of virtually uninterrupted service at the summit of British affairs, starting with the launch of the Transport and General Workers' Union in 1922. The only other national leader who went back that far, indeed much further, was Winston Churchill; Bevin's imprint on his era was in my view second only to Churchill's.

It was just six weeks since Attlee had finally felt obliged to move his friend from the Foreign Office on his seventieth birthday, while keeping him in the Cabinet without portfolio. This wasn't only to sweeten the pill: Clem still relied on Ernie's political nous and heft, right up to the week of his death when he sought to prevent Nye Bevan flouncing out of the Cabinet amid a molten row with

Hugh Gaitskell, who had recently succeeded Cripps as Chancellor. Ostensibly about the introduction of charges into the new National Health Service, the dispute was really a power struggle after Gaitskell's promotion over his older rival. The young Harold Wilson, who resigned with Bevan, believed Bevin would have prevented the split by convincing Gaitskell to cancel the proposed charges. Those charges ultimately raised a tiny sum compared to a defence budget soaring to more than twice the total NHS budget in the wake of the Korean War.

'Bevin asked Nye Bevan and me round on a particular Tuesday in April,' Wilson recalled thirty years later.

> We put the facts, we put the figures. He then said that he was going to side with us, partly I think because he thought Herbert Morrison was behind the machinations and Ernie didn't like Herbert. But on the Saturday he died. He was already very very frail and could hardly talk really because his jaw was all deformed. But his head was clear, his brain was clear.[1]

Bevin thought, probably correctly, that Morrison was yet again scheming to oust Attlee, this time by precipitating a crisis while Attlee was in hospital with an ulcer and he was Acting Prime Minister. Ernie was determined to stamp it out, true to the last to his dictum when told that Morrison was his own worst enemy: 'Not while I'm alive he ain't.'

But it was not to be, and Bevan's resignation ignited bitter left/right Labour factionalism, Bevan vs Morrison/Gaitskell, which helped the Tories win the October 1951 election, seven months after Bevin's death, and then the following two elections in 1955 and 1959.

The loss of Bevin weakened without removing Attlee and possibly cost Labour the 1951 election, Churchill's last hurrah. It was incredibly close. Labour topped the poll with 48.8 per cent of the vote but came narrowly behind the Conservatives in seats. Had Labour won the three post-war elections (1945, 1950 and 1951) in a row, and had the Tories been out of power for more than a decade, maybe Britain today would be less like the United States and more like Sweden, and perhaps Bevin would have been vindicated in his prophecy: 'They say Gladstone was at the Treasury from 1860 to 1930. They'll say that Bevin was at the Ministry of Labour from 1940 to 1990.'[2] Instead, Bevin was evicted by Thatcher in 1979.

Even so, when Churchill re-entered No. 10 on 26 October 1951, few thought he was inaugurating a new Tory era that would see Britain's right-wing triumph in ten of the next seventeen elections until 2019, ruling for two-thirds of the next seven decades. At Bevin's death, post-war Britain appeared to be Labour Britain. It would have astonished him that Labour rule was nearly over and the 1945 landslide would come to look like a freak not a mould. He would have been equally shocked that there would never again – at least not yet – be a trade union leader remotely as powerful as him. He was lionised in his day as the first of a new breed of 'common man' who would manage the British state in a new democratic era. But Bevin wasn't the first of a kind: he was the first and last.

There was talk of another trade union leader taking over as Foreign Secretary in 1951, on the Bevin model. Sam Watson, leader of the Durham miners and chairman of the Labour Party in 1950, was touted, but a weakened Attlee felt compelled to appoint Morrison. Watson was in Bevin's image of massivity, pragmatism and self-educated charisma: as late as the 1959 election he was lined up to become Labour leader Gaitskell's Foreign Secretary had he been elected. But Harold Macmillan won a landslide and the Foreign Office was filled by the fourteenth Earl of Home, who had been Neville Chamberlain's parliamentary private secretary at the Munich conference with Hitler twenty years before and proceeded four years later to become one of Eton's five post-war Tory Prime Ministers, including the present incumbent Boris Johnson. Deflecting an attack from Harold Wilson, 'Alec' Home quipped, 'When you think about it, Mr Wilson is the 14th Mr Wilson.' But everyone knew which was born with the silver spoon in their mouth.

In retrospect, for all his victories on the home front, Bevin was harbinger of a seminal moment when England might have undergone a Scandinavian-style equalisation yet did so only partially. There were two lasting Labour transformations: full, regulated employment, and the National Health Service, a compound of Bevin and Bevan. But it stopped there. Moreover, even this was possible only because of the prior political triumph of Bevin and Attlee, taking Labour into a successful coalition with Churchill in 1940 and winning the 1945 election in its aftermath. A new, more open, classless and equal society in Britain requires a new Bevin as much as a new Bevan.

Only two Labour leaders have won general elections in the seventy years since Bevin: Harold Wilson in 1964, 1966 and 1974; and Tony Blair in 1997, 2001 and 2005. The social democratic achievements of Wilson and Blair were considerable, although lambasted by today's contrarian left much as were Attlee and Bevin in their day. Only the passage of decades converted the left to admiration of the 1945 government. At the time, most of the left was fiercely critical, particularly of Bevin's anti-Stalinist foreign policy, yet Bevin got the measure of Stalin in the way Churchill got the measure of Hitler, and the creation of West Germany and the transatlantic security alliance were as important as the creation of the NHS to the success of the Attlee government.

'People will not look forward to posterity, who never look backward to their ancestors,' said Edmund Burke. This is as true of the left as of the right. Left contrarianism after 1951 had the corrosive effect of making much of the labour movement indifferent or hostile to winning power again on a pragmatic basis. This is the antithesis of Bevin, who grasped the imperative for democratic pragmatism in pursuit of transformational goals. As a result, there have been fewer Labour governments than there might have been and far less social democracy in our national life.

One consequence of the trade unions mostly going into opposition to the Labour Party after Bevin is that Labour's only two successful post-1951 leaders regarded the unions as something to be navigated around, rather than as genuine partners in a shared endeavour of social partnership and change. Blair and Wilson had no Bevin. Gordon Brown and Roy Jenkins greatly strengthened these respective leaders with bold ideas and reformist impetus, in the tradition of the Keynesian transformation of Attlee's Labour Party championed by Bevin. For all his sniping at intellectuals, Bevin was as formidable a thought leader as he was a trade union leader. But ideas are not enough: organisation and social reach are equally vital. The Labour Party needs again to become a genuine labour *movement*, otherwise populism fills the void and the likes of Nigel Farage and Boris Johnson become leaders of the working class. Bevin successfully resisted this in the 1930s; Bevin today would be doing the same again.

The one trade union leader since 1951 who rose towards Bevin's level was Jack Jones, leader of the T&G from 1969 to 1978 and one of Bevin's last appointees as a full-time official in 1939. He was a brilliant organiser in Coventry's motor and engineering factories.

Jack Jones pioneered a few notably Bevinist state institutions, notably the Health and Safety Commission and the Advisory, Conciliation and Arbitration Service (ACAS). After Wilson's re-election in 1974, he initially acquiesced in an incomes policy to tackle rampant inflation. But 'Emperor Jones', as he was known, was distrustful of social democrat politicians, the opposite of Bevin in his heyday, and he mostly kept his distance: his middle name wasn't Larkin, after the Liverpool-Irish revolutionary trade union leader Jim Larkin, for nothing. After his retirement in 1978, which followed Wilson's succession by Jim Callaghan in 1976, collaboration between the Labour government and the trade unions broke down totally. In the ensuing, disastrous 'Winter of Discontent', the unions became as unpopular as in the General Strike of 1926 before Bevin asserted control, leading to Thatcher's election in 1979, which simply made the unions more oppositional still.[3]

In the four decades since 1979 union membership has more than halved from a peak of 13.2 million then to just 6.3 million today, its lowest level since 1939. Yet, even as trade unionism has declined, so too has Labour support among trade unionists, particularly when the party has been badly led. In the 1983 and 2019 elections more trade unionists voted Tory than Labour. Since Bevin's death, the general rule has been a weak, poorly led Labour Party and weak, poorly led trade unions mutually reinforcing each other's weakness.

Bevin today would prioritise an entrepreneurial expansion and recreation of the trade unions, and Labour's social organisation, as much as a modernisation of party policy. It is telling that Tony Blair, in his party modernisation prior to winning the 1997 election, essentially adopted the German SPD's Godesberg programme of 1959, changing the statement of aims and values in Clause 4 of Labour's constitution from a 'nationalisation' to a 'communitarian' view of social democracy. This was much needed; it was thirty years overdue. Yet Germany's SPD was – and is – a warning as much as a model. Commanding huge respect for its stand against both Hitler and Stalin, and providing three outstanding Chancellors after 1969 in Brandt, Schmidt and Schröder, the SPD has nonetheless led post-war Germany for an even shorter period than Labour has led post-war Britain. A key factor has been the weakness of its relationship with Germany's trade unions, because of the historic strength of communism and the deep working-class roots of the Catholic-allied centre-right parties (the CDU and CSU). The SPD is now in precipitate decline, as are the French socialists, whose trade union links have been similarly weak.

There are glimpses of how different it might have been – and might still be – in Australia and Sweden, whose social democratic parties, while under pressure, have long been more successful than Britain's, and better able to counter the populism of right and left because they are more deeply rooted in trade unions and their members and families. Sweden's social democrats have become the largest party in all twenty-nine of the nation's elections of the past century. Labour has managed this in just ten out of the twenty-seven in Britain. The incumbent social democratic Prime Minister, Stefan Löfven, founded a large and successful general trade union akin to Bevin's T&G. When elected party leader in 2012, Löfven wasn't even a member of the Swedish parliament and had to be parachuted in much as Bevin was parachuted into the House of Commons as Minister of Labour in 1940.

Australia, midway between Sweden and Britain in historic electoral success for its Labor Party, has an even stronger tradition of trade unionist political leadership. Not just famously Bob Hawke in the 1980s; seven of the eleven Labor Prime Ministers of Australia between 1904 and 2013 were trade union leaders. Poignantly, the leader who effectively established Labor as a party of government in Australia, Andrew Fisher, was a Scots emigrant who had been a trade unionist alongside Keir Hardie, organising the 1881 Ayrshire miners' strike with Hardie as a nineteen-year-old miner. He was sacked and blacklisted, which is why he emigrated. The story has shades of Bevin in Bristol, who thought of becoming a missionary abroad after his similar experience in 1909.

Lula da Silva of Brazil, Cyril Ramaphosa of South Africa and Lech Wałęsa of Poland all became recent leaders of their nations by first leading trade union movements to bring about fundamental social and political change. They were Bevinist all, in force of personality, in ideas, in pragmatism and in organisational prowess.

The Bevin of Britain today would be organising the millions of low-paid workers, particularly in the 5 million-strong and largely non-unionised social care and 'gig economy' sectors, maybe by creating a new general union on the scale of the T&G. Bevin's union of today would be providing the services and benefits needed today, for example affordable housing for the young – who might then start joining trade unions again – just as Bevin in his day built care homes for retired T&G members and organised excursion and holiday companies for working-class families in the 1930s. And he or she would be allying with an electable Labour leader – like Attlee – to get Labour elected on a pragmatic programme.

For inspiration they might also look to the modern American Bevin: Andy Stern, who turned the Service Employees International Union into a transformational industrial and political force in his fifteen years at the helm after 2005, adding 850,000 members, largely unskilled and low paid, while exerting himself mightily on behalf of Barack Obama. After Obama's election in 2008, Stern was his most regular visitor in the White House and a critical impetus towards 'Obamacare'.[4] Stern went to university, which Bevin wished he'd been able to do, but otherwise he is a modern Bevin.

A reincarnated Bevin might also avoid Bevin's own mistakes. No nostalgia for past empires of any kind, and thoroughly engaged in Europe, its peoples and its politics. Yet he would be equally evangelical in his beliefs. Indeed, he wouldn't have to change much of what Ernie said to an American audience in 1947, making the case for a transatlantic union of free peoples:

> We believe as good social democrats that it is possible to have public ownership, great advance and social development, and with it maintain what I think is the most vital thing of all, liberty. I don't believe the two things are inconsistent, and never have. If I believed the development of socialism meant the absolute crushing of liberty, then I should plump for liberty, because the advance of human development depends entirely on the right to think, to speak and to use reason, and allow what I call the upsurge to come from the bottom to reach the top.[5]

After a year living with Bevin, I keep asking myself this big question: why in twentieth and 21st-century Britain, with all the expectations of a democratic society, did Bevin turn out to be a freak not a mould? Why was he the first and last of his kind?

Maybe because he did not live quite long enough to help win that third post-war election in 1951. Maybe because his partnership with Attlee, while exceptionally close and productive, limited his imprint on the Labour Party since he never became the leader himself. Churchill always regarded Bevin as the more formidable of the Attlee–Bevin duo: 'The most distinguished man that the Labour party have thrown up in my time.' Maybe because Bevin was too much of a loner within the trade union movement: he never built a school beyond acolytes in the T&G and too readily believed his own conceit that he was 'a turn-up in a million'. Maybe because the Conservative Party was just too strong, with its established elites and its success in welding together economic liberalism and English nationalism into a cross-class political machine even as democracy advanced. All these might be thought contributory factors.

Or maybe it is far simpler. Virtually all human lives end in frustration, if not in failure, and Bevin was no exception. 'If only I had had a bit longer,' were among his last words.[6]

Herbert Henry Asquith, the Prime Minister who fatefully took Britain into the First World War, asked of himself, from Robert Browning's 'Christmas Eve':

> T'were to be wished the flaws were fewer
> In the earthen vessel that holds the treasure
> But the main thing is, does it hold good measure?[7]

To which Attlee made reply for Bevin: 'Men recognised in him a national leader, someone to lean on. He attracted power. At a time when the Labour Movement had all the hopes, aspirations, ideas and saints necessary for Utopia, Ernest helped bring its feet to the ground by insisting that these things without power were useless.'[8]

Britain needed Bevin once. Now it needs his kind again.

'United we stand; divided we fall.' Division and disloyalty were cardinal sins in Bevin's union.

ACKNOWLEDGEMENTS

M y greatest debts and heartfelt thanks are to Nathan Lloyd, Patrick Storey and Roger Liddle, and to Ed and Alice, who were with me every step of the way. Olivia Beattie and James Stephens at Biteback were as brilliant as ever. Lucy Stewardson was a superb copy-editor. This is my fourth book in a decade with Biteback, the best political publisher in Britain. Iain Dale and my late lamented friend Ed Victor got me started and I have never looked back.

I write in the footsteps of giants, particularly Lord Bullock, whose three-volume *Life and Times of Ernest Bevin*, published over twenty-three years to 1983, is a work of immense scholarship. As I got to know Bevin intimately, I entered into a continuous debate with Alan Bullock; it is just a pity it could not have been in person. Dozens of other lives and memoirs of Bevin and his associates, and studies of particular themes and episodes, contributed to this portrait, as well as newspaper and manuscript archives and that great unread, Hansard. The House of Lords library was also immensely helpful, which would have amused Ernie.

Roy Jenkins told me that books are never finished, just abandoned. This one was abandoned on the day Boris Johnson announced that Britain would be shut down to tackle coronavirus. It is an emergency of a kind Bevin relished. He would already be thinking and planning beyond, mindful of the Book of Proverbs: 'Where there is no vision, the people perish.'

Andrew Adonis
London, 24 March 2020

NOTES

INTRODUCTION

1 Nigel Lawson's phrase from *The View from No. 11: Memoirs of a Tory Radical* (Bantam Press: London, 1992), p. 613.
2 Lord Attlee, *The Observer*, 13 and 20 March 1960.
3 Francis Williams, *Ernest Bevin: Portrait of A Great Englishman* (Hutchinson: London, 1952), pp. 90, 100.

CHAPTER 1: ORPHAN

1 I am grateful to Jo Johnson for pointing this out to me.
2 Alan Bullock, *The Life and Times of Ernest Bevin, Volume 1: Trade Union Leader 1881–1940* (Heinemann: London, 1960), p. 2.
3 Trevor Evans, *Bevin of Britain* (Allen & Unwin: London, 1946), p. 32.
4 Williams, *Portrait*, p. 13.
5 Ibid.
6 *Picture Post*, 30 November 1946.
7 Graham Goodlad, 'British Liberals and the Irish Home Rule Crisis: the dynamics of division', in D. G. Boyce and A. O'Day (eds), *Gladstone and Ireland: Politics, Religion and Nationality in the Victorian Age* (Palgrave: London, 2010), p. 89.
8 Williams, *Portrait*, pp. 14–15.
9 *Picture Post*, 30 November 1946.
10 Williams, *Portrait*, pp. 9, 16.
11 Evans, *Bevin of Britain*, p. 45.
12 Christopher Mayhew, 'Ernest Bevin, A radio portrait', 24 April 1957, BBC, tape no. CTBS 3066, p. 3.
13 Evans, *Bevin of Britain*, p. 47.
14 Ibid., p. 48.
15 Mark Stephens, *Ernest Bevin: Unskilled Labourer and World Statesman* (SPA Books: London, 1981), p. 126.
16 Evans, *Bevin of Britain*, p. 11.
17 *Bristol Evening Despatch*, 21 April 1945.
18 Giles Radice, *The Tortoise and the Hares: Attlee, Bevin, Cripps, Dalton, Morrison* (Politico's: London, 2008), p. 28.

19 Evans, *Bevin of Britain*, pp. 49–50; *Daily Herald*, 5 June 1952.
20 Evans, *Bevin of Britain*, pp. 53–4; Radice, *The Tortoise and the Hares*, p. 31.
21 Evans, *Bevin of Britain*, p. 59.
22 Text of the Limehouse speech: Lloyd George papers, House of Lords Record Office, LG/C/33/2/11; Edward VII's protest: John Grigg, *Lloyd George: The People's Champion 1902–1911* (Eyre Methuen: London, 1978), pp. 208–11.
23 Bullock, *Trade Union Leader*, p. 17.
24 Williams, *Portrait*, p. 27; Evans, *Bevin of Britain*, pp. 60–62; Bullock, *Trade Union Leader*, p. 21.
25 Williams, *Portrait*, p. 27.

CHAPTER 2: DOCKERS' KC

1 Stephens, *Ernest Bevin*, p. 56.
2 Mayhew, 'Ernest Bevin', p. 5.
3 Williams, *Portrait*, p. 44; Bullock, *Trade Union Leader*, p. 36.
4 Bullock, *Trade Union Leader*, pp. 36–7.
5 Williams, *Portrait*, p. 56; Peter Weiler, *Ernest Bevin* (Manchester University Press: Manchester, 1993), p. 9; Bullock, *Trade Union Leader*, p. 35; Evans, *Bevin of Britain*, p. 88.
6 Bullock, *Trade Union Leader*, p. 45.
7 Ibid., p. 47; Beatrice Webb, *Diaries 1912–1924* (Longmans, Green and Co. Ltd: London, 1952), p. 44.
8 Williams, *Portrait*, p. 58.
9 Weiler, *Ernest Bevin*, p. 32.
10 Bullock, *Trade Union Leader*, p. 48; Weiler, *Ernest Bevin*, p. 16.
11 Bullock, *Trade Union Leader*, p. 56.
12 Ibid., p. 55.
13 Ibid., pp. 53, 56, 61.
14 Alan Bullock, *The Life and Times of Ernest Bevin, Volume 2: Minister of Labour 1940–1945* (Heinemann: London, 1967), p. 265; J. T. Murphy, *Preparing for Power: A Critical Study of the History of the British Working-Class Movement* (Jonathan Cape: London, 1934), p. 172.
15 Williams, *Portrait*, p. 100; J. M. McEwen (ed.), *The Riddell Diaries 1908–1923* (Athlone Press: London, 1986), p. 258.
16 Williams, *Portrait*, p. 75.
17 'Proceedings of a Court of Inquiry into wages, rates and conditions of men engaged in dock and waterside labour', Industrial Courts Act, 1919, pp. 7–9.
18 Stephens, *Ernest Bevin*, p. 37.
19 Weiler, *Ernest Bevin*, p. 28.
20 Williams, *Portrait*, p. 81.
21 Bullock, *Trade Union Leader*, p. 127.
22 Ibid., p. 131.
23 'Minutes of the Triennial Delegate conference, Plymouth, 18–22 May 1920', Dock, Wharf, Riverside and General Workers' Union, pp. 129–36.
24 *The Times*, 6 August 1920.
25 Williams, *Portrait*, p. 83; Dockers Union Triennial Delegate conference, pp. 34–6.
26 Williams, *Portrait*, p. 85.
27 Bullock, *Trade Union Leader*, pp. 137–8.
28 Williams, *Portrait*, p. 86.
29 Bullock, *Trade Union Leader*, pp. 138–40.
30 Mayhew, 'Ernest Bevin', p. 7.
31 Bullock, *Trade Union Leader*, pp. 232–3.
32 Ibid., pp. 140–41.
33 Williams, *Portrait*, p. 99.
34 Bullock, *Trade Union Leader*, pp. 39–40.

35 Francis Williams, *Magnificent Journey: The Rise of the Trade Unions* (Odhams: London, 1954), p. 339.

36 Bullock, *Trade Union Leader*, p. 182; Williams, *Magnificent Journey*, p. 340.

37 Harry Green, 'The Rise of Trade Unionism in North Wales', *Western Daily News*, 3 January 1953.

38 Bullock, *Trade Union Leader*, p. 155.

39 Ibid., pp. 196–7.

40 Ibid., p. 189.

41 Williams, *Portrait*, p. 103.

42 Ibid., p. 109.

43 Richard Hyman, *The Workers' Union, 1989–1929* (Oxford University Press: Oxford, 1971), p. 160.

44 Williams, *Portrait*, p. 113.

45 Ibid., p. 111.

46 Mayhew, 'Ernest Bevin', p. 8.

47 Bullock, *Trade Union Leader*, p. 206.

48 Ibid., p. 473.

49 Lord Attlee, *The Observer*, 13 March 1960.

50 Evans, *Bevin of Britain*, pp. 23–4; Weiler, *Ernest Bevin*, p. 10.

51 Stephens, *Ernest Bevin*, pp. 131–2.

52 David Marquand, 'James Ramsay MacDonald', *Dictionary of National Biography*; Bullock, *Minister of Labour*, p. 378.

53 Bullock, *Trade Union Leader*, p. 246.

54 Williams, *Magnificent Journey*, pp. 357–8.

55 Bullock, *Trade Union Leader*, pp. 236, 244, 257, 260.

56 Ibid., p. 53.

57 Williams, *Portrait*, pp. 100–101.

CHAPTER 3: GENERAL STRIKE

1 Evans, *Bevin of Britain*, p. 146.

2 John Campbell, *F. E. Smith, First Earl of Birkenhead* (Pimlico: London, 1991), p. 773.

3 Beatrice Webb, *Diaries 1924–32* (Longmans: London, 1956), pp. 70–71.

4 Bullock, *Trade Union Leader*, p. 282.

5 Ibid., p. 285.

6 Ibid., p. 406.

7 Ibid., p. 302.

8 Ibid., p. 306.

9 A. J. Cook, *The Nine Days: The Story of the General Strike Told by the Miners' Secretary* (Co-operative Printing Society: London, 1927), pp. 2–3.

10 Bullock, *Trade Union Leader*, p. 310; Campbell, *F. E. Smith*, pp. 172, 770–72.

11 L. S. Amery, *My Political Life, Volume 2* (Hutchinson: London, 1953), pp. 483–4.

12 Bullock, *Trade Union Leader*, pp. 313–16.

13 Ibid., p. 319; From 'A Labour Correspondent', in *Yorkshire Evening News*, 27 May 1926.

14 Cook, *The Nine Days*, p. 6; Robert Taylor, *The TUC: From the General Strike to New Unionism* (Palgrave: London, 2000), p. 36; Williams, *Portrait*, p. 139.

15 Taylor, *TUC*, pp. 34–5; Bullock, *Trade Union Leader*, pp. 323, 326.

16 Bullock, *Trade Union Leader*, pp. 319–20.

17 Cook, *The Nine Days*, p. 8.

18 Bullock, *Trade Union Leader*, pp. 331–2; Taylor, *TUC*, pp. 36–7.

19 Evans, *Bevin of Britain*, pp. 160–61; Cook, *The Nine Days*, p. 9.

20 Bullock, *Trade Union Leader*, p. 356.

21 Chris Wrigley, 'Sir Ben Turner', *Dictionary of National Biography*.

22 Bullock, *Trade Union Leader*, p. 402; Evans, *Bevin of Britain*, pp. 163–4.

23 Bullock, *Trade Union Leader*, p. 590; Taylor, *TUC*, pp. 39, 49; Evans, *Bevin of Britain*, pp. 165–6.
24 Bullock, *Trade Union Leader*, p. 423.
25 Cook, *The Nine Days*, p. 5.
26 Bullock, *Trade Union Leader*, pp. 349, 374.
27 Williams, *Portrait*, p. 125.
28 Campbell, *F. E. Smith*, p. 777.
29 Evans, *Bevin of Britain*, pp. 153–4, 170.
30 Campbell, *F. E. Smith*, p. 775.
31 Bullock, *Trade Union Leader*, p. 369.

CHAPTER 4: KEYNES

1 Brendan Montague, 'The day Thatcher met Hayek – and how this led to privatisation', *The Ecologist*, 10 August 2018.
2 Campbell, *F. E. Smith*, pp. 780–81.
3 Keith Laybourn, *Philip Snowden: A Biography* (Dartmouth Publishing Group: London, 1988), p. 97.
4 *The Times*, 20 October 1922.
5 Kenneth O. Morgan, 'David Lloyd George', *Dictionary of National Biography*; Marquand, 'James Ramsay MacDonald'.
6 Richard Toye, *The Labour Party and the Planned Economy 1931–1951* (Royal Historical Society: London, 2003), p. 34.
7 Peter Clarke, 'We Can Conquer Unemployment: Lloyd George and Keynes', *Journal of Liberal History*, no. 77, 2012–13, p. 49.
8 Ibid., pp. 47–52.
9 Ibid., p. 49.
10 Lucy Masterman, *C. F. G. Masterman: A Biography* (Nicholson and Watson: London, 1939), pp. 345–6.
11 Peter Clarke, *Keynes: The Twentieth Century's Most Influential Economist* (Bloomsbury: London, 2010), p. 100.
12 Lord Skidelsky, House of Lords, Hansard, 18 March 2020.
13 Bullock, *Trade Union Leader*, pp. 427–30.
14 'Minutes of Evidence taken before the Committee on Finance and Industry', vol. 1, 1931, p. 217.
15 A. J. P. Taylor, 'Nobody's Uncle', *Encounter*, October 1960, pp. 76–7.
16 Robert Skidelsky, *John Maynard Keynes, Volume II: The Economist as Saviour, 1920–1937* (Allen Lane: London, 1992), p. 362; Bill Schwarz, 'The Corporate Economy, 1890–1929', in Mary Langan and Bill Schwarz (eds), *Crises in the British State 1880–1930* (Hutchinson: London, 1985), p. 99.
17 Weiler, *Ernest Bevin*, p. 56; 'Final Report', Macmillan Committee, p. 210.
18 Bullock, *Trade Union Leader*, p. 434.
19 James Crotty, *Keynes Against Capitalism: His Economic Case for Liberal Socialism* (Routledge: London, 2019), p. 86.
20 Bullock, *Trade Union Leader*, p. 439.
21 Ibid., p. 446.
22 Ibid., p. 453.
23 Ibid., p. 469; Webb, *Diaries 1924–32*, p. 279.
24 House of Commons, Hansard, 11 February 1931.
25 Weiler, *Ernest Bevin*, p. 70.
26 Bullock, *Trade Union Leader*, p. 480.
27 Ibid., pp. 484–5; Weiler, *Ernest Bevin*, pp. 60–61.
28 Marquand, 'James Ramsay MacDonald'; Evans, *Bevin of Britain*, p. 196.
29 Marquand, 'James Ramsay MacDonald'.
30 Bullock, *Trade Union Leader*, pp. 490–91.

31 Ibid., p. 497.

32 Ibid., p. 494.

33 Evans, *Bevin of Britain*, p. 186.

34 Marquand, 'James Ramsay MacDonald'.

35 Bullock, *Trade Union Leader*, p. 502; Toye, *The Labour Party and the Planned Economy*, pp. 46–7.

36 Skidelsky, *John Maynard Keynes*, pp. 92, 144.

CHAPTER 5: ATTLEE

1   Bullock, *Trade Union Leader*, pp. 499–500.

2   Ibid., p. 527.

3   Roy Jenkins, *Churchill* (Pan Macmillan: London, 2001), pp. 599–600.

4   Evans, *Bevin of Britain*, pp. 189–90.

5   Bullock, *Trade Union Leader*, p. 553.

6   Ibid., p. 509.

7   *The Times*, 27 January 1927.

8   Bullock, *Trade Union Leader*, pp. 562–3.

9   Ibid., p. 566.

10 Ibid., p. 573.

11 For these quotes and accounts of the Brighton debate, I draw on Bullock, *Trade Union Leader*, pp. 566–9 and Hugh Dalton, *The Fateful Years, Memoirs 1931–45* (Muller: London, 1957), p. 69.

12 Bullock, *Trade Union Leader*, p. 567.

13 Ibid., pp. 568–9, incorporating the change of 'taking' to 'hawking' as per most accounts of Bevin's speech.

14 Dalton, *The Fateful Years*, p. 69.

15 Williams, *Portrait*, p. 196.

16 Ronald Blythe, *The Age of Illusion: England in the Twenties and Thirties, 1919–1940* (Faber & Faber: London, 1963), p. 291.

17 Kenneth Harris, *Attlee* (Orion: London, 1995), p. 121.

18 Harris, *Attlee*, p. 122.

19 Henry Pelling, *A Short History of the Labour Party* (Palgrave Macmillan: London, 1996), p. 65; Williams, *Portrait*, p. 7.

20 Bullock, *Trade Union Leader*, p. 601.

21 Ibid., p. 618.

22 Evans, *Bevin of Britain*, p. 197.

23 Bullock, *Trade Union Leader*, p. 605.

24 James C. Robertson, 'The British General Election of 1935', *Journal of Contemporary History*, 1974, pp. 149–64.

25 Ibid., p. 156.

26 Bullock, *Trade Union Leader*, p. 583.

27 *Forward*, 3 October 1936; Bullock, *Trade Union Leader*, p. 584.

28 Bullock, *Trade Union Leader*, p. 585.

29 Ibid., p. 596.

30 Ibid., pp. 631–2.

31 Ibid., p. 617.

32 Ibid., p. 590.

33 Taylor, *TUC*, p. 20; Bullock, *Minister of Labour*, p. 382.

34 Frank Myers, 'Conscription and the Politics of Military Strategy in the Attlee Government', *Journal of Strategic Studies*, vol. 7, 1984, p. 56.

35 Michael Foot, *Aneurin Bevan: A Biography, Volume 2: 1945–1960* (Davis-Poynter: London, 1973), p. 32.

36 Lord Attlee, *The Observer*, 20 March 1960.

37 Lord Attlee, *The Observer*, 13 March 1960.

CHAPTER 6: ERNIE

1   Evans, *Bevin of Britain*, p. 18.
2   Stephens, *Ernest Bevin*, pp. 132–3.
3   Roderick Barclay, *Ernest Bevin and the Foreign Office 1932–1969* (Latimer: London, 1975), p. 61; Nicholas Henderson, *Mandarin: The Diaries of an Ambassador 1969–1982* (Weidenfeld & Nicolson: London, 1994), p. 173.
4   Williams, *Portrait*, pp. 116–17; Harry Green, 'The Rise of Trade Unionism in North Wales', *Western Daily News*, 3 January 1953.
5   'Garrick Club Membership Ledger', 1941. I am grateful to William Keegan for this reference.
6   Weiler, *Bevin*, pp. 165, 76; Michael Foot, *Aneurin Bevan: A Biography, Volume One: 1897–1945* (MacGibbon & Kee: London, 1962), p. 455.
7   Nicholas Henderson, *Inside the Private Office: Memoirs of the Secretary to British Foreign Ministers* (Chicago Press: Chicago, 1987), pp. 26–30.
8   Stephens, *Ernest Bevin*, p. 133.
9   Henderson, *Inside the Private Office*, pp. 30–34.
10 Chris Bryant, *Stafford Cripps: The First Modern Chancellor* (Hodder & Stoughton: London, 1997), p. 387.
11 Henderson, *Mandarin*, p. 140.
12 Stephens, *Ernest Bevin*, p. 132; Barclay, *Ernest Bevin and the Foreign Office*, pp. 67, 78.
13 Patrick R. H. Wright, *Behind Diplomatic Lines* (Biteback Publishing: London, 2018), p. 5.
14 Barclay, *Ernest Bevin and the Foreign Office*, p. 42.
15 Hugh Dalton, *High Tide and After: Memoirs 1945–1960* (Muller: London, 1962), p. 361.
16 A. L. Rowse, *Glimpses of the Great* (University Press of America: Lanham, 1985), p. 36.
17 Rowse, *Glimpses of the Great*, p. 37.
18 Barclay, *Ernest Bevin and the Foreign Office*, pp. 30, 38.
19 Ibid., pp. 83–4.
20 V. L. Allen, 'Arthur Deakin', *Dictionary of National Biography*.
21 Barclay, *Ernest Bevin and the Foreign Office*, p. 88; Arthur Bryant, *The Turn of the Tide* (Doubleday: London, 1957), pp. 35–6.
22 Weiler, *Ernest Bevin*, p. 35; Henderson, *Inside the Private Office*, p. 22.
23 Barclay, *Ernest Bevin and the Foreign Office*, p. 96.
24 Ibid., p. 48. The following quotes are from pp. 48, 49, 91.
25 Bullock, *The Life and Times of Ernest Bevin, Volume Three: Foreign Secretary 1945–1951* (Heinemann: London, 1983), p. 388; Barclay, *Ernest Bevin and the Foreign Office*, pp. 38, 39, 53.
26 Bullock, *Foreign Secretary*, pp. 759, 833.
27 David Owen, *In Sickness and In Power: Illness in Heads of Government During the Last 100 Years* (Methuen Publishing: Yorkshire, 2011).
28 Radice, *The Tortoise and the Hares*, p. 204; Barclay, *Ernest Bevin and the Foreign Office*, p. 51.
29 Bullock, *Foreign Secretary*, p. 833.
30 Henderson, *Inside the Private Office*, pp. 50–54.

CHAPTER 7: WAR

1   Bullock, *Trade Union Leader*, p. 650. This is also the source for the later quote from the speech.
2   *The Times*, 5 April 1940.
3   House of Commons, Hansard, 8 May 1940.
4   Roger Hermiston, *All Behind You, Winston: Churchill's Great Coalition 1940–45* (Aurum Press: London, 2016), p. 25.
5   Williams, *Portrait*, p. 228.
6   John Colville, *The Fringes of Power: Downing Street Diaries 1939–1955* (Weidenfeld & Nicolson: London, 2004), p. 220; Radice, *The Tortoise and the Hares*, p. 112.

7 John G. Winant, *A Letter from Grosvenor Square: An Account of a Stewardship* (Houghton Mifflin Co.: Boston, 1947), p. 155.

8 Bullock, *Trade Union Leader*, p. 654.

9 House of Commons, Hansard, 13 February 1946.

10 Bullock, *Minister of Labour*, p. 20; Radice, *The Tortoise and the Hares*, p. 111.

11 Mayhew, 'Ernest Bevin', p. 11.

12 House of Commons, Hansard, 21 June 1944.

13 House of Commons, Hansard, 22 June 1944.

14 House of Commons, Hansard, 21 May 1941.

15 Radice, *The Tortoise and the Hares*, p. 112.

16 *Manchester Guardian*, 24 May 1945.

17 House of Commons, Hansard, 21 May 1942; Bullock, *Minister of Labour*, p. 127; Evans, *Bevin of Britain*, p. 239.

18 House of Commons, Hansard, 8 October 1941, cols 1078–82; Weiler, *Bevin*, pp. 116–17, 142–3.

19 Taylor, *TUC*, p. 88; Weiler, *Ernest Bevin*, p. 122.

20 Weiler, *Ernest Bevin*, pp. 129–30.

21 Bullock, *Minister of Labour*, p. 80; Weiler, *Ernest Bevin*, p. 136.

22 Colville, *The Fringes of Power*, p. 220.

23 Basil Dean, *The Theatre at War* (G. G. Harrap: London, 1956), p. 134.

24 Ibid., p. 137.

25 Ibid., p. 134.

26 Angus Calder, *The People's War: Britain 1939–1945* (Pimlico: London, 1992), p. 392.

27 Evans, *Bevin of Britain*, p. 215; Weiler, *Ernest Bevin*, p. 136.

28 Bullock, *Minister of Labour*, p. 354.

29 Weiler, *Ernest Bevin*, pp. 125–6; Taylor, *TUC*, p. 101.

30 Weiler, *Ernest Bevin*, p. 135.

31 David Marquand, *The Progressive Dilemma: From Lloyd George to Blair* (Weidenfeld & Nicolson: London, 1991), p. 77.

32 Evans, *Bevin of Britain*, p. 244; Paul Addison, *The Road to 1945: British Politics and the Second World War* (Pimlico: London, 1975), p. 14.

33 Weiler, *Ernest Bevin*, p. 135.

34 Evans, *Bevin of Britain*, p. 235.

35 Bullock, *Minister of Labour*, p. 265.

36 Ibid., pp. 260–61.

37 Evans, *Bevin of Britain*, p. 183; House of Commons, Hansard, 27 November 1940, col. 284.

38 House of Commons, Hansard, 16 April 1951, cols 1467–73; Bullock, *Minister of Labour*, p. 175.

39 Bullock, *Minister of Labour*, p. 108.

40 House of Commons, Hansard, 29 July 1941.

41 Stephens, *Ernest Bevin*, pp. 127–8; House of Commons, Hansard, 16 April 1951, cols 1467–73.

42 Bullock, *Minister of Labour*, pp. 134–6.

43 Ibid., p. 70.

44 Ibid., pp. 152, 178.

45 Ibid., p. 188.

46 Evans, *Bevin of Britain*, p. 222.

47 Bullock, *Minister of Labour*, p. 124.

48 Evans, *Bevin of Britain*, pp. 243–4.

49 Taylor, *TUC*, p. 77.

50 I am grateful to Lord Baker of Dorking for this reference.

51 *The Economist*, 9 December 1944.

52 Bullock, *Minister of Labour*, pp. 343–4.

53 Ibid., p. 347.

54 Ibid., pp. 328–9.
55 Weiler, *Ernest Bevin*, p. 139.
56 Ben Pimlott (ed.), *The Second World War Diary of Hugh Dalton 1940–45* (Jonathan Cape: London, 1986), p. 554; Bullock, *Minister of Labour*, pp. 232–3.
57 Bullock, *Minister of Labour*, p. 381.
58 *Manchester Guardian*, 9 April 1945.
59 Bullock, *Minister of Labour*, p. 378.

CHAPTER 8: VICTORY
1 Harris, *Attlee*, p. 262.
2 Weiler, *Ernest Bevin*, p. 144.
3 Ibid.; *The Economist*, 16 June 1945.
4 Bullock, *Minister of Labour*, p. 385.
5 Martin Gilbert, *Never Despair: Winston S. Churchill 1945–65* (Heinemann: London, 1988), p. 35.
6 Bullock, *Minister of Labour*, p. 391.
7 Nicklaus Thomas-Symonds, *Attlee: A Life in Politics* (I. B. Tauris: London, 2010), p. 134.
8 Bullock, *Minister of Labour*, pp. 392–3; Harris, *Attlee*, pp. 262–3.
9 Harris, *Attlee*, p. 265.
10 Bullock, *Minister of Labour*, p. 393.
11 Barclay, *Ernest Bevin and the Foreign Office*, p. 80; Bullock, *Foreign Secretary*, p. 456.
12 Pimlott, *Hugh Dalton*, p. 410.
13 Barclay, *Ernest Bevin and the Foreign Office*, p. 49.
14 Sir John Wheeler-Bennett, *King George VI: His Life and Reign* (Macmillan: London, 1958), p. 638.
15 Pimlott, *Hugh Dalton*, p. 421.
16 Bullock, *Minister of Labour*, p. 394; Pimlott, *Hugh Dalton*, pp. 414–15; *The Observer*, 23 August 1959.
17 Lord Morrison of Lambeth, *Herbert Morrison: An Autobiography* (Odhams: London, 1960), pp. 246–7.
18 Pimlott, *Hugh Dalton*, pp. 415, 422.
19 Barclay, *Ernest Bevin and the Foreign Office*, p. 84.

CHAPTER 9: STALIN
1 Evans, *Bevin of Britain*, p. 147.
2 Ibid., p. 148.
3 Andrew Roberts, *Masters and Commanders: The Military Geniuses Who Led the West to Victory in World War II* (Penguin: London, 2009), p. 556.
4 Roberts, *Masters and Commanders*, pp. 557, 559; John Barnes and David Nicholson (eds), *The Empire at Bay: The Leo Amery Diaries 1929–45* (Hutchinson: London, 1988), p. 1030; Jenkins, *Churchill*, p. 796.
5 Robert H. Ferrell (ed.), *Off the Record: The Private Papers of Harry S. Truman* (University of Missouri Press: Columbia, 1980), pp. 51, 53.
6 Bullock, *Foreign Secretary*, p. 25.
7 Thomas-Symonds, *Attlee*, pp. 135–6.
8 Robert James Maddox, *Weapons for Victory: The Hiroshima Decision* (University of Missouri Press: Columbia, 2004), p. 111.
9 Richardson Dougall (ed.), *Foreign Relations of the United States: Diplomatic Papers, The Conference of Berlin 1945, Volume Two* (United States Government Printing Office: Washington, 1960), pp. 515–17.
10 James F. Byrnes, *Speaking Frankly* (Harper: New York, 1947), p. 79; Radice, *The Tortoise and the Hares*, pp. 138–9, 176.
11 'The Conference of Berlin', Diplomatic Papers, p. 477.

12 Richard Bessel, *Germany 1945: From War to Peace* (Simon & Schuster: London, 2009), p. 2.
13 John Dietrich, *The Morgenthau Plan: Soviet Influence on American Postwar Policy* (Algora Publishing: Sanford, 2002), p. 64.
14 Lucius D. Clay, *Decision in Germany* (Doubleday and Company: New York, 1950), p. 5; Elliott Roosevelt (ed.), *The Roosevelt Letters, Volume Three 1928–45* (Harrap: London, 1953).
15 Anne Deighton, *The Impossible Peace: Britain, the Division of Germany and the Origins of the Cold War* (Oxford University Press: Oxford, 1990), p. 20.
16 *Tribune*, 8 March 1946.
17 Myers, 'Conscription', p. 60.
18 House of Commons, Hansard, 19 June 1947.
19 Andrew Roberts, *'The Holy Fox': A Biography of Lord Halifax* (Weidenfeld & Nicolson: London, 1991), p. 295.
20 Lord Robertson of Oakridge, 'A Miracle? Potsdam 1945 – West Germany 1965', *International Affairs*, vol. 41, 1965, p. 403.
21 Deighton, *Impossible Peace*, p. 56.
22 Ibid., p. 48.
23 David Robertson, *Sly and Able: A Political Biography of James F. Byrnes* (W. W. Norton: New York, 1994), pp. 379, 387, 445; Ferrell, *Off the Record*, p. 49.
24 Robertson, *Sly and Able*, p. 446.
25 Patricia Dawson Ward, *The Threat of Peace: James F. Byrnes and the Council of Foreign Ministers 1945–1946* (Kent State University Press: Kent, 1979), p. 62; Fraser J. Harbutt, *The Iron Curtain: Churchill, America and the Origins of the Cold War* (Oxford University Press: Oxford, 1986), p. 125.
26 Harbutt, *The Iron Curtain*, pp. 138–9; Robertson, *Sly and Able*, p. 450.
27 Harbutt, *The Iron Curtain*, pp. 141–4.
28 Robertson, *Sly and Able*, pp. 451–3; Harbutt, *The Iron Curtain*, p. 141.
29 Ward, *The Threat of Peace*, pp. 75–6; Robertson, *Sly and Able*, pp. 456–7.
30 Deighton, *Impossible Peace*, p. 62.
31 Ibid., p. 73; Weiler, *Ernest Bevin*, p. 159.
32 Ward, *The Threat of Peace*, pp. 79–80.
33 Harbutt, *The Iron Curtain*, p. 247.
34 Robertson, *Sly and Able*, p. 479; Deighton, *Impossible Peace*, p. 83.
35 Deighton, *Impossible Peace*, p. 89.
36 Ibid., p. 91.
37 Bullock, *Foreign Secretary*, p. 184.
38 Ibid., p. 352.
39 Roy Jenkins, *Nine Men of Power* (Hamish Hamilton: London, 1974), p. 63.
40 House of Commons, Hansard, 22 October 1946; Christopher Knowles, *Winning the Peace: The British in Occupied Germany 1945–1948* (Bloomsbury: London, 2017), p. 101.
41 Knowles, *Winning the Peace*, p. 66.
42 Deighton, *Impossible Peace*, p. 112.
43 Ward, *The Threat of Peace*, p. 170.
44 Deighton, *Impossible Peace*, pp. 121–3.
45 Ibid., pp. 121–5.
46 Ibid., pp. 127–9.
47 Bullock, *Foreign Secretary*, pp. 382–3.
48 Ibid., p. 375.
49 Ibid., p. 382.
50 Ibid., pp. 386–7.
51 Ibid., p. 391.
52 Deighton, *Impossible Peace*, pp. 156–7.
53 Williams, *Portrait*, pp. 263–4.

54 Bullock, *Foreign Secretary*, p. 404.
55 Ibid., p. 403.
56 Ibid., p. 406.
57 Ibid., pp. 406–7.
58 House of Commons, Hansard, 19 June 1947.
59 Barclay, *Ernest Bevin and the Foreign Office*, p. 89; Radice, *The Tortoise and the Hares*, p. 177.
60 Weiler, *Ernest Bevin*, pp. 164–5.
61 Bullock, *Foreign Secretary*, p. 413.
62 Deighton, *Impossible Peace*, p. 187.
63 Ibid., p. 197.
64 Ibid., pp. 203, 210–11.
65 Ibid., pp. 208–9.
66 Ibid., pp. 218–19.
67 Ibid., p. 201; House of Commons, Hansard, 22 January 1948, cols 383–409.
68 Radice, *The Tortoise and the Hares*, p. 178.
69 Alex Danchev, *Oliver Franks: Founding Father* (Clarendon Press: Oxford, 1993), p. 107; Henderson, *Inside the Private Office*, p. 51.
70 Stephens, *Ernest Bevin*, p. 135; Barclay, *Ernest Bevin and the Foreign Office*, p. 74.
71 Bullock, *Foreign Secretary*, p. 90.
72 Ibid., p. 764.

CHAPTER 10: FAILURES

1 Evans, *Bevin of Britain*, p. 251.
2 Weiler, *Ernest Bevin*, p. 67; Nicholas Owen, *The British Left and India: Metropolitan Anti-Imperialism, 1885–1947* (Oxford University Press: Oxford, 2007), pp. 292–3.
3 William Roger Louis, *Imperialism at Bay: The United States and the Decolonization of the British Empire, 1941–1945* (Oxford University Press: Oxford, 1978), pp. 18, 555–6; Weiler, *Ernest Bevin*, p. 147.
4 Evans, *Bevin of Britain*, pp. 149–50.
5 Simon Schama, *A History of Britain: The Fate of Empire 1776–2000* (BBC Books: London, 2002), pp. 540–42.
6 Myers, 'Conscription', p. 68.
7 Harris, *Attlee*, p. 425.
8 Pimlott, *Hugh Dalton*, p. 577; Benjamin Grob-Fitzgibbon, *Imperial Endgame: Britain's Dirty Wars and the End of Empire* (Palgrave Macmillan: London, 2011); Weiler, *Ernest Bevin*, p. 175.
9 Stephens, *Ernest Bevin*, p. 134.
10 Bullock, *Foreign Secretary*, p. 32.
11 Earl Attlee, *Empire into Commonwealth* (Oxford University Press: Oxford, 1961), pp. 1, 53–4.
12 Weiler, *Ernest Bevin*, pp. 172–3.
13 Jenkins, *Nine Men of Power*, p. 79.
14 Dalton, *High Tide and After*, p. 146.
15 Ibid., p. 147.
16 Raphael Langham, 'The Bevin Enigma: what motivated Ernest Bevin's opposition to the establishment of a Jewish state in Palestine', *Jewish Historical Studies*, vol. 44, 2012, p. 169.
17 I am grateful to Sir Ronald Cohen for this reference.
18 Dalton, *High Tide and After*, p. 147; Langham, 'The Bevin Enigma', p. 168; John Bew, *Citizen Clem: A Biography of Attlee* (Riverrun: London, 2016), p. 427.
19 Langham, 'The Bevin Enigma', p. 169.
20 Bullock, *Trade Union Leader*, p. 623; Langham, 'The Bevin Enigma', pp. 173–4.
21 Bullock, *Foreign Secretary*, p. 169.
22 Weiler, *Ernest Bevin*, p. 171.

23 Martin Gilbert, *Churchill & The Jews* (Simon & Schuster: London, 2007), pp. 275–6; House of Commons, Hansard, 22 January 1949.

24 House of Commons, Hansard, 21 February 1946.

25 Radice, *The Tortoise and the Hares*, p. 204.

26 Barclay, *Ernest Bevin and the Foreign Office*, p. 67.

27 Radice, *The Tortoise and the Hares*, pp. 205–6; Nicholas Henderson, *Channels and Tunnels: Reflections on Britain and Abroad* (Weidenfeld & Nicolson: London, 1987), p. 151.

28 Radice, *The Tortoise and the Hares*, p. 207.

29 Dan Jackson, *The Northumbrians: North-East England and its People* (Hurst: London, 2019), p. 200.

30 David Reynolds, *Island Stories: Britain and Its History in the Age of Brexit* (William Collins: London, 2019), p. 48.

31 Bevin to Attlee, 1 January 1947, in Nicholas Mansergh and Penderel Moon (eds), *Constitutional Relations Between Britain and India: The Transfer of Power, 1942–1947, Volume IX* (Her Majesty's Stationery Office: London, 1980), p. 236.

32 Henderson, *Mandarin*, p. 65.

33 Barclay, *Ernest Bevin and the Foreign Office*, p. 72.

34 John Colville, *Footprints in Time: Memories* (HarperCollins: London, 1976), pp. 213–14.

CHAPTER 11: BEVIN TODAY

1 Harold Wilson, transcript of 'A Prime Minister on Prime Ministers: Clement Attlee, Part 2', ITV, 22 February 1978.

2 Evans, *Bevin of Britain*, p. 244.

3 Geoffrey Goodman, 'Jack Larkin Jones', *Dictionary of National Biography*.

4 Matt Bai, 'The New Boss', *New York Times*, 30 January 2005.

5 Bullock, *Foreign Secretary*, p. 92.

6 Henderson, *Inside the Private Office*, p. 51.

7 H. H. Asquith, *Letters to Venetia Stanley* (Oxford University Press: Oxford, 1985), p. 503.

8 Lord Attlee, *The Observer*, 13 March 1960.

INDEX